...ress Cataloging in Publication Data

...k Giants: yesterday, today, tomorrow.

...ty). Football club (National

...

796.33'264'097471   73-6466

...hed by Henry Regnery Company
...llinois Street, Chicago, Illinois 60610
...ared in the United States of America
...ngress Catalog Card Number: 73-6466

th

GIA
ye
TO
TO

Da

Library of Con

Klein, Dave.
The New Yo

1. New York (
League)—Histo
GV9 56.N4K55

HENRY REGNERY

This is for twelve years and too many faces that whizzed by too quickly. It is for the few faces that stopped and became friends. That may not sound like much, but it is.

And especially, this is for Willie, who took the same route and understands all the things that can't be explained.

Contents

Foreword

The Giants are an old-fashioned family, old-fashioned in the best sense. They are enormously loyal, patriarchal in organization, proud of their tradition, difficult to penetrate, and uncompromising in their principles, and they are the least contrived group I've ever been associated with.

The Giants family is not only the Mara family founded by the late, beloved Timothy J. Mara, but every player who ever wore the uniform. The family also includes the ticket manager, the equipment man, the secretaries, the players, the coaches and ex-coaches, the scouts, and among many, many others, the broadcaster.

As part of the family you are expected to conduct yourself as a Giant on and off the field. The rules of conduct are rarely spelled out, but you know them.

The Giants family is forthright and blunt yet difficult to know. Dave Klein knows them.

Dave knows them because he has worked at it, worked

hard. I started broadcasting their games in 1949, but my association with them began ten years before that, when I played with their farm team, the Jersey City Giants, coached by Bill Owen, Steve's brother. It wasn't long after Dave started covering the club that even I began to look to him for information and insight into the team. He dug, he asked questions, he persisted, he took time to investigate deeply. He made it a point to spend time not only with the coaches and the stars and the management, but with the men on the taxi squad, the reserves, the scouts, the lesser figures among the Giants. It was common practice for all of us who covered the club to "ask Dave" when a situation was blurred. Dave Klein focused the issue.

As a broadcaster I well know that each of us sees a game in his own manner. There are many issues in this book that I see differently than Dave. However, I value his opinion no less than I do my own.

This is a book for Giants fans, of course. But it is also a book that transcends sports. It is a book about people—the people who have made up the Giants family.

Marty Glickman

Preface

I have covered the New York Giants for the last twelve years, which is equivalent to more than one-third of my life. I am sure there were better things I might have done, but once bitten by the newspaper virus, one finds recovery incredibly difficult if not entirely impossible. Antibiotics are no match for ribbon ink.

During this time, I have made a good number of friends. Of course most of these relationships have been with other newspapermen, but others have been with jocks who have had more on their minds than football. It would serve no purpose to list them all, for they know who they are, and, more important, I know who they are.

I would, however, like to express special words of thanks for the two Als—Sherman and Webster—who have done so much to educate and entertain this typewriter type.

Allie Sherman, for many reasons, is the most impressive man I have met during my association with professional football. He is warm, intelligent, considerate, articulate, and sincere. We first met in 1961 during an interview held in his dormitory room at Fairfield University, where the Giants were conducting their summer training camp. Both of us were rookies in a sense. It was his first year as head coach and my first year as the team's correspondent for the *Star-Ledger*.

A friendship grew and deepened, and for the eight succeeding years in which Allie remained as head coach, we met socially as often as we did in the coach-reporter situation. Since his firing, that has not changed at all. I am most thankful for that.

When Allie was fired in the autumn of 1969 I was personally disturbed, as I would have been had he been an engineer released by Lockheed or a counterman dismissed by the local eatery. Friends are friends, regardless of what they do to support a family.

A great deal of information to be found in these pages has come from Allie, but there are some confidences I have kept, and not at all reluctantly. He is in many ways and for many reasons a private person. I would do nothing to disturb his aura of dignity.

I am grateful to him, and although I have said that in person, it's nice to have the chance to say it once more in print. For the record, he deserved better from the Giants.

Alex Webster is different. He is roughly hewn and similarly polished. He is a man's man, a player's player, and now a player's coach. Having settled into his new role, Alex has dropped away to a degree from his old image and is now becoming more "coachly," but that comes with the job these days.

Alex and I are from the same area of New Jersey, and though he is a decade my senior, it never seems that way. With Alex the talk and the scotch are always plentiful. He is easy to like, and being his friend, one can also feel embarrassment for him, though not as much now as when he was first thrust into his job. He does not speak with Sherman's grace and ease, nor does he possess the same mastery over words, but he makes up for all of that with refreshing honesty and a John Wayne-like determination. He is genuine, and that counts.

A word to Wellington Mara, or about him, is necessary. We have established a cordial relationship during these dozen years, and most of the time he has been more than gracious. He is a complex man, seemingly caught up in the intensity with which he guards his inheritance, the Giants; the team has directed and controlled his actions since boyhood.

We are of different worlds and different eras, of course, and although no sourness has entered our dealings, Wellington is difficult to know. There is no denying the presence of a protective shield, as though to open himself would be some sign of weakness. He has been fair with me, which is all anyone can expect.

Well Mara prefers beer to scotch. He prefers to sit in the tourist section of the planes he charters for the team rather than up front in the first-class cabin that houses the coaches, the press, the doctors, the publicity people, and the ever-present Father Dudley, team chaplain and amateur interviewer (often Father Dudley's attempts at the latter have come at the worst times to the annoyance of those who have to talk to players and beat a deadline).

I am more than neutral about Well Mara. I want to like the man, and I hope he can say the same about me when he finishes this book. If what he reads about himself is not altogether flattering, it is an altogether honest attempt to portray him. I am sure he will recognize honesty as a far more valuable commodity.

Timmy Mara? I don't know him because he has never wanted to be known by one of our craft. As I understand it, his first real assumption of responsibility with the team came in 1972, at the age of 39, when he began firing front-office employees. He might have chosen his victims with more care since Don Smith greatly enhanced the team's image and is still missed. But Timmy, the son of the late Jack Mara and nephew to Well, has had a hell of a good time with his life. One assumes he is pleased over that.

Generally, the experience of traveling with the Giants has been gratifying. I have seen much of the country. I have a brainful of memories. I have seen many historic NFL games. To many this might not seem equal payment for the expenditure of a dozen years. But I might have spent that time sitting behind a desk, which would have been far worse. Even Saturday nights in Cleveland have more to offer.

Finally, I would like to remember Phil King.

He was one of the few close friends who came from the ranks of the players. He was perhaps the one man I knew who lived his life with a constant full-throttled gusto. He laughed when he felt it, which was mostly all the time.

In January 1973, when he was successful, healthy, and 36 years old, he accidentally shot himself in the head while cleaning a pistol in Memphis, Tennessee. He died instantly.

Carole and I were vacationing in San Francisco at the time. I read the story early one morning, and before I could get home his funeral had been held. He was a good friend, and what I'll remember most is his laughter.

Perhaps, after a dozen years with basically the same people, it is the laughter that is most precious.

Dave Klein

1

Before There Were Giants

On September 17, 1920, the American Professional Football Association held its organizational meeting.

Pete Rozelle had not yet been born, nor had Jim Brown, Y.A. Tittle, Bart Starr, or Johnny Unitas. Vince Lombardi was a seven-year-old boy in the Sheepshead Bay section of Brooklyn, wondering whether to become a priest or a prize fighter.

There were 11 men gathered in an automobile agency showroom in Canton, Ohio, and their ambition was to found a league of professional football teams. Each man was awarded a franchise for the sum of $100. The teams included the Akron (Ohio) Steels; the Rochester (New York) Jeffersons; the Chicago Tigers; the Cleveland Panthers; the Dayton (Ohio) Triangles; the Rock Island (Illinois) Independents; the Decatur (Illinois) Staleys; the Hammond (Indiana) Pros; the Canton Bulldogs; the Buffalo All-Americans; and the Columbus (Ohio) Panhandles. During the Association's first season, two more teams were added — the Detroit Heralds and the Chicago Cardinals — and they, too, had to find the $100 entrance fee.

Jim Thorpe, the immortal running back from the Carlisle Indian School, was named commissioner of the league, an honor accorded him because of his reputation, not his administrative abilities. Thorpe and his Association had footballs and vacant lots and unused high school fields and a collection of men who loved the game of football. Thus they had themselves a league.

The American Professional Football Association was to be the forerunner of the National Football League, but no one present that day in Canton would have imagined or dared to speak aloud any prediction of financial success. Most of the men who became owners did so only to become players.

There was no formal schedule, no formal standings, no crowning of a league champion. Rosters were erratic, and men played for more than one team, schedules permitting. Salaries were of a will o' the wisp nature; if money was there, the players were paid, and often the money was raised by passing hats through the crowds during the games. Most of the players considered $50 a game handsome reward; several made considerably less, and a few even played for free. Only those name athletes who had captivated college audiences dared ask for more. Occasionally, for the truly outstanding college All-American, a team would provide a sum ranging from $100 to $300 per game, but the star would be expected to lend his name to this half-baked endeavor and to make publicity and ticket-selling appearances as well.

The Association was the brainchild of a young man named George Halas who played football and baseball with equal competence. Halas had been hired as the physical director of the Staley Starch Works in Decatur and had organized a company football team. He needed other teams for his company team to play, and so he interested other men in his idea of an organized league.

The idea of professional football was not a new one, but Halas's idea of an organized league smacked of originality. For many years, though, it remained a matter of conjecture as to whether the league really was organized. There were times when the league's staunchest supporters, even Halas himself, were tempted to scrap the project. That they fought this temptation, that somehow they came up with additional funds and teams strong enough to survive, has given today's NFL its foundation of strength and its aura of permanence.

The problems Halas and his Association encountered can be better understood if one considers the sport they were trying to organize. Professional football in its early days was both provincial and chaotic.

Professional football's beginnings can be traced back to 1895, when the Latrobe, Pennsylvania, Young Men's Christian Association fielded a team in Westmoreland County, 45 miles southeast of Pittsburgh. The Latrobe team made its competitive debut on August 31, 1895, defeating the township team from Jeanette, 10 miles away, by the score of 12-0. For the next decade Latrobe maintained a powerful team that played hit-and-miss football. The team played when it could, where it could, with whatever players could be found, and against whatever teams could scrape together the 11 men needed to offer competition.

The idea of touring teams caught on, especially in the coal country of western Pennsylvania, where the men were as hard and as unyielding as the anthracite veins they mined, where they resorted to totally disorganized brawling on Sunday afternoons for lack of any better distraction. Teams flowered in Jeanette, Greensburg, Pittsburgh, and McKeesport, in Pottsville and Pellstown. Soon the sport spread to upper New York State, where such towns as Buffalo, Syracuse, Corinth, Auburn, Clayton, Watertown, Alexandria Bay, Oswego, and Ogdensburg sponsored teams before the advent of the twentieth century.

The games were well attended. Indeed, the passions of the

locals often became so aroused that the contests ended earlier than planned, with several hundred fans milling with the players on the field in a dandy display of mayhem.

It was rough, violent, Neanderthal football. No one wore helmets, and shin guards were rarely seen. Only the man who respected the conformation and future of his nose and teeth showed up with a rudimentary face guard. In lieu of helmets the players grew their hair long and then parted it down the middle, hoping that the added cushion of tresses would protect their craniums from cuts, bruises, and knocks.

Some of the finest collegiate athletes of the day played for these teams in search of spending money, often under assumed names in order to protect their tenuous guise of amateurism. These players included Fielding "Hurry Up" Yost of West Virginia, Doggie Trenchard and Arthur Poe of Princeton, Walter Okeson of Lehigh, Walter Howard of Cornell, Pudge Heffelfinger of Yale, Bemus and Hawley Pierce of the Carlisle School, G.H. Brooke and P.D. Overfield of Pennsylvania, Fred Crolius of Dartmouth, and Phil Draper of Williams College.

Dr. John Brallier, who later opened a successful dental practice in Latrobe, has been acknowledged as the first confessed professional football player on record. He admitted to taking ten dollars plus expenses to play quarterback for Latrobe against Jeanette in their inaugural game, after which he returned to Washington and Jefferson College to play quarterback until the end of the season. He came back to Latrobe and played professionally for the next several years.

During the middle of the 1896 season, Latrobe's sponsors ran into financial problems. Brallier, end Eddie Wood, and halfback Dick Ely, the team's stars, had to play the final three games for a total of $50 and expenses. But the next season Latrobe found new money, recruited additional college talent, and claimed the high point of its season as it defeated the great Greensburg team.

It is possible, however, that professional football predates even the brawling Pennsylvania teams. According to Dr. Harry March, who became the secretary of the New York Giants in their first season of 1925, semi-pro football really began in 1890 when several athletic teams in and about New York City played each other on weekend afternoons. The teams were composed of well-known local college men who played regularly at school and then participated for money on Sundays. These men played for the Manhattan Athletic Club, the Orange (New Jersey) Athletic Club, the Crescent Club of Brooklyn, the Staten Island Athletic Club, and the Knickerbocker Athletic Club. (March, however, gives credit to the state of Ohio as the cradle of organized professional football.)

With the subsequent growth of the game came the emergence of common sense. The pros ruled that only those no longer eligible for college football or other amateur competition in any sport could be admitted to the ranks of the professionals. And then the professionals began to shake off their provincialism.

On December 28, 1902, the Syracuse professional team played a challenge game against the Philadelphia Nationals in New York City's Madison Square Garden and won 6-0. It was pro football's first metropolitan exposure, and to dignify the occasion the officials worked in full dress: high silk hats, gloves, morning coats, high-fashion spats, and knickers.

Also in 1902, Connie Mack organized a team named the Athletics, after his famous American League baseball team in Philadelphia. Mack inserted his star pitcher, Rube Waddell, into the line-up, an action that was met with great reluctance and displeasure by Waddell. Mack later claimed the championship of the world after his squad defeated the reigning champion — unofficial, of course — from Pittsburgh. The Pittsburgh team had a fullback named Christy Mathewson, far better known as one of baseball's greatest pitchers. But Mathewson had been a linecrasher (an early-day linebacker) during his undergraduate years at Bucknell and, unlike

Waddell, had never lost his taste for the physical contact of football.

Professional football in New York and Pennsylvania was lively and popular, but until the formation of the APFA, Ohio remained the bloodiest of battlegrounds for the loosely knit professional teams. Such cities as Canton, Akron, Massillon, Columbus, and Dayton offered teams made up of valiant and violent men, ready for the hand-to-hand combat featured in that early style of play. Jim Thorpe played professionally for Canton in 1911, and Thorpe's presence alone was enough to lend something special to Ohio football.

The ruthlessness of those early Ohio teams is evident in the story of Willie Heston, an All-Time All-American running back from the University of Michigan and the star of Fielding Yost's "Point-A-Minute" offense. When, after his graduation, Willie dropped several hints that he might consider playing for cash, Canton, Massillon, and Akron found themselves locked in a bitter bidding struggle. Heston lifted his demands to ridiculous heights and thereby alienated all three teams, who refused to hire him at any price. A year later, slightly cowed and still casting covetous eyes on some of the pro money, Heston agreed to play for Canton at the fabulous figure of $600 a game.

Heston's first professional appearance was against Massillon, and on the first play of the game he was savaged by half the team, so much so that he could not play for much of the remainder of the season. When he had sufficiently healed he tried to perform against the Chicago Bears, but they left him with a shattered leg that marked the end of his career.

Despite the unusually brutal treatment accorded him, Heston was only one of many prestigious players on the Ohio teams. Charlie Moran, later a major-league baseball umpire, played for Massillon in the same time span. From the Carlisle Indian School came the Pierce brothers, Albert Exendine and Frank Mt. Pleasant. The famed Indian settlement school in

Duluth, Minnesota, later achieved even greater distinction when Thorpe formed a team composed entirely of its graduates and entered it in the NFL under the name of the Oorang Indians. They played the regular league schedule in 1923, 1924, and 1925.

As time progressed, other Ohio cities acquired their own teams, notably Columbus and Shelby. Joe Carr, who later became the league's commissioner, was the owner of the Columbus team, which boasted the most prolific football family in the history of the game. Seven of the eleven Columbus starters were members of the Nesser family, six of them brothers and the seventh, Fred, the son of the oldest brother, Ted. None had played college football, having spurned several scholarship and cash offers. This amazing family tradition continued into the National Football League, and it wasn't until Al Nesser retired from the Cleveland Rams in 1931 that the dynasty finally petered out.

Still another unusual aspect of Ohio football was the presence of Knute Rockne and Gus Dorais, who had taken Notre Dame to national football supremacy with the first efficient use of the forward pass. Rockne and Dorais played with many teams, often jumping from one high bidder to another in the space of a week. They appeared for so many teams that it is impossible to chronicle their professional careers. It has been reported that the Columbus team found itself facing Rockne and Dorais on six different occasions during the same season, as members of six different teams. Rockne, of course, went on to become Notre Dame's head coach, whereas Dorais kept his finger in the professional pie and, from 1943 through 1947, coached the Detroit Lions.

Other men who were destined to become famous as coaches appeared in the line-ups of the early pro teams as ordinary players. They included Jock Sutherland, Greasy Neale, Charlie Brinkley, Tuss McLaughry, and Fido Kempton.

With the outbreak of World War I, professional football

moved into a more glamorous and competitive period. In 1918 the team representing the Great Lakes Naval Training Station was chosen to play in the Rose Bowl, where it devastated the Mare Island squad. On the Great Lakes roster were Halas, Jimmy Conzelman, Paddy Driscoll, Harold Erickson, Hughie Blacklock, Jerry Jones, and Emmett Keefe, all of whom were later to play or coach in the NFL.

But only Jim Thorpe stood out as a superstar in those days before pro football's national acceptance. Thorpe was a gallant, brooding warrior who stalked the coal fields of Pennsylvania, the flatlands of Ohio, and the frozen tundra of upper New York State. He was intensely proud of his Indian heritage, and he once admonished a coach for his superior bearing. "You white men outnumbered us and also had the press agentry," he said. "When the white men won it was always a battle; but when we won, it was a massacre."

Jim, a Sac and Fox Indian, weighed 190 pounds. He was equally adept in track and field, baseball, and football. His baseball exploits eventually led to tragedy after Thorpe emerged as the American hero of the 1912 Olympics in Stockholm, where he won gold medals in the shot put, the high jump, the broad jump, and the hurdles.

When a newspaper in Connecticut revealed that Thorpe had played professional baseball for a team in Rocky Mount, North Carolina, in 1911, all his medals were taken away and dispensed to those men who had finished second in the Olympic events. The fact that very few participants in those days — as today — were simon-pure amateurs did nothing to salvage Thorpe's pride. He quickly signed contracts to play professional baseball and football, but when the athletics were done he became a disconsolate, forgotten, and penniless man, ravaged by disappointment and whisky.

Thorpe's finest sport was football. In 1912, when Carlisle trimmed Army 27-6, the game was written up this way in the *New York Times*:

Standing out resplendent in a galaxy of Indian stars was

Jim Thorpe, recently crowned the athletic marvel of the age in the Olympics at Stockholm. The big Indian captain added more lustre to his already brilliant record, and at times the game itself was almost forgotten while the spectators gazed on Thorpe, the individual, to wonder at his prowess. . . . He simply ran wild while the cadets tried in vain to stop [him] . . . It was like trying to clutch a shadow. He did not make any of the four touchdowns credited to his team simply because the brilliant Arcasa was chosen to carry the ball on three of the four occasions, when a plunge meant a score. . . . Thorpe went through the Army line as if through an open door. His defensive play was on a par with his attack. . . . Thorpe tore off runs of 10 yards or more so often that they became common. . . . In the third period he made a run which will go down as one of the greatest ever seen on the Plains. . . . Catching a punt on the Army 45-yard line, Thorpe, zigzagging first to one side and then to the other, wormed his way through the entire Army team.

It was the wild, Midwestern variety of this chaotic sport that Halas tried to organize with his league. Somehow, the American Professional Football Association staggered through its first season of 1920. Some teams even made money. Halas's Decatur Staleys netted $1,800 after expenses, and the 22 players shared in the profits. "The men voted me 2 full shares," Halas recalls, "because I was both a coach and a player. It was hard work. We practiced every day, 6 days a week, and on Sundays we played our games."

As the 1921 season approached, there were some noticeable changes. Thorpe was fired as commissioner and was replaced by Joe Carr, who stayed on the job for 18 years until his death in 1939. The original 11 teams expanded to 13 by 1921. The Decatur and Hammond franchises disbanded and were replaced by the Chicago Bears and a pickup team from Cincinnati. In addition the league awarded membership to the Acme Packing Company of Green Bay, Wisconsin, which quickly named its franchise the Green Bay Packers.

Halas, who had operated the Staleys, moved his men to Chicago and renamed them the Bears. A top-flight semi-pro team in Chicago that had been organized ten years earlier, the Racine Cardinals, changed its name to the Chicago Cardinals and also joined the Association.

The Cardinals should not be mistaken for the Racine, Wisconsin, club that joined the league in 1922. The Cardinals derived their name from the fact that most of the players lived near Racine Street in Chicago. The rivalry between the Bears and Cardinals was to continue through 1959, when the Cardinal's owners, Charles and William Bidwill, sought a city of their own and moved their franchise to St. Louis.

Halas owned the Bears; he still does. He is today the sole surviving member of the original 11 owners, and for most of the Bears' 52 years he has served as their president, head coach, chief stockholder, and general manager.

Halas, who had had a fling with the New York Yankees as an outfielder in 1919, quit baseball when it became apparent that he was destined to remain a bench-rider. So he went home to Decatur and began working for the Staley Starch Company. The football team he put together for the company became the original APFA (NFL) member, the only one to survive.

In 1921 Halas's team won ten games, lost one, and tied one. The loss was administered by the Chicago Cardinals, but four days later the Bears avenged that defeat 10-0. Charley Dressen, later a baseball player and manager, was the quarterback for the Cardinals.

The Bears, champions of their league, did not retain that distinction the following season. An unexpected number of 18 teams crowded the league, and the title was won by the Canton Bulldogs, with a 10-0-2 record. Perhaps the most significant development of the 1922 season, though, was the decision to change the name of the APFA to the National Football League.

Halas recalls the reasoning: "We did it because American Professional Football Association was just too damned difficult to spit out. Besides, we wanted to give the impression we were the only league worth following in the country, and the word *national* always meant that to me. It was kind of impressive, I guess, and it sounded right. I would say we made a pretty good choice, wouldn't you?"

The 18 teams of 1922 included such new entries as Racine, Wisconsin; Louisville, Kentucky; Milwaukee, Wisconsin; Marion, Indiana; Toledo, Ohio; Minneapolis, Minnesota; and Evansville, Indiana. But even 18 did not remain as a maximum, for the idea of organized professional football had spread rapidly. Everybody wanted a piece of the action. With cities all over the country clamoring for franchises, the total hit 20 in 1923, reached 20 again in 1925, and flooded to an all-time high-water mark of 26 in 1926.

Teams drifted in and out of the league. Some tried to grab fortune and glory with little working capital and a lot of nerve. Others attempted to build a champion by buying top players or raiding other teams and universities. But a natural weeding process eventually took hold, bringing the NFL to a workable number of entries by the early 1930s, when the total ranged between 8 and 11 teams each year.

There was no doubt that the league was growing, if not in profit margins then in popularity. Enough money was being made to entice prospective owners into bidding for franchises, but most of the cash had to be directed into the acquisition of name players, men whose college reputations could guarantee the sale of tickets.

No player attracted more attention during this period than did Ernie Nevers, who had starred at Stanford University. No college player of his time had received more publicity; no player was better known. When Nevers graduated, the bidding was on.

In the fall of 1925 the city of Jacksonville, Florida, had just completed a new municipal stadium in order to get the jump on other Florida cities anxious to land a pro football franchise. The first thought on the part of the stadium operators was to start a team with Red Grange, the great running back whose rushing records at the University of Illinois stood until the 1960s. But Grange already had signed to play with the Bears, and the Florida entrepreneurs cast about hurriedly for another player to spark the acceptance of their team.

A newspaperman in Jacksonville came up with the answer. "Get Nevers," he said. "He's the best player in the world, even greater than Grange."

Negotiations were begun, and after two weeks of dickering Nevers signed a contract to play with the Jacksonville team for $15,000. The money was deposited to Nevers's credit in a California bank, after which he climbed on a train and wheeled to Florida.

Nevers played in two games for Jacksonville, a team with nothing more in the way of talent than local volunteers. But Jacksonville was not ready for pro football, Ernie Nevers or not, and attendance figures were dismal.

The team died after those 2 games. Nevers, who was to go on to an outstanding career with the Chicago Cardinals (he still holds the single-game scoring record of 40 points), had his $15,000, and the citizens of Jacksonville had their new stadium — unused, unwanted, and prohibitively expensive.

The Jacksonville team's failure was all too typical of this era of the NFL. Another team a thousand miles up the coast was about to begin a much different story. That team had just completed its first season. It had a winning record of 8-4 on the field, but success was only on the gridiron. All else was bleak.

No one could have predicted the extraordinary success that lay in the future of this franchise. But George Halas correctly sensed that for his league to gain national popularity, it had to be represented in the country's largest city.

The franchise was the New York Giants. Its success kindled a rebirth of professional football and paved the way for today's multimillion-dollar NFL.

2

Timothy J. Mara

Don Smith: "I remember he didn't like a story I had written for my newspaper. He really got angry, yelled at me when he saw me next and then had me barred from the team's locker room. The next week he came to me and apologized. Then a few months later I was hired to be the Giants' publicity man, and I stayed in that job for 12 years, a good 12 years. He was a very strange and unpredictable man, but when you were around him, you knew something was always happening. You could hear it."

Toots Shor: "The big thing about Tim was his imagination. You could tell him he had to make germs the most popular thing in town, and he'd find a way. He'd get everybody in New York absolutely nuts to have the most germs on their block. The man was a promotional genius . . . and a very close and dear friend. Did he ever try to sell me germs? Nah, he knew the alcohol would have killed them all."

Jack Mara: "Once in a while he'd come up with a really wild idea, like parading lions on the field because we were

going to play Detroit or trying to find somebody named
Davy Crockett and have him hunt a bear on the field before
we played Chicago. What we had to do usually was agree with
him and then wait until he saw himself it wouldn't work. If
we laughed or argued he'd get stubborn and insist on doing
it."

It was 1925, and New York City was at its gaudiest. After
all, there were no Roaring Twenties in Tuscaloosa. They were
born in New York City, a place with a life-style all its own,
with a pulse and a beat that were distinctly feverish. New
York was the center of entertainment, politics, high finance,
and industry; its frantic night life bred con men, high-rolling
gamblers, get-rich-quick schemers, showy women and their
pistol-packing, diamond-stick-pinned men.

And sports. Sports always carried a high premium of
interest in New York City because of the hero factor. New
York City was very big on heroes, and if none were present,
several could be manufactured.

Those who dabbled in penny stocks and hit it big became
celebrities because of their sudden riches. Political scandals
made folk heroes of their perpetrators, benevolent bandits
who had beaten the bosses and who received envy rather than
public condemnation.

The hero worship carried over to sports. A well-timed
home run or a fortunate right cross to the jaw of an opponent insured lifelong income and fame. He who did well in
sports found his name in headlines, and he whose name
appeared in headlines was eagerly pursued. He who found
success in the glitter-world of big-time sports found much
more in the world of the idolaters. The Great White Way
opened milky-white arms and toasted its new hero.

It was the time of the Lucky Generation, and lucky was
proper for many reasons. Lucky because grass and trees still
grew in the city; lucky because the country was still there,
just outside the factory walls; lucky because the air was still
pure and the highways still winding roads.

The writers of the day told the world that America was discovering its own identity, bold and brassy, loud and lavish, proud and powerful. We had come through "the war to end all wars," and because we were victors there was reason for national jubilation. The words of F. Scott Fitzgerald and Carl Sandburg told the rest of the world that America was here, was ready, was bigger and better and dirtier and more savage, more colorful and somehow more desirable than any other country.

Sports was part of this social celebration. Legends grew from men, and the superstars achieved adulation that would be impossible today. The New York Yankees had Babe Ruth, Bambino, the Sultan of Swat, a gargantuan bad boy with a bloated belly and a booming bat who caused his teammates and his manager uncounted agonies as well as providing them with uncounted heroics and indelible memories.

The New York Giants, the National League's answer to the Yankees, had two-fisted, foul-mouthed, tobacco-chewing John J. McGraw. As a manager, McGraw was more tyrant than teacher. His days off were spent at the race track winning or losing thousands of dollars. The National League also housed the Brooklyn Dodgers, who won not at all but whose antics and penchant for losing with a flair captivated a borough that today would be the country's fourth largest city.

There was Jack Dempsey, who made New York his and became the most celebrated heavyweight champion of them all. Big Jack — the Manassa Mauler, the bon vivant of Broadway who trained on champagne and cheesecake, who became as much of a New York City landmark as the Empire State Building. He opened a restaurant that became one of the most popular spots in Manhattan, right up there with El Morocco, the Stork Club, the Cotton Club in Harlem, and Tony Pastor's in the Village.

There was big-time college football at Manhattan College, New York University, City College, Fordham, and St. John's.

The Jewish-Italian segment of this burgeoning, mixed metropolis gave its young men to prize fighting and basketball. There was bicycle racing, prehistoric professional basketball, and thoroughbred horse racing. The year was a sequence of sports, gambling, and excitement.

Into the midst of all this clamor strode Timothy J. Mara, as much a part of it as anyone. Mara had quit school when he was 13 years old because school got to be too much for a boy with a vivid imagination. Schoolwork was a burden, too, since Mara sold newspapers in the morning and afternoon and worked at night as an usher in a movie theater, all in a dedicated but unproductive attempt to help support his widowed mother.

But the larger reason for Mara's leaving school was that he enjoyed the life, the hustle and tinsel and glitter, of the Lower West Side of Manhattan. His eyes twinkled at the sight of the finely dressed, free-spending gamblers and bookmakers and their lavishly accoutred women. He itched for the big money, for recognition, the access into the right clubs and circles. Mara was a New York City person, as distinct a type as an Oklahoma dirt farmer or a Maine lobsterman. The pulse of the night-life and the action was in his blood.

Eventually Mara became a bookmaker, which was, if not an honorable profession, at least a legal one. He set up shop at the most exclusive sections of the New York thoroughbred tracks, and despite catastrophic early losses he became one of the most popular bookies in the city, known at Saratoga and Jamaica and Belmont. Mara was known as T.J., a ruddy-faced, beefy, brash six-footer, never at a loss for a smile, always quick to pay off losses, often understanding when his clients came up with too much week and not enough money on Friday. With his promotional endeavors, bookmaking, business efforts, and the selective cultivation of friends from the elite of New York's moneyed flamboyancy, T.J. Mara became a well-known man, a celebrity in the brightly lit night.

"I never passed up the chance to promote anything," Mara

once said, "not just because of the profit I might have made but for the challenge of promoting something. But you have to remember that New York City in the twenties was virgin area for a smart promoter. There was money around, and people would buy anything, or at least come to see or hear it."

It was in this rousing atmosphere that Tim Mara, unknowing and unaware, met up with professional football.

One of Mara's closest friends was Billy Gibson, a fight promoter and, at the time, the manager of heavyweight Gene Tunney. One day Tim called on his friend Gibson with the thought of buying a piece of the Tunney contract.

It was early August 1925 when Mara entered Gibson's office. "I remember that it was a hot, steamy day," Mara later recalled, "and it was so damned uncomfortable I wasn't sure I could sit there for very long to deal. I had to keep moving, but I went because I had already started out for his office and I wanted some of Tunney. I really did."

Mara found Gibson occupied with two strangers. Gibson was shaking his head, clearly in the act of refusing something, when he saw Tim walk in. He quickly introduced Mara to the men — Joe Carr, the commissioner of the fledgling National Professional Football League, and Dr. Harry March, one of the leading proponents of what had come to be called "postgraduate football."

The men had come to Gibson, a known plunger, in the hopes that he would purchase a franchise for New York City. The new league desperately needed the exposure and prestige of New York, and Gibson was one of the best-known sports and entertainment promoters in the city.

But Billy shook his head at them. "No, no, I just don't think it will promote," he said. Then he turned to Mara. "Maybe my friend Tim here would like to buy it," he said.

"Buy what?" Mara asked.

"A franchise for New York City in a professional football league," said Carr.

"How much?" Mara asked.

"Five hundred dollars," said Carr.

Tim smiled. "Sure," he said. "Any sports franchise for New York ought to be worth 500 bucks. Even football. I'll take it."

And so the New York Giants were born.

Or, to be more accurate, the New York Football Giants, Inc., a name necessary to differentiate between the new, risky venture and the safely established baseball team of the same name. The team's official corporate name remains the same today, even though the safely established baseball Giants had to move to San Francisco in 1958 in search of new money.

Now Tim had to learn about football. "I founded this club on strength and ignorance," he used to say. "The strength of my players and my own ignorance. I don't think I had seen more than two football games in my life, but here I was with a team, and I had to do something."

Mara's first move was to hire Dr. March as the team secretary. March became more than a secretary. He was player scout, business manager, accountant, general manager, and bill collector. March's first move was to hire a man named Bob Folwell as the head coach. Folwell had been an All-American at the University of Pennsylvania and then a coach at Lafayette, Washington and Jefferson, and the U.S. Naval Academy. March then signed players, mostly local names with what was hoped would be built-in fan appeal.

The organization soon included Billy Gibson as a partner-in-debt; Gibson had reconsidered and decided that he did, after all, want a piece of professional football in New York. But the Giants belonged to Tim Mara, who freely, readily, and repeatedly admitted to an appalling lack of knowledge of the game. Happily, Tim did not need any expertise to become successful.

"I was betting on the city of New York," he would say later when the Giants were an unquestionable success. "Sports have always been important in New York, and the franchise was worth that money even if it would have been in a shoe-shining league."

Choosing to leave the administration of the team to Dr. March and a handful of others hired to help him — which included his 17-year-old son, Jack, and the 9-year-old Wellington, who served as ball boy — Tim went about the business of promoting the Giants.

"Tickets were a problem," he used to laugh. "They must have been, because nobody wanted to buy them."

The fans of New York City, who until then considered "postgraduate football" something to be played in the sticks of Latrobe, Canton, and Orange, had to be educated to the delights of this new game. How better to educate them than to get them into the stadium? Of course a companion question arose — how, indeed, to get them into the stadium? It was a challenge to a promoter of Mara's reputation.

"I can remember," says Wellington Mara, today's team president, "how he used to walk around the streets handing out free tickets and half-price tickets. And if he couldn't get half price, those became free, too. All he wanted was to get some people into the stands. He had to do that before he could hope to get their money, I suppose. Outside of the football played by the New York colleges, people here knew only about Notre Dame and Army and Navy. Besides, the professionals had an unsavory air about them, much like professional baseball players had when they first started touring the country."

Tim soon found that his $500 investment had ballooned considerably. The same lesson has been learned at greater expense by many modern-day owners of expansion teams chasing a pot of gold at the other end of sports-television promises. By the time the first season was concluded, Tim had written checks totalling nearly $25,000. The money went for such diverse expenses as uniforms and footballs, ticket and program printing, the hiring of a coach and front office personnel, the players' payroll, team transportation, room and board, rental of a stadium (the Polo Grounds, which was used by the baseball Giants as well), and other miscellaneous expenses, not the least of which included "favors and gifts" for a few select members of New York's sporting press, an investment made in the hopes of keeping the Giants' name and exploits in the all-important newspaper headlines.

Jack Mara once estimated that his father gave away, "Oh, at least five thousand tickets to every game, and sometimes our crowds didn't add up to that many, which meant people didn't even want to come for nothing. At first no one knew what team we were talking about. Most of our friends wouldn't even come around. They thought we meant the baseball Giants, and then they'd look at us like we were crazy, because they knew the baseball Giants didn't play football, and even if they did they knew we sure as hell didn't own them."

Tim began to care about the money he was spending. He could no longer afford to toss it around with the same flair as he dispersed free tickets, and in some cases his economy measures were extreme. John F.X. Condon, who used to do the public address announcing at the Polo Grounds games and who now promotes boxing for Madison Square Garden in New York, remembers a particular incident:

"We were playing a game late in December, and it started to get dark," Condon says. "The officials wanted the lights turned on, but when they looked for the stadium electrician, the man who had to do it, he wasn't to be found in his regular location. So they asked me to page him. I did. And as soon as I did, Mr. Mara came running to where I was sitting, looking very angry.

" 'What the hell are you doing, Condon?' he asked. 'Who told you to get the lights turned on?' I told him the officials had made the request because they couldn't find the electrician to tell him themselves. 'Of course they couldn't find him. I sent him away. Do you know it costs me a thousand bucks to turn those damned lights on?' But we had to do it anyway, and for a week or so he wouldn't talk to me."

For many years, with an occasional exception, the Giants drew few paying customers, and the losses continued to mount on the ledger. There was no logical explanation for T.J.'s insistence that professional football in New York could be profitable. But there was no denying Mara's devotion to the sport.

Until his death in 1959, Tim continued to promote. With the increasing success of his Giants, his efforts became single-minded, and he found the other businesses and endeavors he once had loved to be time-consuming and dreary. His heart remained in prize fighting and thoroughbred racing, however, so much so that with the advent of pari-mutuel betting machines in 1935 he was moved to forecast publicly and bitterly "the collapse of racing everywhere" if the "honest bookmaker" was removed from the scene in favor of "those idiot machines."

Once Mara was asked why he held on so stubbornly, especially during the late 1920s and early 1930s when the Depression stripped even his wealthy friends and backers. "I wondered myself at the time," he replied. "I was giving up the other enterprises to give more time and more money to the team. The answer was the boys [Jack and Wellington]. They got a great pleasure out of football and were deeply interested in it. I could see the future of it grow clean and good."

Mara kept in his desk until the day he died a treasured letter written by Wellington in 1930, when his younger son was 14. It was a comprehensive scouting report on the Staten Island Stapes, detailing how the Giants could beat them if the Maramen "were not seized by overconfidence." With his budding front-office eye, young Well also noted the prices the team could charge for tickets and the reaction of the fans to such an increase.

"You can see," T.J. commented, "that Well was a pretty good scout then, and now there isn't anybody better."

Jack, meanwhile, was Tim's pupil from a business and promotional aspect. Jack absorbed front-office operations and technique, and he later proved to be the business mind behind the team; Well found contentment in manipulating players, making trades, and offering assistance in the fields of coaching and scouting.

T.J. kept a personal financial log, or ledger, in his desk, across which he had printed "The NFL at a Glance." The ledger contained his own study of crowd and money figures over the years as well as some carefully thought out projections. Presumably the book served another purpose—it was a textbook for Jack, and it did its job well. After Tim's death and at the entrance of big-money television into the NFL scene, Jack quickly grasped the enormous potential of the televised game and forced himself to learn, at a crash-program pace, the intricacies of television, its cost factors and its potent effect not only on the fans but on the game itself.

Tim's Irish stubbornness, then, was all that stood between the Giants and financial disaster. He was prepared to fight down to his final dollar to keep the franchise afloat, and this quality was never more valuable than in the middle 1940s, when, backed by baseball riches, a new league appeared and threatened the existence of the NFL.

The league was called the All-America Conference, and among its strategies was to put teams into Yankee Stadium in the Bronx and Ebbetts Field in Brooklyn, thus mounting attractions on both sides of the Giants and the Polo Grounds. By the time the ashes were sifted, the AAC had been forced into bankruptcy and the NFL, although scarred and nearly drowning in red ink, had survived. Most of the owners of the league gave the credit for ultimate victory to Tim Mara.

"He was in New York, where we had to be strong," said George Halas, the founder, president, and then head coach of the Chicago Bears. "If we had a weaker man in the key city, the whole league might have gone down."

Whatever shortcomings Mara had in his knowledge of football, he still earned, and deserved, the label of professional.

Don Smith, who was the Giants' publicist for a dozen years until being fired in 1972 by T.J.'s grandson, Timmy, remembers an incident that clearly explains Mara's feelings about his team:

It was in 1956, and I was a young reporter working for the Long Island Press. Covering the Giants was my first major assignment, and I took it seriously. Also, I guess, I took it a bit personally, and when they lost I would get upset.

Well, one day we went to Washington and the Giants played a purely lousy game. I mean, the Redskins were terrible, and the Giants had no business even letting them stay close. But Washington won. When I wrote my story, I got a little nasty. Among other things, I said the Giants had quit right there on the field.

Some of the players brought in copies of my paper the next day, and one copy reached T.J. The following Sunday they were home, playing the Chicago Bears, and after leading 17-3 in the final few minutes, Harlon Hill caught two sensational touchdown passes and it finished in a 17-17 tie. I went down to the locker room to interview the players, and that's when it started.

T.J. saw me come in, and he ran at me. "You," he screamed, "you get the hell out of here." I thought he was kidding, so I walked over to another part of the room, but he followed me, screaming and yelling and getting red in the face. I finally had to walk out. I waited a few minutes and then came in again. This time it was Jack who spotted me. "Didn't you hear what my father said?" he roared. "Get out of our locker room."

So there I was, out in the hall for the second time. After a while I decided to sneak in through the coach's office. But as soon as I hit the players' locker room, Wellington saw me. I figured he was reasonable and wouldn't throw me out, but he grabbed me. "You heard my father and my brother," he said. "Do I have to throw you out, too?"

Well, that convinced me, so I went home, wrote my story of the game without player quotes, and then worried.

Tuesday was the weekly press luncheon day in Yankee Stadium. I really worried all weekend because I didn't know if I should go, if I'd be allowed to stay. Finally I decided I had to try, so I went.

I walked into the Stadium Club and nobody talked to me. The other writers seemed to know I was tainted, and they gave me a wide berth. T.J. walked right past me. Jack turned his back on me. Well stared at me for a long minute, and then he turned away, too. Well, it got to be time to sit down at the tables, and in the rush to find seats, plus my own confusion, I suddenly realized everyone was seated and there was no extra chair for Don Smith. Nobody looked at me.

That was it, I figured. I went back to the coat room and started to put my coat on. I was going to leave. As I did, I had to pass the small corner table where T.J. always sat by himself. He looked up at me.

"Where the hell do you think you're going?" he said.

"Home," I said. "It's clear that nobody wants me around."

"Just a minute, Smith," he said. "Sit down here with me. And you sit with me for the rest of the season. I'm sorry I blew up at you Sunday. You write whatever you want to write. You're a young man with a lot of ability. But do me a favor. Never use the word *quit* when you talk about the Giants. These are professional people, proud people, and nothing hurts a professional more than the word *quitter*."

He was a big man, T.J. Mara. He had a knack for enjoying life. He could go to parties, race tracks, sit in saloons with guys. He was a big, ruddy man; he looked like the stereotyped Irish politician. He always wore a derby hat and those coats with the velvet collars. He and George Halas and George Preston Marshall and Bert Bell made this league work. They sure weren't sophisticated, but they knew promoting.

I think in Jack, T.J. saw his kind of guy. Jack would be able to relax, to walk away from the pressures of the team. He could take a day and go play golf, or he could suddenly decide to go to the track and leave the office at 11 in the morning. But in Well, T.J. saw the kind of a man who would work, who would dedicate himself to the team, who didn't really have many outside interests. I don't think Well can really relax. He's constantly thinking about the team, even today. I think T.J. wished he and Jack were more like Well, but they were different types.

Until the day he died [February 17, 1959] he was close with the team, but he had started to tail off. He left the running of it to the sons, and he had time for the track and for relaxing. I was hired the same year he died, just a few months before, in fact, and I know he had a lot to do with my hiring. I really respected that man. It's a shame some of the things that happened later on had to spoil so much.

When T.J. Mara died, the New York Giants were a fixture in his city. Jack was the team president and Wellington the vice-president. A Fordham pal of Well's, Ray Walsh, was the general manager. T.J.'s grandson, Timmy, was named as the team's secretary-treasurer at the age of 25.

The Giants had played in more championship games than any other NFL team. They made more money than any other NFL team. They had more Hall of Fame members than any other NFL team.

T.J., too, was in the Pro Football Hall of Fame as a charter member. He had seen a $500 investment become a way of life for his sons and for their sons, and he had played an integral role in bringing the NFL through its stormy, shirt-tail beginnings.

3

The First Giants — 1925 - 1929

Although the first five years of the Giants' franchise in the National Football League had some important and satisfying dates, one overriding problem remained—no one, or at least very few, wanted to buy tickets.

One game drew a paid audience of 80 fans, several others resulted in gates under 1,000, and an infrequent crowd of 10,000 was enough to be hailed as a major breakthrough.

For Tim Mara and his sparse but loyal supporters, the first season of 1925 brought with it one spectacular date, one game that convinced the bulky Irishman that his town did indeed have the ability and the desire to make professional football a smash hit.

It was December 6, 1925, and the opposition was George Halas and his Chicago Bears. What kindled the furious demand for tickets was the presence of the Bears' star, the legendary Red Grange.

Grange recently had concluded his college career at the University of Illinois, where he had given new meaning to the term All-American by capturing the imagination of football fans across the country. He was a runner of extraordinary skills, a solidly built, flashy ball-carrier with a flamboyant, roughneck, brawling nature.

Indeed, Grange's name had appeared on the Giants' lists from the day Mara began planning the first roster. When Mara sat down with his general manager, Harry March, and his head coach, Bob Folwell, they decided they needed men whose names and reputations would sell tickets. More important, they determined that one supername was necessary.

"There is only one such player today," said March. "He is Red Grange."

There was, in Mara's mind, no alternative, no second choice who could have approached Grange's crowd appeal. So T.J. packed a bag and set out for the Illinois college town of Urbana, prepared to "spend whatever had to be spent" to secure the signature of Grange on a New York Giant contract.

Unfortunately, he was too late. Grange, expressing disappointment because Mara had offered more money, explained that he had only recently signed to play with the Bears.

Well, not exactly with the Bears. He had signed a contract to play professional football, and the contract he had signed was a personal services agreement with one C.C. "Cash and Carry" Pyle, a youngish movie-house owner from Champaign, Illinois. Pyle then had gone to Halas, showed him the contract, and forged his own deal with the Bears, whereby both Grange and Pyle would receive fat salaries plus a percentage of the game receipts each time Red played for Chicago. Clearly, Grange's athletic powers on the field did not carry over to his reasoning powers off it.

Mara, unsuccessful in his attempt to sign Grange for the Giants, tried the next best move. He located Pyle and Halas and arranged for a game in New York. Both men, envisioning a huge crowd and realizing the prestige of playing the Big City, readily agreed. Pyle, a man motivated by the scent of greenbacks, even suggested that Mara double the ticket prices for this game.

T.J. refused. "Those people who have been attending our games deserve to be treated fairly," he insisted. "I will not hold them up, Red Grange or no Red Grange." It was an attitude that was to live on; the Giants continually tried to treat their fans right, even to the extent of being the last modern-day team to raise ticket prices.

The game was scheduled and publicized, and by the day of the game the Polo Grounds was sold out. The game brought the Giants a unique experience—people were fighting to get inside. Mara, who had optimistically printed 70,000 tickets, saw them sell out in 2 days, and he discovered that their prices (most of them sold for between 50¢ and $2.50) had increased tenfold in the hands of the city's scalpers.

By the time the Fire Department was ordered to lock the gates, more than 74,000 people were jammed inside the old stadium. "It looked like an invasion," Mara recalled. "People had bought ladders and were scaling the walls, and for every one who was caught and ejected, ten more made it in and saw the game for free standing in the aisles."

Thousands more, denied access, stationed themselves on the cliffs and boulders surrounding the Polo Grounds—the stadium was set in a bowl-shaped hollow at Coogan's Bluff— and from all reliable police estimates a crowd of nearly 85,000, both inside and out, saw Red Grange and the Chicago Bears that afternoon.

The Giants lost the game 19-7, but that was not the day's most significant development. The total of the gate receipts was. The event had attracted a record crowd, which had earned the Giants and the Bears the unprecedented sum of $143,000.

Even after paying the exorbitant Pyle-Grange-Halas fees

and after settling with the Polo Grounds employees and his own people, Mara realized a profit of $18,000. The Bears, after paying Grange and Pyle, came away with $56,000.

The game, even though the Giants were beaten, was an athletic success, laced with excitement and drama. The fans were there to see Grange perform his magic, and they rooted for him as much as for the hometown Giants. Red did not disappoint the hero-worshipers, although it took him a while to get into action.

Realizing that the Giants were hell-bent to stop Grange, Joe Sternaman, the Chicago quarterback and an early partner of Halas's, resorted to a commendable strategy. He faked the hand-offs to Grange, and while the Giants gang-tackled the legend, Sternaman kept the ball and ran it himself. This resulted in two Sternaman touchdowns in the first half for a 12-0 Chicago lead; it was not 14-0 because Sternaman missed both extra-point kicks.

The Giants scored in the waning moments of the first half when Jack McBride rushed across for the touchdown. McBride added the extra point to cut Chicago's lead at the intermission to 12-7.

There was plenty of time and more than ample opportunity for New York to win the game in the second half, but the Giants failed to capitalize on their ability to keep Grange at bay. Then Red finally went to work, and the Giants folded. With the Galloping Ghost doing his thing, the Bears scored again and put the game out of reach.

Grange scored that final touchdown not as an offensive player but on defense, at which he also excelled. The Giants, deep in their own territory, had decided on a gamble. They sent in kicker Doc White with instructions to fake a punt and then pass to quarterback Mike Palm, who had been a sprint champion at Penn State. The key to the success of the play was McBride. He was to run a deep pattern down the sideline and thus decoy Grange, who was playing defensive halfback.

It worked, to an extent. The Bears did not expect anything

but a punt, and they dropped back into a deep punt-receiving formation. As expected, Grange stayed with McBride when the latter took off downfield. Sternaman, the punt-rusher, was deposited on his sitting apparatus by Lynn Bomar. But White panicked when the Bears began to rush him, and he did not wait for Palm to get into the open. Instead, he threw a long pass down the sideline to McBride.

McBride never caught the ball. The alert Grange did, and he returned the pass 35 yards for Chicago's final touchdown. The interception and touchdown were enough to wrap up the game, and no further scoring ensued.

Palm defended his call after the game. "I figured it would make no difference if we lost 19-7 or 12-7," he said, "and the play had all possible chances of resulting in a Giant victory."

Regardless of the defeat, the game and its immense crowd gave Mara solace through the next five years, when pro football in New York reached a dismal and, today, inconceivable low point. But Mara was certain of eventual success, and he went so far as to call New York City "the professional football center of the country."

The professional football center of the country soon settled into other diversions, leaving the Giants begging for customers. Chick Wergeles, the team's first publicist, once recapped those lean years: "I can remember touring the city's newspaper offices, and then New York had about a dozen papers. I'd bring a stack of tickets and offer a dozen, two dozen, a hundred, anything the boys wanted. They didn't want any. It was like I was trying to sell dollar bills for two dollars. We'd give away four or five thousand tickets for each game and we couldn't count that many people in the seats. Our highest price ticket was two bucks, while the colleges were getting as high as six, yet they'd pack the stadiums and we couldn't fill it for free."

Wergeles himself became something of an institution in New York before his death in May 1972 at the age of 80. If it had anything to do with sports, Chick promoted it. He did publicity for the two local harness racing tracks, Yonkers and Roosevelt. He worked the college basketball programs at Madison Square Garden. He publicized local boxing events and managed the Goodall Golf Tournament, now defunct but then one of the top spots on the tour. Wergeles managed fighters, notably Beau Jack, and in his later years he had a piece of the Rocky Marciano contract.

Even Wergeles's death was a tribute to New York color. He was found in the parking lot at Yonkers, having collapsed after leaving his car on the way to work that night. An attendant found him, rushed over, and asked, "Mister Wergeles, what's wrong?"

Chick replied, "I'm dying. It's my heart. Reach into my pocket, take two bucks, and play me a 5-2 daily double." Then he died.

When Mara bought the franchise and hired March, he said he was lost as far as what the next step should be. "I asked Harry what do I do next," T.J. once said, "and he told me to leave it to him. I did." Mara did not impose any financial restrictions on March's efforts to put a team together, and so the good doctor was free to sign as many big-name All-American players as he could find.

Among the players on the Giants' first roster were Jim Thorpe, the aging but still legendary Carlisle Tech hero; Joe Alexander, a center from Syracuse; Lynn Bomar, an end from Vanderbilt; Ed McGinley, a tackle from Penn; and Century Milstead, a tackle from Yale. Another All-American player, Walter Koppisch, a runner from Columbia, was purchased from the financially ailing Buffalo Bisons.

March did not stop there. By canvassing All-American lists and by extensive travelling, he turned up "Nasty Bob" Nash and Heinie Benkert of Rutgers, Art Carney of Navy, Jack McBride of Syracuse, Warren "Dutch" Hendrian of Pittsburgh, and Henry "Hinkey" Haines of Penn State. Other original Giants were Al Bednar, Lafayette; Phil White, Okla-

homa; Paul Jappe and Jim Frugonne, Syracuse; Owen
Reynolds, Georgia; Fred Parnell, Colgate; Mike Palm, Penn
State; Henry Nordstrom, Trinity (Connecticut); and Larry
Walbridge, Fordham.

The arrangement with Thorpe was unique in that the
Giants agreed to pay him $200 per half. He was never able to
collect $400 since his legs had long since betrayed his heart
and he could not play much at all.

Thorpe's finish in the East was pathetic. He had played
parts of two games on successive days against the Frankford
(Pennsylvania) Yellow Jackets and had received $400. An old
Indian friend from Carlisle had recently returned from serving with the Moors as an aviator in an uprising against
French rule in North Africa. The friend wanted money, and
Jim promised him a loan. They had dinner together and,
when the friend asked for money again, Thorpe handed him
five dollars. It was too little from the receiver's point of view,
and words became punches. A frantic brawl followed, no
holds barred, and the police had to separate them. Both left
without arrest, but the next day Thorpe's "friend" showed
up with a revolver and looked for Jim all over town. For-
tunately, he could not find him.

The Giants fired Thorpe after that because, according to
Dr. March, "he abused us to other people, claiming we had a
racial hatred for all native Americans. We would have been
glad to keep him for his advertising value, but not the kind of
advertising he was inclined to furnish, through the police
courts."

Unlike today's lengthy and profitable preseason schedules,
the Giants of 1925 had just one exhibition game before their
initial year in the NFL. It was played against Ducky Pond's
All-Stars in New Britain, Connecticut, and the Giants won,
26-0, as McBride and Thorpe each scored two touchdowns in
the first quarter.

The next week the season opened, and the Giants suffered
a shutout defeat 14-0 at the hands of the Providence Steam-

rollers. Both touchdowns came in the second period, the first on a 95-yard kick-off return by Anthony Golembeski, the second on Stretch Garvey's 51-yard return of a blocked New York punt.

Despite the loss, the Giants' starting lineup—Bomar, Parnell, Joe Williams, Joe Alexander, Carney, Milstead, Jappe, Hendrian, Benkert, McBride, and Haines—had been established. A trend toward stingy defense soon was seen.

The next weekend the Giants had their Polo Grounds home opener in a double-header against Frankford. The Giants lost 5-3 and 14-0 before a crowd of 25,000 fans. The large turnout gave Mara a false sense of security since the crowds were not to approach that figure for some time.

Standing at 0-3, the Giants turned it around and won their next seven games. Five of the wins were shutouts, one of them registered against the world-champion Cleveland Rams.

One home game remained, and the Giants were in a $40,000 hole. At that point Mara and March attempted to lure Grange, failed, and instead booked what became their biggest game ever, the December 6 clash between the Bears and the Giants. It salvaged a profit for the season of some $18,000, and the first year ended with the Giants in fourth place in the NFL with an 8-4 record.

After that Bob Folwell retired, and Joe Alexander was named as a playing coach. Much more important developments were about to arise, though, concerning Pyle and Grange. Pyle was so impressed by the 80,000 fans who wanted to see the Giants and the Bears that he decided to make a permanent home for his star in New York. He did not, however, believe he had to join the NFL. Instead, he secured a three-year lease on Yankee Stadium, within sight of the Polo Grounds on the north bank of the Harlem River, named his new team the Yankees, and announced he had joined the NFL.

That was not the case at all. The NFL owners had to approve any new franchises, and since Pyle was invading the

Giants' territory, they particularly had to agree to the intrusion. T.J. Mara, already burdened by an empty stadium and a nearly empty coffer, was not about to grant approval to any competition for the scarce New York football fan. Some of the owners, however, wanted Pyle in the league because of the apparent fan-appeal of Grange. Others backed Mara, realizing that he had been there first, had expended thousands of dollars in an attempt to get the franchise on solid ground, and could supply "sane and responsible" leadership in the all-important New York area.

Pyle was asked to make a presentation, and it was then that his brash and brassy attitude soured even those who had favored his inclusion. "I have the biggest star in football. I have a lease on the biggest stadium in the country. And I am coming into your league whether you like it or not." Like it they did not, and by a unanimous vote Pyle was refused admittance.

He was enraged, and he determined to make good on yet another ultimatum. He had threatened to form his own league if the NFL did not welcome him. Now he set about to organize. Pyle's first step was to lure Folwell out of his premature retirement, and his next step was to raid the Giants' roster for Century Milstead. He put both of them at the head of his team in Philadelphia, the Quakers. He then organized a team in Brooklyn, which made three for New York City, and he hired former Notre Dame All-American Harry Stuhldreher, one of the famed Four Horsemen, as its coach and running star.

Calling his organization the American Football League, Pyle set up teams in Chicago, Boston, Newark, and Rock Island, Illinois. There was a final, desperate plea for peace from Mara and the NFL, and a midnight conference was arranged. But it quickly degenerated into a fearful argument, and according to March, "Mister Pyle's chin narrowly missed a massaging several times."

That ended any hopes for a peaceful settlement of their

differences, and Pyle's AFL began play the following season, 1926. It was an undertaking doomed to defeat, but the war proved costly to both sides. "We had to spend much more money to get players," March said, "and we had to pay them far more than they were worth just to keep them out of Pyle's league."

It was disaster for Pyle, his Yankees, and his league. Five of the seven Sunday games he scheduled for New York had to be played in teeming rain and clutching mud. None of his AFL teams showed a profit, although all of them tried to sign the biggest-name players. Even the Yankees, who had Grange, were box-office failures, and in two months Pyle's league was out of business.

The war exacted a heavy price. The Giants, who had set up shop on Broadway and 103rd Street, were hard pressed to pay the rent for their one-room office. Top-quality players, too, were no longer readily available, although March was able to turn up a few. The best of them were Earl Potteiger of Ursinus, Steve Owen of Phillips College in Oklahoma, Jack Hagerty and George Murtaugh of Georgetown, Glenn Killenger of Penn State, Riley Biggs of Baylor, and Al Nesser of sandlot fame in New York. Bednar, Bomar, Carney, Koppisch, McBride, Parnell, Haines, and White returned.

The 1926 season under coach Alexander was a duplicate of the first. The team finished with an 8-4 record, but they ranked no better than seventh in what was an unwieldy 22-team league. But having driven Pyle out of business, plus having built a winning team, gave Mara unchallenged stature in Eastern professional football.

Yes, Mara continued to lose money, but he had a winning team, and his athletes were far superior to most other teams'. The 1927 season produced the first of many legendary New York Giant teams, as it resulted in Mara's first championship. The record for 1927 under Potteiger, who had replaced Alexander as coach, was 11-1-1. The Giants beat the Chicago Bears for the league championship 13-7. During the season,

New York shut out 11 of its 13 opponents, limited the enemy to a total of 20 points, and scored 172.

Owen was the leader of the rough-and-ready defense. He teamed with Milstead, Indian Joe Guyon, Cal Hubbard, Charlie Corgan, Tut Imlay, Jim Kendricks, Dick Stahlman, and Red Badgro. Many of them, of course, played offense, too. The two-platoon theory that rules today was far too expensive to be considered in 1927.

The Giants were favored to win the championship after their remarkable season. Any team that had been able to register 11 shutouts, still a league record, and manage 6 of them in a row was deemed invincible.

As the championship game progressed, however, the Bears became menacing. They had reacquired the services of Grange (sans Pyle), who had helped them amass an impressive 9-3-2 record. Now the Bears, with Grange and Jack Driscoll running relentlessly, managed a 7-7 tie. Late in the game they drove to the New York 1-yard line and seemed headed for the go-ahead touchdown.

But the Giants held somehow and took over on downs. They had very little chance of moving the ball, and in those days a punt on third down, or even on second down, was commonplace. So when, on second down, the Giants sent Fay Wilson deep into the end zone in punt formation, the Bears were not at all surprised.

The snap of the ball did not go to Wilson. It spiraled into the waiting hands of Hinkey Haines, the blocking back, who threw a forward pass to Corgan. The end was alone, and he made it to the Bears' 42 before being tackled.

From there the Giants marched in for the winning touchdown, setting off a citywide celebration and prompting Mara to call his Giants "the best professional football team in the world."

He was right, but for just one season. In 1928 the team slumped badly, and although they retained many of the 1927 players, they limped in with a 4-7-2 record. There would be no championship, of course, but Mara and his associates became deathly afraid that there would be no team, either.

Never had revenue been as low. The 1928 Giants were a joke on the field, but the gate problem was hardly a joke. Mara lost more than $40,000 that season and began to think about disbanding the team or selling it off. His conviction that professional football and New York were a match kept him involved, but he did effect some changes.

The players, world champions in 1927, had grown spoiled, coddled, self-impressed, and downright lazy. They refused to practice, sulked when criticized, and often played at a level well below their abilities.

It was embarrassing and frustrating, and perhaps a small part of the blame may be found in T.J. Mara's newly imposed economic retrenchment. When the team travelled to Pottsville, Pennsylvania, to open the season, it was not on a first-class Pullman car but on a rented bus. And when the bus broke down in the hills of Pennsylvania in a teeming rainstorm, the players—world champions, mind you—had to get out and push.

They won the game the next day 12-6, but they hardly looked like champions. March berated the players and threatened to cut or trade anyone who failed to respond to his censure with better play.

"It was," said Century Milstead, "the first time we had to realize we were not pampered college boys but hired hands."

The shock treatment worked for a while, and the Giants beat the strong Green Bay Packers the following week 6-0. But it was not to last, as evidenced by a trip the third week of the season to Chicago. Instead of staying in a hotel, the world champions were housed in a local YMCA, and they spent a sleepless night in the cramped, overheated rooms. They lost to the Bears the next day 13-0, and the next week brought a 28-0 defeat at the hands of the Detroit Wolverines.

The Detroit game was the worst defeat a Giant team had ever absorbed, and on the way back to New York March and coach Potteiger sulked and scolded and plotted ways to jolt the team out of its apparent apathy. Back at home the Giants snapped out of their slump. They beat the New York Yankees 10-7, played a scoreless tie with Frankford, and beat Pottsville 13-7. Then they tied Detroit 19-19 after holding a 19-7 lead in the fourth quarter. The tie marked the big slip, the slide into mediocrity. The team lost its next two games, 16-0 to Providence and 7-0 to Stapleton. After that was a game with the Yankees, and when the Giants fell behind 6-0 after the first half, Mara decided to take the responsibility for chastising them on his own.

Angered because one of the stars had arrived late—and so drunk he could not play—T.J. stormed into the dressing room and delivered a pep talk liberally sprinkled with abuse and ridicule.

The situation had gotten out of hand, and dissension soon split the team. A rookie running back, Bruce Caldwell, became the scapegoat in the second half of the game. "You haven't blocked all season when you were supposed to," said a veteran lineman in the huddle, "so we are not going to block for you. We're awfully sorry, but this is pro football. You don't block for us, we don't block for you."

The next three times Caldwell carried he was smothered for embarrassing losses, and the Giants lost the game 19-13. They wrapped up the season with losses to Frankford (7-0) and the Yankees (7-6).

Mara, placing a good share of blame at the feet of March, decided to run the team himself. He fired Potteiger, the coach, and traded or released 18 veterans. It was a spectacular shakeup of what had been a championship team, but the House of Mara was devoid of spirit and drive, and its hot-tempered owner had to fill the vacancies with players who wanted to become stars on a winning team.

The man Mara wanted most was Benny Friedman, a 5-foot-11, 185-pound quarterback from Michigan, who was a forward-passing master in a day when the forward pass was still looked upon by the majority as a novelty.

"We need Friedman," Mara told March. "Spend what you have to spend, but get him." It was an order, but orders cannot always be obeyed. The Detroit Wolverines—who had named their team after the Michigan team in order to impress the All-American Friedman—would not sell or trade. Mara made four offers, each one considerably higher than the last, but Leroy Andrews, the promoter and coach of the team, would not let Benny leave Detroit.

Finally, Mara had no choice—he bought every one of the Detroit players, including Andrews. Friedman received an unheard-of $10,000 salary in a day when the highest-paid stars earned $125 per game, and Andrews was hired as the new head coach.

Friedman was the first man to revolutionize pro football. He was such a prolific and devoted passer that he began throwing on any down, not just on the occasional third down his peers felt was proper for a forward pass. "If it works, why wait until they are expecting it?" he asked Mara. T.J. agreed.

Friedman arrived at the Giants' summer training camp in Asbury Park, New Jersey, with a good idea of what to expect. The Giants were a team with few veterans and even less pride. They had to be bound together, and he was the leader to accomplish the task. He gathered around him the six remaining veterans—Steve Owen, George Murtaugh, Jack Hagerty, Mule Wilson, Tony Plansky, and Dale Moran—and promised them an exciting, winning season if they agreed to play at their best level in each game.

"He made us believers," Owen remembered. "He was a natural leader who came to us with a great reputation, someone we were able to respect right away because he had already proven himself."

An improbable 18 rookies were in training, and although Andrews ran a stern and demanding camp, the players became accustomed to going to Friedman with their problems.

One such incident is worth recounting. Plansky was a 6-foot-1, 220-pound fullback, a natural and gifted athlete. He was the United States decathlon champion, a golfer whose scores stayed fixed in the low 70s, and the fastest man on the Giants. But Plansky was constantly getting hurt. He had broken his leg the previous season as a rookie, and in the first week of the 1929 training camp he was injured again. He couldn't understand how Friedman, who was constantly tackled from all sides during the games, could avoid even minor injuries.

"You just don't know how to play this game," Friedman said.

That stunned Plansky, who considered himself a pro in every sense of the word. "Oh, really? How do you mean that, star?" he countered.

Friedman then launched into a detailed lecture, which he had heard from his coach at Michigan, the famed Fielding Yost, on the proper way not only to tackle but to be tackled. "You should run low, but always with your head up," Friedman told Plansky. "To protect yourself, you must brace your neck. When you're tackled, you should fall in a compact ball with your legs and arms drawn in. That's how to stay away from getting hurt."

Perhaps it was only coincidental, but Plansky spent the entire 1929 season as a healthy player.

Other players had come with Mara's purchase of the Detroit Wolverines, and those who stayed were Les Caywood, Ed "Tiny" Feather, Joe Westoupal, Bob Howard, and Lyle Munn. It was Munn, a rangy end, who was Friedman's favorite target in Detroit and the man he insisted on having with him in New York.

An attempt to land NYU star Ken Strong, a runner-kicker of All-American abilities, fell short—$1,000 short. Mara had instructed Leroy Andrews to offer Strong $4,000, but the hard-headed coach felt it was too much for a rookie. He offered Strong $3,000, an amount Strong rejected. Strong signed with Stapleton, and although he later became a Giant star, Mara never really forgave Andrews for going against instructions.

The Giants regrouped under Andrews and Friedman and turned from a 4-7-2 team to a near-championship 11-1-1 squad. Unfortunately, the only loss was to undefeated Green Bay, and the defeat cost the Giants a shot at the league title.

Despite a scoreless tie with the Orange Athletic Club in the opening game, Mara soon saw the improvement in his new team. Rules in those days prevented a quarterback from throwing from closer than 5 yards behind the line of scrimmage, and the unwieldy, melon-shaped football added to the woes of prospective passers. But nothing could stop Friedman, who performed with a sometimes uncanny skill, throwing long, spiraling bombs downfield as the Giants befuddled opponents and thrilled the fans.

The 0-0 tie with Orange was followed by a 7-0 victory over Providence, and that led to a 19-9 victory over Stapleton before 20,000 customers in the Polo Grounds, the Giants' first-ever opener success. A week later the crowd had increased to 30,000, and New York beat Frankford 32-0.

That game really kindled excitement in New York. After Gerry Snyder dropped a first-quarter pass in the end zone, Friedman hit Moran, Flaherty, and Hagerty for second-period TD passes. Friedman rested on the bench for most of the second half, and the Giants never allowed Frankford to mount even a token threat.

Then in mid-season another development, unrelated to football, threatened the team's well-being. The stock market crashed, and Mara was hurt deeply. He had invested heavily in a far-ranging selection of speculative stock issues, and when the Great Crash hit the nation, signaling the beginning of the decade-long Depression, Mara was faced with the Giants' bills and expenses—and little resources. The Giants, in turn, were faced with the necessity of making money quickly.

The Giants next traveled to Chicago and beat the Bears 26-14 after trailing at halftime 7-6. The secret to the second-half comeback was Benny Friedman's halftime analysis of the situation. Chicago's George Trafton, a defensive center, had pulled out of the line to become an early-day middle line-backer. Then Trafton changed that tactic and began rushing on almost every play. The rush forced Benny to hurry his passes, but it also left the Bears' middle wide open.

When the second half started, Friedman keyed his game plan on Trafton's actions. When Trafton rushed, Benny passed over him. When Trafton held back, Benny handed off or had time to pass long. Benny's plan resulted in three touchdowns in the first ten minutes of the third quarter, two of them going to ends who were free and clear in Trafton's unprotected middle area.

En route home the Giants had a game scheduled in Buffalo on a Tuesday. They won handily 45-6, but in the fourth quarter a Bison player, skidding on a muddy, rain-slicked field, accidentally slashed open Friedman's shin with his cleats. Friedman hobbled off the field, hurt.

His leg sore and badly torn, Friedman visited the team's physician, Dr. Joe Alexander, a former Giant and the team's 1926 head coach. After an examination Alexander determined that Friedman would be able to play, but he prescribed a most unusual solution to keep the ripped shin protected. "Get smart," he told Benny. "Take a copy of *Liberty* magazine and rip it in half. The halves make two perfect shin guards." It worked wonders, and Friedman starred that next weekend as the Giants blanked the Orange Athletic Club 22-0.

The shin guards episode led to a comical confrontation between Friedman and a woman fan after the season. At a dinner party, Benny was approached by the woman with a request for advice. "My son would never play anything as violent as football," she said, "but in soccer he keeps banging up his shins. What do you do to avoid this problem?"

"Madam," Friedman said, "we football players tear *Liberty* magazine in half and use the halves as shin guards," he intoned.

"Thank you," she said, but the look of puzzlement remained on her face. "By the way, Mr. Friedman," she asked, "we don't subscribe to *Liberty*. Do you think *New Yorker* would work?"

Following the victory over Orange, the Giants played a key game with the Bears in the Polo Grounds. Once again, Friedman's aerial mastery came through. The Bears could not solve the riddle of when he would pass and when he would call for a running play. When Benny did pass, he did so with remarkable accuracy, and in the ensuing 34-0 slaughter he completed 12 of 23 attempts for 4 touchdowns ranging from 30 to 55 yards.

With no defeats and just one tie to mar an otherwise perfect record, the Giants found themselves looking up at their next opponent—Green Bay, who also was undefeated. Since this was before there were two divisions in the NFL, all the teams were lumped together, and in order to win the 1929 championship New York had to finish ahead of everyone. In this case *everyone* translated into Green Bay.

"We had no problem with anyone else," Friedman remembered, "but the Packers were special. They were so big, and yet they were so fast, that they almost won their games before they took the field. They won many of them on their reputation."

It would be the Giants' only meeting with the Packers during the season, and it was a game the Giants clearly had to win. Their fate apparently was decided prior to the game. Standing in the center field area of the Polo Grounds during pregame warm-up drills, center Saul Mielznier was staring at the green-and-gold-clad Packers. Finally, he turned to Friedman and said, "Benny, did you think they were that big? Just look at them."

Indeed, the Packers presented a formidable appearance. In

days of 200-pound linemen and 175-pound runners, Green Bay offered a line averaging 220 pounds per man, anchored by former Giant Cal Hubbard, who later became a famous baseball umpire. Hubbard weighed 245 pounds.

Coach Andrews fiddled with the idea of reducing his eight-man defensive line to a six-man alignment, which would give Green Bay perhaps more of an advantage on short runs but which would, on the other hand, enable the Giants to prevent long breakaway gains and equally long and crippling passes.

Ultimately Andrews chose not to change. "We had gotten as far as we had by doing the same things," he said, proving that coaching theory has remained unchanged for fifty years, "and I didn't think we could help ourselves by trying something new and possibly confusing now."

The Packers were by far the superior team, outcharging the Giants' line, outfoxing the Giants' defenders, and outhustling the Giants' proud offensive players. But when Friedman passed to Plansky for a third-quarter touchdown, New York trailed by only 7-6.

Then it all collapsed. On a crucial punting formation, with Green Bay on its own 31-yard line, the Packers gambled. Instead of kicking the ball, Verne Lewellen took the snap and passed to Johnny Blood, who had slipped behind the hard-charging Giant line. Blood took the pass to the New York 43, and 6 plays later fullback Bo Molenda, a teammate of Friedman's when both were Michigan undergraduates, scored to make it 14-6.

Shortly thereafter, in the waning moments of the game, a frantic Friedman pass was intercepted and returned for a touchdown.

"What else could I do but pass?" a disconsolate Friedman asked in the quiet team dressing room. "We had to score quickly, and passing is the only way to do that."

Nevertheless, the Giants were losers. The score was 20-6, and their record had slumped to 6-1-1. They were faced with the necessity of winning their remaining 5 games, and even then coming up short if Green Bay did the same.

The Giants did win their final 5 games, defeating Stapleton, the Chicago Cardinals, the Bears, and Frankford twice. But their worst fears were realized. Green Bay also won its 5 remaining games, and with a 12-0-1 record was better than the 11-1-1 Giants.

So the fire that had started in 1925 had burned at least through the remaining years of that first decade. By the end of the 1929 season, the Giants were established. Perhaps they were not founded on a solid rock base, and undeniably they had financial worries that would escalate before they would abate, but quietly—and sometimes sensationally—they had become part of the New York scene.

As 1930 approached, the team looked ahead at its second decade, not knowing of the many developments that soon would color and affect not only their present but their future.

Through it all, the one constant remained T.J. Mara. His bulldog stubbornness would keep the team going through its rocky years and through some of his own most troubled times.

As Decade Two entered, the prime concern was still financial. The solutions to the problem were varied and often foolish, but the team went on.

GIANTS OF THE TWENTIES

Alexander, John	Tackle	Rutgers	1926
Alexander, Joseph	Guard	Syracuse	1925-27
Allison, Jim	End	Texas A&M	1928
Ashburn, Cliff	Guard	Nebraska	1929
Badgro, Morris (Red)	End	Southern California	1927-35
Bednar, Al	Guard	Lafayette	1925-26
Benkert, Henry	Back	Rutgers	1925
Biggs, Riley	Center	Baylor	1926-27
Bloodgood, Elbert	Back	Nebraska	1928

Bomar, Lynn	End	Vanderbilt	1925-26
Brennan, Matt	Back	Lafayette	1925
Burkhardt, Art	Guard	Rutgers	1928
Caldwell, Bruce	Back	Yale	1928
Campbell, Glen	End	Kansas Teachers	1929-33
Capps, Wilbur	Back	Central Oklahoma	1929
Carney, Art	Guard	Navy	1925-26
Corgan, Charles	End	Arkansas	1927
Eckhardt, Oscar	Back	Texas	1928
Feather, Elwin	Back	Kansas State	1929-30, 1932-33
Flaherty, Ray	End	Gonzaga	1928-35
Friedman, Benny	Quarterback	Michigan	1929-31
Frugonne, Jim	Back	Syracuse	1925
Gallagher, Ed	Tackle	Washington & Jefferson	1928
Garvey, Art	Guard	Notre Dame	1927-28
Grigg, Cecil	Back	Austin	1926
Guyon, Joe	Back	Carlisle	1927
Haggerty, John	Back	Georgetown	1926-30
Haines, Henry	Back	Penn State	1925-28
Harms, Art	Tackle	Vermont	1927
Harris, Oliver	End	Geneva	1926
Harrison, Ed	End	Boston College	1928
Hartzog, Howard	Tackle	Baylor	1928
Hendrian, Warren	Back	Pittsburgh	1925
Henry, Wilbur	Tackle	Washington & Jefferson	1927
Hill, Charles	Back	No College	1926
Hill, John	Back	Amherst	1926
Hogan, Paul	Back	Washington & Jefferson	1926
Howard, Bob	Guard	Marietta	1929-30
Hubbard, Cal	Tackle	Geneva	1927-29, 1936

Imlay, Talma	Back	California	1927
Jappe, Paul	End	Syracuse	1925, 1927-28
Kendricks, Jim	Tackle	Texas A&M	1927
Kenyon, Bill	Back	Georgetown	1925
Killenger, Glenn	Back	Penn State	1926
Koppisch, Walter	Back	Columbia	1925-26
Levy, Harvey	Guard	Syracuse	1928
Lyons, George	Tackle	Kansas State	1929
McBride, John	Back	Syracuse	1925-28, 1932-33
McGinley, Ed	Tackle	Pennsylvania	1925
McMullen, Dan	Guard	Nebraska	1929
Marker, Cliff	Back	Washington State	1927
Mielznier, Saul	Center	Carnegie Tech	1929-30
Milstead, Century	Tackle	Yale	1925, 1927-28
Moran, Dale (Hap)	Back	Carnegie Tech	1928-34
Munn, Lyle	End	Kansas State	1929
Murtaugh, George	Center	Georgetown	1926-32
Myers, Tom	Back	Fordham	1925-26
Nash, Bob	Tackle	Rutgers	1925
Nesser, Al	End	No College	1926-28
Nordstrom, Harry	Guard	Trinity (Connecticut)	1925
Owen, Steve	Tackle	Phillips	1926-36
Owen, William	Tackle	Oklahoma A&M	1929-37
Palm, Mike	Back	Penn State	1925-26
Parnell, Fred	Tackle	Colgate	1925-27
Plansky, Tony	Back	Georgetown	1928-29
Potteiger, Earl	Back	Ursinus	1926-28
Reed, Max	Center	Bucknell	1928
Reynolds, Owen	End	Georgia	1925
Rice, J.	Back	No College	1929

Rooney, Cobb	Back	Colorado	1925
Rosatti, Roman	Tackle	Michigan	1928
Schuette, Paul	Guard	Wisconsin	1928
Sedbrook, Len	Back	Oklahoma City	1929-31
Snyder, Gerry	Back	Maryland	1929
Stahiman, Dick	End	DePaul	1927
Stevens, Ted	Center	Brown	1926
Thorpe, Jim	Back	Carlisle	1925
Tomlin, Tom	Guard	Syracuse	1925
Voss, Walter	End	Detroit	1926
Walbridge, Lyman	Guard	Fordham	1925
Webber, Howard	End	Kansas State	1926
Wesley, Cecil	Center	Alabama	1928
Westoupal, Joe	Center	Nebraska	1929-30
White, Phil	End	Oklahoma	1925-27
Williams, Joe	Guard	Lafayette	1925-26
Wilson, Fay	Back	Texas A&M	1927-32
Wycoff, Doug	Back	Georgia Tech	1927-31

4

Steve Owen, the Renewable Coach

In 1931 Tim Mara fired Leroy Andrews as the head coach of the New York Giants. He needed a new man.

"What I needed was a man's man. What I wanted was a man who could manage other men, a man other men would respect. What I got was even more than I bargained for."

What Tim Mara got was Steve Owen.

There is this about Stout Steve—he was a brute. He was tough and two-fisted and a chewin' man. He was schooled in the bloody tradition of early professional football, and he knew more about the effect of a straight right cross than he did about a power-sweep or a flea-flicker. He was a player first, a Marciano man who would take a smashed nose if it meant getting a chance later to return the blow. He played football with a verve and a determination that put fear into other men, and he found, after he began coaching, that he could teach his players to put that fear into others.

"No doubt he was the toughest man I ever knew," Tim

49

Mara remembered. "He was bigger than most of the players then, and he loved to mix it up. If you liked that kind of football, you just had to love watching Steve in action."

Owen was a man of humor, the basic, direct humor that came from his unique combination of Oklahoma boyhood and New York football. He was a man of strong convictions, too. "If a boy doesn't have the guts to get off the ground and hit back harder than he took, no coach in the world can help him. He'd be better off quilt-sewing."

This, then, was the man Tim Mara chose to salvage his New York Giants, to build them into a championship team, to make his men supermen.

"I remember Steve pretty well," says Frank Gifford, one of the Giant immortals. "He was rough. He wouldn't listen to complaints. But he knew football players, and he knew discipline, and you had to do it his way or you wouldn't do it at all for the Giants."

One day another of the Giant immortals, Hall of Fame safety Emlen Tunnell, found himself in a shouting argument with Steve. "Emlen, you shut your mouth, or it's going to cost you $100," Steve warned.

Tunnell, beyond the point of reason, snapped back, "Go ahead, make it 100."

"Okay, that'll cost you 100," Steve said.

"Make it 200," screamed Tunnell.

"Fine. It's 200," said Steve.

"Don't stop now, you big fake. Make it 300."

"Okay, Emlen."

"You're still a slob. Make it 500."

At this point Owen drew himself up to his considerable height, which was 6-feet-4, and with a booming voice that spoke of his 250 pounds ended the argument.

"Don't be stupid, Emlen," he said. "You don't have that much money, and if it came to a fight I'd kill you."

Emlen laughed. Owen laughed. No fine was ever levied.

Steve Owen came to the Giants from Cleo Springs, Oklahoma, a frontier town on the banks of the Cimarron River.

He was a cowboy in every sense of the word, riding herd on cattle, roping horses, and working as a rigger in such oil-boom towns as Burkburnett and Enid.

Owen was born in Cleo Springs on April 21, 1898, and the fact that he carried with him just a grade-school education was a tribute to his school-teaching mother. "I didn't want even that," he said, "but she made me finish. She made us go to school in a tent she had set up in a neighbor's yard, and at night we all learned to read and write. It wasn't that common, and it kind of set us apart, even from the adults."

At the age of 16 Steve was 6-feet-1 and 220— "but aside from rasslin' we didn't have much time for any sports. My dad was always finding chores for us to do, but he knew I was a good rassler and some nights he'd bring home some old boy who had whupped everybody else and wake me up and make me rassle the man until I finally beat him. I never let him down, but one night it took me more than an hour to throw a fellow and my dad was a little annoyed with me."

When Steve was 18 he entered the Student Army Training Corps at Phillips University in Enid, where he and football conducted their ferocious first meeting. "I was just sittin', mindin' my own business," Steve once recalled, "when the team coach came over to me. His name was Johnny Maulbetsch, and he asked me why I wasn't playin' football. I said it was because I didn't know how. He said he'd teach me and I said okay, but I didn't know what the hell he was talkin' about."

Maulbetsch, an All-American fullback at Michigan in 1914, proceeded to deliver a perfunctory lesson in line play and then set himself up opposite young Owen and hit him. "He kept knockin' me down and I kept gettin' up, wonderin' what I was supposed to do," Steve remembered. "But he wouldn't say nuthin', just keep grinnin' and hittin'. Finally I caught on and knocked him one. He was kinda slow gettin' up, but he had a big grin and he told me I had learned the game."

Owen earned a position as an offensive and defensive

tackle on the Phillips team. In his first game the man across from him smashed him in the face, opening Steve's nose. Wiping off the blood, Steve got back up and said, "Okay, if that's the way you want to play this game, let's go."

Maulbetsch, watching carefully, knew he had a gem. "That big old boy was just knocking everybody down," he said. "I never saw a man get that angry, and I knew he'd be a great player."

In 1922 the Phillips team scored at the incredible rate of a point a minute and went undefeated for the season. The total points scored by the opposition numbered six. After college, however, Steve despaired of being able to play his "favorite game" again. But a wave of roughly organized, semi-pro teams had hit the Southwest, and Steve joined a few of them on barnstorming tours through Texas, Oklahoma, Arkansas, Missouri, and Louisiana. In Kansas City Steve and a team-mate, Dutch Strauss, were hired by the pro team, the Cowboys.

"We played for $50 a game," Steve said, "but pshaw, I'd have played for 5 bucks."

By 1925, though, the Cowboys were broke and stranded in Duluth, Minnesota. Then a wire came from New York. Tim Mara had heard about the team and wanted it to play his Giants in the Polo Grounds. Would they come?

"We all wanted to go," Steve said, "but nobody had any money. So we wired back to Mister Mara and told him that, and he sent us enough expenses for travel. Man, it was terrific. We all bought sandwiches and had a hell of a time on the day coach to New York."

Upon arrival the Cowboys found out that Mara had rented cowboy uniforms for the team. They changed in the Giants' offices and paraded down Broadway before a wild and de-lighted crowd.

The Cowboys lost the game 9-3, but Owen had impressed Bob Folwell, the head coach that first year with the Giants. When the next season was to start Steve reported to Kansas

City, but he was told there was no room for him there. "We've sold you to the New York Giants," reported Leroy Andrews, then coach of the Cowboys. Dr. March, influenced by Folwell, had purchased Owen's contract for $500, a princely sum in 1925 for a football player.

Upon his arrival in New York Steve began disrupting bodies all over the practice field. It was enough of a display to earn him a regular position as a tackle. In 1931 he and Friedman acted as co-coaches on an interim basis after Andrews was fired, or chose to retire. Then in 1932 Steve became the head coach.

Why?

"I wasn't sure then," Tim Mara would say much later, "but he seemed to get along with all the players, and he seemed to take his work seriously. He was the kind you could have a lot of confidence in. Besides, he had worked as a foreman for my coal company [the Harlem River Coal Co.]. He knew how to handle rough customers with tact. He was sincere, honest, and never made any trouble. He always gave his best. Hell, if he didn't know enough football by then to be a coach, he had wasted a lot of time in the game, right?"

It wasn't that easy to get Steve to take the job. Each day for a month Tim and his son Jack would call Owen at the coalyard and ask him for a recommendation. Steve stuck with a man named Guy Chamberlain who had played and coached at Frankford.

"He's a good man," Steve said. "I think I'd like to play for him."

A few days later it was Mara on the telephone again.

"Steve, we've finally made up our minds on a coach," he said.

"Good," Owen said, hoping it was Chamberlain.

Silence.

"Come on," Owen said, "who is it?"

"It's you," said Mara. "I'm tired of buying you new uniforms. You're the coach."

Owen was 34 years old. He was to stay on for 23 years as the team's head coach, and during that time his squads would win 8 championships. His record for the 23 years would be 150-100-17. Most important, during Owen's tenure many of the most famous players in the history of the Giants would be developed, and the Mara family is quick to credit Steve with much of the responsibility.

Included among Owen's more talented players were Mel Hein, Ken Strong, Eddie Danowski, Johnny Dell Isola, Harry Newman, Dale Burnett, Red Badgro, John Cannella, and Leland Shaffer. Once he took the Giants into the 1940s, Steve's stars had names such as Jim Poole, Jim Lee Howell (who would succeed him as head coach), Hank Soar, Johnny Mellus, Willie Walls, Frank Reagan, Chet Gladchuck, George Franck, Lou DeFilippo, Len Younce, and Ward Cuff. Steve's last championship came in 1946, and on that team were Bill Paschal, Joe Sulaitis, Frank Filchock, Jim White, DeWitt Coulter, and Frank Liebel. At the very end of his regime the Giants already had welcomed such modern-day stars as Emlen Tunnell, Frank Gifford, Kyle Rote, Charley Conerly, Al DeRogatis, Arnie Weinmeister, Tom Landry, and Otto Schnellbacher.

For the first two years on the job, Steve was both a coach and a player; in 1934 he retired to the sidelines. "It got plain to me that I wasn't able to play regular any more," he said, "and as the coach, I wanted to see what some of the younger players could do. Besides, if I wasn't doin' the job, I wouldn't have wanted another coach to keep me on the field. Yessir, I guess you could say I fired myself."

But he continued to work out with the players, to partake in scrimmages and practices, and to get down in the dirt to make a point, to employ his experience and considerable skill as a teaching aid.

Then in 1937 he realized it was time to curtail even that. "We were practicin' one day without pads, and Cuff hit me a shot in the thigh. I didn't let anybody see it hurt, but for two days I could hardly walk. My leg got stiff, and I think I had a blood clot or somethin'. Anyway, that was the end of physical contact with younger men. It was a tough decision, but from that day on I was on the bench, and I did all my coachin' from the sidelines."

Owen, who became distinctive for the wad of snuff he always seemed to carry between his lower teeth and his lip—and which caused him to speak with a pronounced burr—soon became equally distinguished as a defensive mastermind.

It was all in his philosophy of the game. "I'd rather win by 3-0 than lose by 43-42," he once said. "If the other team has a great offense, or a superstar athlete, we have to stop him."

Steve's special defenses for such as Sammy Baugh, Sid Luckman, Don Hutson, and later Otto Graham and Ollie Matson, earned him a reputation as a "policeman." It was not a label he enjoyed.

"That makes me sound dull," he said. "I'm not dull as a coach. I'm careful, and I try to be smart. I mean, if we're playin' Washington, we know Baugh is going to throw the ball better than anyone else we've seen throw it all year. Why should we just let him do it? Why should we stay in the same kind of defense we'd use against a team that doesn't throw as well? That's not smart. That doesn't make sense. If there's something to try, I'll try it, if I think it has a chance of workin'. That doesn't make me dull or cautious. Hell, that makes me a gambler, doesn't it?"

Owen's dedication to defense was the hallmark of the Giants. It continued after his retirement, since Jim Lee Howell, who played for him, had been schooled in Steve's philosophy and was fully prepared to take over by the time he assumed the head coaching position.

Owen was the first coach in professional football to exhibit a pronounced desire to kick off at the start of a game rather than receive. Although he drew much criticism for this, he was able to justify it in his own mind—and since he was a man who had very much his own mind, that was his sole consideration. "The teams are usually nervous before a game starts," he said. "They are more prone to make errors. I want us to be able to capitalize on their mistakes. You will find that very often interceptions or fumbles occur on a team's first or second series in a game. Besides, if we can hold them and make them punt, we'll have the ball a hell of a lot closer to midfield than if they kicked off to us and we fielded it at our 20."

Owen was never more effective than when he plotted special defenses for another team's star or flair. Don Hutson, for example, a superb receiver for the Green Bay Packers for a decade, presented unique problems, which Owen, more often than not, was able to solve. When the Giants had to play the Hutson teams, Owen had the defensive halfbacks force Hutson to the outside, toward the sidelines. "We knew we couldn't stop him from catching the ball," Steve explained, "but by catching it near or at the sidelines his chances of breaking away were greatly reduced. We could stop him from scoring touchdowns, even if we couldn't do a thing about his catching passes."

Another classic conception was Owen's style of defending Baugh, Washington's great quarterback. Baugh was yesterday's Joe Namath or Y.A. Tittle or Johnny Unitas. There was no adequate way to stop his passes from finding their targets, and his release time was so quick that rushing him—as today when playing Namath—resulted only in frustration. A rush also would leave gaping areas of the field waiting unprotected for Baugh's receivers.

"We didn't rush him much at all," Owen said. "There was no point in it. We couldn't get that old boy anyway, we just couldn't get to him in time. He got rid of the ball too goddamned fast. So we used some of those rush men to cover his receivers. I think we must have had two or three men covering every one of his receivers. His best pass patterns were short ones, and he'd use three or four of them to move up the field. But if all his men were covered, he couldn't hit those short ones, and he was never much good at throwing very long. He lofted the ball too high, made it too easy to bat down or intercept."

This early theory of defending Baugh came to fruition in 1950 as the famed "Umbrella Defense," a tactic that deserves some explaining because it revolutionized the game of football.

In 1950 Owen had such versatile defensive players as Tom Landry, Emlen Tunnell, Otto Schnellbacher, and Harmon Rowe, four backs with great speed, range, size, and intelligence. That same year Otto Graham at Cleveland had destroyed every known defense with his precision passing. The Browns had won nearly every game since coming over from the defunct All-America Conference, where they were virtually invincible. Now it was up to Owen and his Giants to find a solution.

The Giants had come to use a 6-1-4 defense, which translates into a 6-man front line, 1 roving linebacker, and 4 deep backs. It was effective, but not against Graham.

So the Giants reversed it into a 4-1-6, which with relatively minor adjustments and refinements grew into the 4-3-4 modern defense, which only now is beginning to undergo some changes.

The defensive ends for the Giants, Ray Poole and Jim Duncan, shifted off the line, slid back, and became outside linebackers. This put them in position to cover the Browns' receivers coming out of the backfield. When Poole and Duncan dropped off, the Giants were left with the four-man rushing line of Al DeRogatis, Arnie Weinmeister, Jon Baker, and John Mastrangelo. Poole and Duncan, in effect, joined the deep four to form an "umbrella" pass defense.

In 1950 the Umbrella worked so well that the Giants were able to pin the first shutout ever on Cleveland, a magnificent 6-0 victory in which Graham was held without a completion in the first half. Moreover, Graham threw three first-half interceptions, and for the first time in his career he did not click on a touchdown pass.

The Giants' defense, though, was not perfect. Sometimes there were breakdowns in coverage assignments; other times teams decided to eschew the pass entirely and concentrate on running slant and belly plays into the four-man line. When in 1952 the Pittsburgh Steelers registered a stunning 62-7 victory over the proud, defensive-minded Giants, Owen had no choice but to resort to his well-known sense of humor.

"It's a damned good thing I am known as a genius of defense," he said, "or else the score might have been 100-7."

Owen's sense of the comic was always present. When in 1932 he gathered the team in a town called Magnetic Springs, Ohio, for the first summer training camp after becoming head coach, he addressed the squad for one of his infrequent rallying speeches.

"Men," he said, his chaw of tobacco moving from one cheek to the other, "I've never been one to say a lot, and I'm not going to change that. There are two things I want to say, and then we can get back to football. First, I never thought of myself as being a coach, and I'm surprised Mister Mara did. Second, I am not goin' to expect miracles from you. But I am goin' to expect effort. I want you to hit them harder than they hit you, and the winnin' will come. Anybody who doesn't see things my way is playing for the wrong team."

He continued to coach that way. His way was the only way, although he was always open to suggestions from the players. For example, Eddie Danowski, the gutsy running back from Fordham, once told the quarterback to use a certain play and let Eddie carry wide. The quarterback gave Eddie the ball, and Eddie was slammed down for a 5-yard loss on what was a critical play late in the game.

As the team trudged off the field, Owen was screaming at the quarterback. "What kind of dumb play was that?" he demanded.

He was told that the play was Danowski's and that Eddie had said it came from the bench.

Striding up to Danowski, Owen began to berate him. "But coach," Eddie said, "it's a good play and it will work. I didn't get one block I needed, or I'd have made 20 yards."

Owen thought about it. Then he went to the quarterback and instructed him to use "Danowski's play" the next time the Giants had the ball. Eddie got the block he needed and gained exactly 20 yards.

Danowski was one of Owen's favorites. When Eddie joined the Giants in 1934, having been an All-American runner at Fordham, he brought with him to the Polo Grounds a formidable rooting section. But in his rookie year he didn't log much playing time, and his fans began to chant, "We want Danowski, we want Danowski." Eddie, itching to play, was pleased with this development, hoping it would spur Owen to use him more often. Finally, at a time when the chanting was unusually fervid, Owen called out for Danowski. Eddie quickly stripped his cape and ran up to the coach.

"Eddie," Owen chuckled, "it seems a bunch of your friends are yelling for you over in that section of seats. Go over there and see what they want."

Later on Danowski became the team's quarterback, and he found a young, ambitious halfback much in his mold named Tuffy Leemans.

Signed out of George Washington University, Leemans had been discovered by the young Wellington Mara and quickly became a Giant star. But Tuffy always had a play better than the one Danowski had called, and he'd chatter and plead in the huddle for its use.

Finally, Owen approached Leemans at practice. "I've decided to make you the play-caller," he said. "From now on, you call the play in the huddle."

Leemans, confused and shaken, protested. "But I've got enough to do blocking and running the ball," he said.

"That's what I thought, too," responded Steve. "So from now on you keep your mouth shut in the huddle. I've told Danowski that the next time you ask for a play, you are to call the rest of them for the entire game."

Owen was obsessed with discipline, but he fought a losing battle with his spirited and fiery Giants. Once, however, he was forced to make a stand.

It was 1935, and the Giants were closing in on their third straight Eastern Division championship. Steve noticed many of the men reporting to weekday practices either tardy or tipsy, or both. Steve decided to follow a group of them around town one night, and they hit every spot known to the swinging man of the day.

Owen called a team meeting the next afternoon and upbraided the players for their irresponsible actions. "Not only is it bad enough that you're becoming a bunch of drunks," he said, "but you're goin' to places where there are friends of Mister Mara. It has got to stop."

But it did not, and when he caught one of the players sneaking a keg of beer in through a side door of the hotel where many of them stayed, Steve raided the room and found nearly a dozen Giants in various stages of nonsobriety.

The next day, he issued a rule called "Owen's Order": "Any player found to be drinking hard liquor during the season will be dismissed without a hearing. You men must conduct yourselves like gentlemen, and I will not accept any excuses. Any player who makes himself, the Giants, his coach, and Mister Mara look bad with the public has no place here. I don't plan to give anyone a second chance."

It was enough to discourage even the most reckless curfew-breaker, and the Giants pulled themselves together to win that third consecutive championship with a minimum of further incidents.

Losses always disturbed Owen, and he often found that he had to balance disappointment with humor. In a particularly depressing performance in Detroit one day, as the Giants were absorbing a dismal 38-0 defeat, halfback Leroy Gutowsky missed a block in front of the Giants' bench, stumbled off the field, and booted a bucket of ice water all over the coach. The water froze.

"I didn't know what to do," Gutowsky remarked. "It was so funny I wanted to laugh, but I was afraid to."

Owen considered his plight. His clothes had become encrusted with a sheet of ice. His hair turned icy and hard. Icicles formed on his eyebrows. Finally, he looked at the team, smiled, and said, "You're absolutely right in doing this. If I played for a man who wasn't any smarter than to coach you bunch of jackasses, I'd throw water at him, too."

Steve never had any real difficulty with the sportswriters of the day since most of them had in one way or another partaken of the Mara largesse, but Steve never put much respect or credence in their ability as football experts.

In 1939 the most feared team in the NFL was the Chicago Bears, the Monsters of the Midway. When one particularly vital late-season game with Chicago was due, the New York sportswriters spent the week composing messages of dire fortune for the Men of Mara. The Giants won the game 16-14.

Afterward, Owen called for a press conference in the Giants' locker room. When all the sportswriters were assembled, he proceeded to congratulate them for the part they had played in the victory.

"I've got to thank every one of you for this victory," he grinned. "The Bears really believed all those stories you wrote about how wonderful they were. I could tell by looking at them when they came on the field that they didn't see how they could lose. You boys really convinced 'em. All I had to do to get my men ready was to say, you know, kinda easily, 'I see by the papers that you boys don't have a chance, that you're goin' to get your ears knocked off by the Bears.' It was better than a pep talk, fellas. Thanks a lot."

As Owen's colorful career continued, he began more and more to affect the history and fortunes of the franchise. He went scouting with Well Mara to Mississippi, and they came back with a quarterback named Charley Conerly. Steve developed the Umbrella Defense and saw it become a league force. He guided the development of such players as Leemans and Cuff, Strong and Soar, Paschal and Danowski, Landry and Tunnell.

Perhaps his most satisfying accomplishment, though, was the simple selection of a slip of paper from the hat of league commissioner Bert Bell in 1951.

As was the custom for several years during that period, a bonus pick was awarded to the team that drew a specially marked slip of paper at each draft. The bonus pick was to be used before any other team had a chance to draft a player, and traditionally the choice went to the most coveted athlete available from the country's crop.

In the 1950 college season no player was more coveted than Kyle Rote of Southern Methodist University. The Giants, because of their fine record that year, had no chance to select him in their normal first-round position since they were to draw next to last. Their only hope was to wind up with the bonus pick.

At the annual draft pick that winter, Jack Mara approached the slip-filled hat with his brother Well. Before they picked, however, Jack said, "Well, why don't we let the left-hander pick? He might change our luck."

So Owen, the left-hander, was called up to the head table. He drew a slip from the hat held high above Bert Bell's head and took it down. It had the special mark on it.

"Kyle Rote," yelled Owen. "The Giants have Kyle Rote."

Rote, a 6-foot, 190-pound tailback, would play with the Giants for 11 seasons, first as a running back, then as a flanker. He, along with Conerly and Gifford, was to play a large role in the Giants' incredible run of championships and winning seasons in the 1950s and early 1960s, and he set many club records that stood for years after. Rote caught 301 career passes for 4,808 yards and 52 touchdowns. He scored 312 career points, 54 career touchdowns, and added thousands more yards as an all-purpose running back.

"With Rote and Gifford, I'd put only a few men in the

same class as running backs and receivers," Owen said after he retired and before Ron Johnson, of course, came to New York.

"It was the luckiest thing I ever did, picking that slip of paper and yelling out Kyle's name. I guess after all those years it was time for me to do something right."

Rote was to play for Steve for just three seasons. Then the Giants had to come to one of the toughest decisions in their history of family management.

In 1953 the Giants were 3-9. Most of the blame fell at Owen's feet as one who had refused to change with the times. "Football is a game played down in the dirt," he insisted, "and there's no sense in gettin' fancy about it."

But it was no longer a game played down in the dirt. The new coaches had brought about an evolution. The game had grown increasingly sophisticated. Offenses were complex, and defenses were becoming intricate as a result. The Maras knew a change was necessary, but none of them had the heart to fire Steve. He had coached their team for 23 years, and he had never signed a formal contract. "I never knew how much I'd get paid," he said. "I left that up to Mister Mara. A handshake was good enough for the both of us."

Finally, the decision to replace him was made. The three Maras—Tim, Well, and Jack—summoned Steve to their offices.

Steve had no inkling of what was to transpire. "What's up?" he asked casually, sauntering in and seating himself in a vacant armchair.

"We've decided to replace you with a younger man," said Jack Mara, acting as the family spokesman. "But we hope you'll stay with us as the head of our scouting department. You know, Steve, you've got a place with the Giants as long as you live. I hope you know that."

Owen was bitter and hurt. He stayed on the payroll for more than a year but never once showed up at the team's office or at any of the games. Finally, he broke all ties with the Maras, tried to get back into coaching, and held a handful of jobs, including positions with Baylor University, the Philadelphia Eagles, and the Canadian League.

"It was," recalled Jack Mara, "the most difficult thing I had ever done with the Giants. It hurt me and my father and my brother as much as it hurt Steve. But it had to be done. It was necessary."

After a total of 29 years with the team as a player and coach, Stout Steve Owen was gone. He left, with his passing, memories of glory. He had as much as anyone a hand in the creation of this franchise's golden history and tradition. But he could not tolerate being fired.

"I never thought they'd do that," he once remarked. "It was like being fired by my family, my brothers."

Steve Owen had resisted change too long in a world of professional football that lived by constant change.

Even the Umbrella had sprung a leak.

5

The Second Decade – 1930 - 1939

It could never happen today, but when it did on December 14, 1930, it spurred new interest in professional football in New York City and entrenched the Giants as an integral part of their community.

What happened was a charity game between the Giants and a team of All-Time Notre Dame All-Stars, a roster that called back the memories of legendary Fighting Irish heroes.

In 1930 New York City was agonizing through the first acute throes of the Great Depression. Men who had earned thousands of dollars months before were selling apples in the street for 5 cents. Many more had taken the easier way out via a plummet from a skyscraper window. Even Tim Mara had financial worries, not the least of which was a great personal loss in the stock market plus an action brought against him by the County Trust Company of New York to collect on a $50,000 note he had signed for his friend Al Smith's Presidential campaign. In addition, Mara had pending a suit for $526,812 against his former friend Billy Gibson and heavyweight champion Gene Tunney for promotional services rendered.

Worried that all these financial difficulties might result in his loss of the Giants, T.J. signed over ownership to his sons — 22-year-old Jack and 14-year-old Wellington. The Giants, despite the troubled times, had made some money. They had enjoyed a productive 1930 season, finishing with a 13-4 record that fell just a few percentage points short of beating Green Bay for the NFL championship.

Mara, all too well aware of the effects of the Depression, felt he had to do something to help Mayor Jimmy Walker's Committee on the Unemployed. He responded to a call from Walker to all the city's sports teams, both collegiate and professional, to attempt to raise money. Spurred on by a suggestion from his publicity man, Bill Abbott, Mara proposed a charity game between the Giants and Notre Dame. Walker was wildly enthusiastic, but Notre Dame coach Knute Rockne was cool.

Since the game would have to be played the week after the Giants ended their season, Notre Dame would have to travel from California, where they closed their season against the University of Southern California. The idea of all that travel and back-to-back pressure did not appeal to Rockne. But he understood the value of the game and the notoriety it would bring to Notre Dame. He suggested that he bring in a team of former Notre Dame stars. This time it was Mara who was wildly enthusiastic, for that meant reuniting some of the most storied names in college football before New York City fans, many thousands of whom made up—and still make up—the famed Subway Alumni.

The game, from the day it was announced, created a furor in the city until then rivaled only by the 1925 Red Grange appearance. Somehow local residents found the money to purchase tickets. Their interest was understandable, for the Irish alumni team included the legendary Four Horsemen of

Elmer Layden, Don Miller, Jim Crowley, and Harry Stuhl-dreher, plus other former All-Americans such as Rip Miller, Ed Hunsinger, Adam Walsh, Jack Cannon, Johnny Law, and Joe Bach.

Rockne sent out word to his stars, many of whom had not played football for several years, and they all responded. They gathered in South Bend, Indiana, the Tuesday before the game and were whipped into shape by four days of relentless practice.

"I can remember," Crowley said later, "being stiffer and more sore than in all the years I played regularly lumped together."

The alumni had considerably more than just the semblance of a team by the time they boarded a train and headed for New York. They arrived on a Saturday morning and went directly to the Polo Grounds, where Rockne insisted on a strictly secret practice, with even newspapermen and Mara and the team's secretaries locked out. This accomplished, among other things, an even greater heightening of local interest.

"We have several surprises for the Giants," Rockne said, "and we don't want to spoil any of them."

The game had already sold more than $100,000 worth of tickets. More than 50 still-affluent New Yorkers had donated $100 each for the privilege of a field-level box seat. Charles Stoneham, president of the baseball Giants and owner of the Polo Grounds, had donated the use of the stadium to bring as much cash to charity as possible.

Mayor Walker made great use of the visiting Irish. They were formally welcomed at a ceremony on the steps of City Hall, and Walker was interviewed with Rockne and Mara by three national radio networks. By the day of the game more than fifty thousand customers were in the stadium, alternately singing "Cheer, Cheer for Old Notre Dame" and "The Sidewalks of New York."

Rockne, who would be coaching his last Notre Dame team

(the legendary coach would be killed in an airplane crash before the start of the next season), was less than confident. His bravado aside, he knew what to expect from the New York juggernaut, and he was concerned that his team would not only be beaten but humiliated. Before the game started, Rockne visited with Benny Friedman, who with Steve Owen doubled as coach of the Giants. "Benny," he said after warm pleasantries had been exchanged, "my team thinks it knows a lot about football. I'm afraid the boys have a lot to learn. How about taking it easy on us? I have to go back to Notre Dame, you know."

Friedman promised to do what he could but explained that the Giants were determined to win—and win big.

To his team, Rockne imparted a final bit of strategy. "The Giants are big but slow," he said. "Go out there, score two or three quick touchdowns, and then play defense."

It turned out to be a mismatch of enormous proportions. The Giants were far too big for the Notre Damers to contain. On the first play of the game the 170-pound Law, an Irish lineman, looked over at his adversary, the 240-pound Owen. Blanching, Law turned to referee Tom Thorp: "Can you tell me, sir," he asked, "how much time is left?"

At one point in the game, when Notre Dame was on defense, guard Noble Kizer sidled up to teammate Adam Walsh and said, "I'm going to pull out on this play and take the back on pass defense. Cover for me."

"What?" yelped Walsh, who already had absorbed a fearful beating. "And leave me all alone? Not on your life, or mine."

Sure enough, Kizer pulled out when the ball was snapped— with Walsh right behind him. They kept running until they reached the safety of the Notre Dame bench.

"They weren't scared," cracked Crowley. "They were smart, that's all."

Stuhldreher, speaking candidly some years later, recalled the game. "It wasn't much of a football game," he said.

"Rock had the idea that we could beat the pros, and I guess he sort of got carried away in the pregame publicity. But we did drum up a real good crowd for the game, and that was great . . . except that he got the Giants sore at us. I don't think I'll ever forget the opening kick-off.

"Layden caught the ball and was belted by all 11 Giants. They really whammed him. He staggered to his feet, took a dazed look at me in the huddle, shook his head, and asked, 'Is this game over yet?' "

Later in the game, Stuhldreher remembered, he retreated to the end zone to pass. A lineman named Butch Gibson barreled in and smeared him for a safety. "He really smothered me. But he was a gentleman. He helped scrape the dirt off me and checked for broken bones. 'I want to ask you something,' he said. 'I went to a small school called Grove City. You went to a big one, Notre Dame. Now do you know which one played better football?' I couldn't do anything but agree with him. I was afraid not to for fear I'd get him even angrier. As it was, he got me many more times in the game."

The Giants had their 2-0 lead on Gibson's early safety. By halftime New York led 15-0. Friedman had run for 2 touchdowns, and Notre Dame had been limited to no first downs and not a single yard of net gain.

"I came to New York to help a charity, and I'm getting a lot of embarrassment," Rockne complained to Harry March at halftime. "You're making us look bad. I don't want to go home and be laughed at. Let up on us, will you?"

March was touched by the plea, and Friedman agreed. When the second half began most of the Giants' regulars were on the bench. Only halfback Turtle Campbell remained of the starters, and he promptly intercepted Notre Dame's first pass and returned it for another touchdown and a 22-0 lead. Friedman quickly yanked Campbell, too, and there was no further scoring.

Rockne was bitter. "That was the greatest football machine I ever saw," he said. "I'm just glad we got out alive."

The game drew a total gate receipt of $115,153. When Mara, Rockne, and March went into Stoneham's office to settle up, Rockne had a sour surprise in store. Although he had agreed to travel to New York at his own expense, and although the university had agreed to pay for the team's travel and living costs, the coach submitted a bill of "miscellaneous" expenses that amounted to $5,000.

Mara complained, but Rockne was adamant. Friedman, who was in the office as well, suggested that Tim deduct $15,153 for all expenses and present a check for $100,000 to New York City. But Tim just shook his head, handed Rockne $5,000, and 4 days later handed Mayor Walker a check for $115,153. He had taken $5,000 from the paltry profit of the team, which in 1930 amounted to just $23,000 after expenses and salary.

By and large Mara had reason to be satisfied. His team had played well, had beaten the Notre Dame All-Stars, and had made money. Once more professional football was at a peak of interest in New York City. A decade of success and championship beckoned.

In the 1930s the Giants were to achieve their first sustained level of championship quality. They were to play in five league title games, easily their most productive period till then. But each championship had to be earned without Benny Friedman, who quit, bitter and disappointed, when he was turned down by Tim Mara after asking for part ownership in the team in lieu of a salary for the 1932 season.

Friedman, a budding entrepreneur, saw great and glorious promise in the franchise, and assumed that his greatness on the field plus his deep friendship with Mara would enable him to accomplish more than if he were simply a hired hand.

Mara turned him down, perhaps for the first time giving sign of the fierce family pride and exclusivity the sons would expand upon in later years. "I'm sorry, Benny," Tim said. "You're a good friend and a great quarterback, and I hope you come back to us for years. If you cannot play any longer, we'll always have a place for you here. But this is a family business. The Giants are for my sons."

Friedman was disconsolate; he could not tolerate the rejection. He had thought his value to the team and his prior service warranted special consideration. When he was turned down he quit the Giants and joined the crosstown Brooklyn Dodgers.

The loss of the quarterback, although spectacular in its significance, was soon absorbed. The Giants had been busy signing stars out of college and had turned up Red Badgro, Dale Burnett, Chris Cagle, Shipwreck Kelly, Hap Moran, Ray Flaherty, Len Grant, Ken Strong, Harry Newman, Bill Morgan, Tex Irvin, Hank Reese, Potsy Jones, Butch Gibson, John Cannella, and Bill Owen, Steve's younger brother.

The biggest star of them all—a player who was to become one of the most effective and influential in the history of the team and the league—was almost lost because of the tardiness of the United States Post Office (clearly, some things never change).

The player was Mel Hein, a 6-foot-4, 250-pound All-American center from Washington State University. His undergraduate football career had been a succession of superb games, All-American nominations, and testimonials from the professional scouts, all of whom correctly predicted instant success for him once he was ready to play for pay.

The Giants wanted Hein badly, as did several other teams, and in those days before the player draft the offers were rolling in. Hein, who had met and become friendly with several Giants after Washington State traveled to Philadelphia for a game with Villanova, hoped that New York would send him a contract.

He waited and waited, and despite assurances from Mara that a contract was in the mail, all he received were offers from the Providence and Portsmouth franchises. Telephone calls placed at his expense across the country to New York resulted in further assurances from the Giants that a contract was en route. Nevertheless, nothing showed up at his dormitory mail box, and after a month of anxiety he decided he had no choice but to sign with Providence. The Steamrollers had been contacting him weekly, and he decided that the Giants were giving him nothing but a stall.

So Hein signed the Providence contract, mailed it from Pullman, Washington, and, although disappointed, felt some relief that his professional career was guaranteed.

The night Hein mailed back the Providence contract he had a date to play basketball for Washington State against Gonzaga University, whose coach was Ray Flaherty, a Giant who spent his off-seasons in that capacity. As the teams headed for their dressing rooms at halftime, Flaherty caught up with Hein and congratulated him on signing with the Giants.

"You'll like it in New York," he said, "and we sure can use a player of your talent. How was the contract? How much did you get?"

Hein was stunned. "I never got one," he said. "I never heard from the Giants, so I figured they didn't want me. I signed the Providence contract this afternoon and mailed it back."

Flaherty was incensed. "What a stupid thing to do," he said, meaning not Hein's action but the Giants' delay in mailing out a contract. "I know they were going to offer you $150 a game, plus a bonus for signing."

Now it was Hein's turn to be upset. The contract from the Steamrollers had promised $135 a game, with no bonus.

When Hein told Flaherty the terms of the agreement, Ray offered what turned out to be good advice. "I'll get in touch with the Giants tomorrow," he said. "Meanwhile, you try to get that letter back from the post office. Tear it up and don't do another thing until you hear from me or the team."

Hein ran to a telephone and called the Pullman postmaster, but it was too late. The letter had been dispatched. The postmaster, who should somehow be honored by the Giants, promised to wire ahead to Providence and request the return of the letter, undelivered and unopened.

Remarkably, it worked. The letter was returned three days later. That same day Hein signed with the Giants.

"I had no idea what to expect from New York or pro football," Hein remembers. Now the Supervisor of Officials for the American Conference of the NFL, Hein recalled that first trip east: "I had just married, and we piled into a 1929 Ford and set out for New York. When we got there I had 14 bucks in my pocket, no place to live, and no assurances I'd be able to make the team. It was a chance, of course, but it was worth it. I wanted to play football, and New York seemed to be the most attractive place to do it. As it turned out, I never regretted coming to New York. It led to a long career, and even now I'm still in the game, which is a result of my years with the Giants and the fortune I had to play well and for a long time."

Hein had no need to worry about making the team. He was a two-way player with amazing quickness for his size, with great blocking and tackling ability, and with a knack for pass defense, of all things. In a college game against Idaho he had intercepted eight passes. He had it all—size, quickness, talent, determination, attitude—and yet as a rookie in 1931 he seemed destined to remain on the bench.

The regular Giant center was George Murtaugh, an All-Pro veteran and a formidable opponent for any rookie, even one named Mel Hein. Mel remained inactive through 2 exhibition games—one-sided victories, 32-0 and 53-0—and was on the bench when the Giants won their season opener against Providence. But in the second game, against Portsmouth, Murtaugh was injured.

Steve Owen, himself a rookie head coach, turned to his rookie center and sent him in for his first taste of professional football. The team lost that game, lost the next week to Green Bay, and then went to Chicago to meet the Bears. That was the first NFL game Mel Hein would start.

No one noticed, nor would they have had any way to be aware of it, but that game began one of the most enviable "ironman" careers in the history of the league. By the time Hein retired in 1945 he had established team records for longevity that still stand: 15 consecutive years of service as an active player, and 172 consecutive games played. Only in 1972 did Joe Morrison surpass the total of 172 games played, though not consecutively.

But without a quarterback, the 1931 team floundered. The Giants finished the season with a 6-6-1 record, no better than fifth in the league standings, and the next year the Giants were 4-6-2.

Clearly, fresh blood was in order, but even Tim Mara would not have believed the number of stars the Giants would get in one short year. Some organizational changes made the new players all the more effective.

First of all, the NFL in 1933 would have a new look. George Preston Marshall, the owner of the Boston Redskins (who would move in 1937 and become the Washington Redskins), proposed splitting the league into two divisions, with a championship game to be played between the division champions in December. Despite some determined opposition, the move was approved. The alignment for 1933 showed the Giants, Brooklyn, Boston, Philadelphia, and Pittsburgh in the Eastern Division; the Chicago Bears, Chicago Cards, Portsmouth, Green Bay, and Cincinnati were in the Western Division.

At the same time the Giants were able to acquire not only a new batch of husky linemen such as Bill Morgan, Hank Reese, Tex Irvin, and John Cannella but also quarterback Harry Newman and runner Ken Strong.

It was the beginning of a dynasty.

Two key rule changes, also sponsored by George Marshall, were to play a part in the success of the new Giants. The goal posts were moved up to the goal line from the back line of the end zone (which would make field goals easier to kick), and quarterbacks were allowed to throw from anywhere behind the line of scrimmage. Until then, they could throw only from five yards behind the line of scrimmage.

Marshall's reasoning was sound. "I don't know a thing about technical football," he said, "but I do know what the spectators want, and our game has become dull. They want excitement. Face it, we're in show business and entertainment as well as sports. If people don't buy tickets, we'll have no business at all." Marshall, who in later years faced charges of prejudice because he would not allow blacks to play for his Redskins, had nevertheless changed the face of the professional game, and no team had more reason to be thankful than the Giants.

Despite the Giants' run of good fortune, they still were suffering from Friedman's loss. "What we needed was a quarterback," remembers Well Mara, then a teenager but already deeply involved in the operation of his father's team. "The quarterback we wanted was Newman. He had everything we needed. He could throw and run, he was smart, and he had played at Michigan under Benny Friedman. We knew he was well coached."

To get the "tiny" Newman, who was just 5-feet-8 and 170 pounds, Tim Mara broke a personal precedent and offered him a percentage contract. It was based on attendance, and Newman stood to earn as much as $8,000 for the season if his performances attracted paying customers. Newman accepted, and Mara solved one of his major personnel problems.

Now he was able to go about solving the other—a runner. Five years earlier, when Ken Strong had graduated from NYU, he had chosen to sign with the Staten Island Stapletons rather than with the Giants because coach Leroy Andrews had refused to offer him as much money as Mara had instructed.

Now Strong had become available through a roundabout route. He was as adept at baseball as at football, and he had so impressed the Detroit Tigers after signing with the New

York Yankees and playing minor league ball in Toronto that they acquired him for $40,000 and 5 players. But Strong injured his wrist in a collision with a wall in the Buffalo stadium, and in 1932, when the Tigers sent him to a hospital for a bit of corrective surgery, the doctor removed the wrong wrist bone. Instead of removing the smaller bone, which had been fractured, he took the larger bone and left Strong's wrist far too weak to swing a bat forcefully.

So Strong was done with baseball, and he returned to New York to find that the Stapletons had gone under, no longer able to swim through their annual river of red ink.

Now he had no choice—it was football or nothing, and the Giants, still anxious to sign him, knew they had him at a disadvantage. Mara, always one to capitalize on such situations, offered him no more than what he had originally offered—$250 per game. Strong had no choice but to accept and to rue the day 5 years before when he had spurned Tim Mara for the Staten Island Stapletons.

So the Giants had Hein, Newman, and Strong to lead their 1933 team. "We trained in Pompton Lakes, New Jersey, that summer," Hein recalls. "It was a big boost when Strong joined the club. I had read about him in Grantland Rice's stories and, frankly, I was a little doubtful when he was compared to Ernie Nevers and Bronco Nagurski. But when I saw him in action I became a believer. He was that good."

The 1933 Giants ran away from their rivals in the Eastern Division. They won 11 games and lost only 3, and the closest pursuer was Brooklyn with 5-4-1 record. The New York offense was a unique machine for that time since it scored 233 points. The next highest total was 170 by Green Bay, but the Packers managed just a 5-7-1 record.

In the West the Bears had amassed a 10-2-1 record, and thus the combatants for the first NFL championship game between division kings were decided. It would be the Giants and the Bears, and a paid crowd of 26,000 was on hand in Wrigley Field, Chicago.

Newman, tricky and partial to unusual plays, explained to the officials in advance the unusual plays the Giants would use. In the first quarter he sprang the first surprise play, and but for Hein's impatience it would have resulted in a touchdown.

When Hein snapped the ball to Newman, the quarterback handed it right back to the center, who had become an eligible receiver because a line shift had stationed him at the end of the line. Hein was to walk downfield casually until the blockers could get in front of him. It worked perfectly. Newman carried out his fake, pretended to slip, and was slammed to the ground by the Bears' George Musso.

Meanwhile, Hein's impatience proved to be his undoing. After walking for 12 yards unnoticed and untouched, the sight of all that open acreage got the best of him, and he began to sprint to the end zone. That, of course, was enough to attract attention, and he was tackled by a Bears safety named Carl Brumbaugh on the Chicago 15. The defense stiffened, and the Giants could not score.

Later in the opening period "Automatic" Jack Manders kicked a 16-yard field goal for a 3-0 Chicago lead. In the second period, Manders booted one from the 40, and Chicago had a 6-0 cushion.

But Elvin Richards broke away for a 30-yard run to the Bears' 39, after which Newman passed to Badgro for a touchdown. When Strong converted the Giants took the lead 7-6.

That was the halftime score, but Manders struck for the Bears from the 28 in the third quarter, and Chicago again was in front. Then Newman took New York on a 61-yard thrust that resulted in Max Krause's diving over from the 1. Again Strong converted, and the Giants held a 14-9 lead.

Then the Bears cashed in on some razzle-dazzle plays of their own, including a play in which Nagurski bucked into the line, suddenly straightened up, and threw a jump pass to Bill Karr. It was Chicago's first touchdown, and it gave the

Bears a 16-14 advantage as the third quarter ended.

Another spectacular New York play gave the Giants a 21-16 lead: Strong faked a reverse, drew the Chicago defenders to the sideline, then handed the ball back to Newman and tore for the other side of the field. Newman threw the pass, Strong was all alone in the end zone, and the Giants had dealt an embarrassing blow to Chicago's pride and prospects.

Chicago, however, used one more trick play, and it provided the Bears with the final margin of victory. From the New York 36 Nagurski took the ball and tried his jump pass again. It worked this time, too, as he found Bill Hewitt on the New York 25. As soon as Hewitt caught the ball, he lateraled back to Karr, who sprinted the final 25 yards for a 23-21 Chicago lead.

There was not enough time for the Giants to regroup, and they lost the championship game. But it had been the start of a long string of championships.

There was precious little financial reward for the teams. The winning Bears earned $240.22 each, while the losing Giants settled for $210.34 per man. It was a far cry from later winners' and losers' shares, and it cannot even compare with the Super Bowl shares of $15,000 for each winning player and $7,500 for each loser.

The 1934 season produced another championship team in the Polo Grounds and perhaps the most dramatic championship game on record.

The Giants had once again captured their division title easily, playing to an 8-5 season with Boston the runner-up at 6-6. In the West it was Chicago, and the Bears had captured the imagination of the country by completing the NFL's first undefeated season. They had won all 13 of their games, many by one-sided routs, and they had scored 286 points while surrendering just 86.

So these two teams again met for the NFL crown, this time in New York.

A few new faces had been added to the Giants, most

notably running back-quarterback Eddie Danowski of Fordham, his college teammate, guard-tackle Johnny Dell Isola, end Ike Frankian of St. Mary's, guard Bob Bellinger of Gonzaga (signed at Ray Flaherty's urging), and tiny quarterback Willis Smith of Idaho, a man who weighed just 147 pounds.

Three weeks before the championship game, the Giants had been battered by the Bears. Such key performers as Newman and Badgro had been seriously injured, Newman with three cracked vertebrae in his neck, Badgro with a splintered kneecap. Their availability for the title game was questionable; the evening before the game Strong suffered a sprained ankle, and he, too, was listed as doubtful.

To complicate matters, New York City had been battered by an ice storm, and when morning broke the field was covered with a glaze of ice encouraged by ten-degree weather and howling winds.

Jack Mara, the young president of the team, was the first of the official family to get to the Polo Grounds that morning. When he saw the problems, he phoned coach Owen in the hotel where the team had spent the night.

"It's bad," he said. "You can't even walk without slipping. I don't know what we're going to be able to do."

Owen was distressed. Finding Danowski, who would replace the injured Newman that day, he asked, "Eddie, do you think you can pass to someone sliding downfield on his belly?"

It was then that Flaherty spoke up. "When we played at Gonzaga," he said, "we had ice in a game in 1925 and we beat Montana by wearing basketball shoes. You know, sneakers. They kept slipping, but we were able to hold our footing."

Owen was intrigued, but it was Sunday morning and the chances of finding 30 pairs of sneakers were understandably remote.

"Maybe Abe Cohen can help us," Danowski suggested.

Abe Cohen, it should be explained, was the Giants' self-proclaimed Number-One Fan. He was a tailor, and his only connection with sports was the fact that he made the uniforms for the Manhattan College basketball teams. But that meant he had a key to the school's gym and locker room.

Owen put in a call to Abe, who quickly agreed to try. "I'll get there as soon as I can," he promised. "But it's slow going on the streets today."

The Giants still had no word from Abe when they arrived at the Polo Grounds, and nothing had been heard when the game began.

There was nothing to do but start the game, and after a Strong field goal gave the Giants a 3-0 lead, the bulk and ferocity of the undefeated Bears began to take the expected toll.

Late in the first quarter, with Chicago leading 10-3, a clubhouse boy raced up to Owen. Abe Cohen was on the phone, he said, and he was having trouble finding enough sneakers. What should he do?

"What should he do?" roared Owen. "Tell him he should keep trying. What the hell else is there to do?"

It was halftime, and the Giants were dispirited as they waited for the second half to begin. They were trailing, beaten on every block. They were slipping and sliding, and the Bears seemed less affected than they were by the treacherous footing.

A miracle was needed, and suddenly a miracle happened. In walked little Abe Cohen, laden down with pairs of sneakers tied together by their laces.

"I don't know if it's going to work," he said, "but here they are."

Bill Owen, Steve's brother, was the first to find a pair that fit. He jogged out onto the field and came back moments later with a promising report. "It seems better," he said. "It's pretty good."

Moments later the second half began, and the Giants were now outfitted in basketball shoes.

As the Giants took the field, Bears lineman Walt Kiesling

pointed out to coach Halas, "Look, they're wearing sneakers." The dour Halas shot back, "Good, step on their toes."

Chicago increased its lead to 13-3 on a Manders field goal. There was no further scoring in the third quarter, and, sneakers or no, the Giants seemed doomed.

Then the miracle began to work.

Danowski suddenly found new confidence in the sneakers and in the surer footing they provided, and he began to shower the Chicago secondary with passes to Burnett, Flaherty, Strong, and Frankian. The Giants' momentum could not be stopped, and soon the Fordham rookie had brought the Giants closer with a touchdown pass to Frankian.

Three plays later Danowski handed off to Strong, who hit left tackle, veered off to the sideline, and kept going. His sneakers gripped the slick field while hopeful Chicago tacklers slipped and fell. Brumbaugh was the last Bear with a chance, but he, too, slipped and hit the ground. Strong continued to the end zone, a 40-yard dash, and his touchdown and conversion put the Giants ahead 17-13.

Later Strong added another touchdown on an 11-yard sweep and added the conversion for a 24-13 lead. After the police had cleared the field of delirious fans, the Giants piled on yet another score. This time it was Danowski, who intercepted a Gene Ronzani pass to provide the opportunity. When the Giants' offense lined up, Danowski pitched out to Burnett for a 30-yard gain, then kept the ball twice, scrambling over for the touchdown the second time.

The Giants had scored 27 points in the final quarter, which stands today as an NFL record, and they had dismantled the mighty Bears 30-13, thanks to Abe Cohen and his 30 pairs of sneakers.

"Halas," said Brumbaugh, "told us to step on their toes. Dammit, we couldn't get close enough to even see their feet."

By 1935 the nation was aware of the powerhouse that had been built in New York, and the Giants disappointed no one but their rivals in the Eastern Division as they swept to a third straight championship. They played to a 9-3 record with Brooklyn the runner-up at 5-6-1.

There was a slight alteration in the script, however, as the favored Bears suffered a season-long slump and were able to finish no better than third in the West. Detroit won the division with a 7-3-2 record, closely pursued by the 8-4 Green Bay Packers. So the Giants were to play the Lions for the NFL championship.

Basically, it was the same Giant team that had won the two previous Eastern Division championships. But some new men had been added, men who would soon become stars.

One of them was Tod Goodwin of West Virginia, perhaps the first "flake" to play for the Giants. He did the unexpected. He acted more cocky and arrogant than the veteran All-Pros. At West Virginia, coach Greasy Neale made him wear a sign around his neck that read: I AM COCKY. After a while, sure that his brash young receiver had learned his lesson, he gave him permission to stop wearing the sign.

The next day at practice Goodwin showed up with his own, new sign. It read: I AM STILL COCKY.

With Goodwin came Leland Shaffer from Kansas State and Tony Sarausky from Fordham, both of whom proved to be valuable additions.

But Newman had retired after being turned down on his request for a sizable salary increase, and All-Pro guard Butch Gibson had decided to retire just days before summer training camp opened. In addition, Strong became a long holdout and missed some of training camp before finally coming to terms with Tim Mara. He had hired a lawyer to negotiate with the Giants, and that had so angered Mara that he insisted that his son Jack, then 27 and a first-year lawyer, be present at all meetings.

The loss of Newman was hardly felt as Danowski came into his own as a passer, and Dell Isola, who had wasted on the bench in 1934, suddenly was turned into a guard and ably replaced Gibson.

The highlight of the regular season was a 3-0 victory over the Bears in the Polo Grounds, a game played in sticky mud. The winning field goal had to be kicked three times by Strong since the first two, which were good, were nullified by Giants' offsides penalties.

When the third field goal went through the crossbars there was a wild scuffle for the ball. Who should emerge with it but Tim Mara, his fancy clothes plastered with mud, his shoes ruined, and a big grin on his face as he cradled the sloppy ball to his chest.

"Now I know I'm some kind of crazy Irishman," he said. "I give away hundreds of new footballs every year, and here I am fighting for a muddy one."

That victory signaled the Giants' championship push. They followed the 3-0 success with 4 more victories, 3 by shutout scores, to close out the season. The rookies had performed admirably—Goodwin led the league in receiving with 26 catches for 432 yards; Danowski was first in passing with 57 completions in 113 attempts, and he was sixth in the league in rushing; and Richards, nicknamed "Kink," was second in rushing with 449 yards.

Such heroics were convincing, and the Giants were heavy favorites to beat Detroit and win their second straight league championship. After all, the Lions were 7-3-2, token winners in the West because of Chicago's internal problems.

The Giants were victimized by their own arrogance. They called practice sessions only for the two days prior to the game in Detroit, while the Lions, prodded by coach Potsy Clark, worked out for a week in secret sessions.

"The thing that worries me the most," Clark told a Detroit sportswriter, "is not our passing and running. It's our defense, because we have to stop the Giants' passing and running."

A snowstorm following a heavy rain took care of the New York offense, and the Lions showed enough defense to win the game 26-7. The 15,000 fans at the University of Detroit Stadium were overjoyed, but even the defeat did not overly distress the proud Giants. "Upsets will happen," said Owen. "We were upset. That's all there is to it."

The defeat turned out to be a precursor of two straight years of disappointment. The Giants' mighty machine stalled in 1936 and 1937, finishing third and then second in the Eastern Division and failing to reach another championship game until 1938.

During that time of hibernation, the Giants found new players to replace the fading veterans. The most illustrious of them were Tuffy Leemans, a runner from George Washington; tackles Art Lewis of Ohio University and Jack Haden of Arkansas; center Len Dugan of Wichita; Ed Widseth, an All-American lineman from Minnesota; Ward Cuff, a fullback from Marquette; ends Jim Poole of Mississippi and Jim Lee Howell of Arkansas; guard Tarzan White of Alabama; backs Jim Neill of Texas Tech and Hank Soar of Providence College; and tackle Owen "Ox" Parry of Baylor.

These were young, towering, and talented players. It would be only a matter of time before this new edition of the Giant machine would make its presence felt on the NFL fields.

The 1937 Giants had a near-miss in their attempt to win the Eastern Division championship. They battled all season with the Washington Redskins, and in the next-to-last game of the regular schedule their 13-13 tie with Brooklyn, coming after a 10-0 victory over Green Bay, seemed to lock up the division title.

Indeed, after the tie game someone rushed into the locker room with the word that the Redskins had been beaten by Green Bay 6-0. That caused jubilation, for it meant the Giants had clinched the title, and their season-ending clash with the Redskins would be meaningless.

Moments later the same man crept into the locker room with a stricken look on his face. "I'm sorry, fellows," he said. "The score I gave you was after three quarters. The Redskins won the game 14-6."

Dejection quickly replaced the jubilation, but the Giants were confident of victory the following Sunday. "We may have lost to them early in the season," Owen said for the newspapermen, "but right now we are a much better team. I don't think they are in the same league with us."

There was a budding feud between the teams as well since in voting for the All-Pro team, Owen admitted he had not chosen any of the Redskins stars, who at the time included quarterback Sammy Baugh, runner Cliff Battles, and lineman Turk Edwards.

George Preston Marshall, who had foresaken Boston for the gold of Washington, was an inveterate showman, and he brought 10,000 fans up from the nation's capital. He hired a 55-piece band, dressed it in Indian costumes, and led a Sunday morning parade up Eighth Avenue from Penn Station to the Giants' offices at Columbus Circle.

It was a showman's masterpiece, but the Redskins' success in the entertainment business was not expected to rub off on their football efforts. The burly Giants were 3-2 favorites by game time.

Still, New York had its problems containing the brilliant passing of Baugh and the slither-hipped running of Battles, and midway through the third period the Redskins held a tenuous 21-14 lead. Then it exploded. Baugh completed 11 of 15 passes from that moment to the end of the game. Battles added 165 yards rushing (not including 75 with an intercepted pass), and the Redskins scored 4 crushing touchdowns to win the game and the Eastern Division championship 49-14.

Battles, still bitter and carrying a massive grudge, told New York sportswriters they could blame the defeat "on Owen's big mouth. You can blame it on him because he opened his big mouth and we made him pay for it. Maybe next year he'll put a Redskin or two on his All-Star team. We would not have piled up the score if he hadn't made trouble."

Next year came, and since it was 1938 Owen thought his new team was one season away from reasserting its NFL superiority. The squat, muscular man was wrong. The 1938 Giants were as good as any team he had ever produced.

They had Danowski at quarterback, Leemans and John "Bull" Karcis running the ball, and linemen Howell, Goodwin, Hein, Dell Isola, and Poole. The Giants were a formidable team, and as soon as they could be convinced of that, Owen felt, they would take off. He thought the convincing would take all of the 1938 season. It did not; they began to believe right away.

They crushed almost every opponent en route to an 8-2-1 record, scoring 194 points and allowing just 79, the latter being the lowest figure in the league. They evened their score with Washington, twice beating the Redskins by scores of 10-7 and 36-0. A 28-0 victory over the Cleveland Rams in midseason brought the Giants a 6-2 record and, coupled with a Washington loss to the Bears, gave them undisputed possession of first place.

Again the final game of the season was to pit the Giants and the Redskins, and this clash, set for the Polo Grounds, stirred up the fiercest emotions not only in the team but in the city.

As the Giants entered their dressing room on Monday to begin drills for the Washington game, they were greeted by a huge sign hanging over the door. It read simply: REDSKINS 49, GIANTS 14.

Marshall again invaded the city with more than 10,000 fans, chartering 11 railroad cars for the trip to New York. Again there was a parade up Eighth Avenue, and again Marshall and Tim Mara exchanged thinly disguised unpleasantries.

"George," Tim said, "your stadium holds only 37,000. Where are you going to add extra seats for your championship game?"

Marshall, unaware he was being needled, replied, "Well, we can put up a few thousand out in right field and maybe some temporary seats in both end zones and . . ."

Mara interrupted, "On the other hand, George, you may not have to worry about it at all. You can just take a train up here and pay your way in to see the Giants play. In fact, I'm sure of it."

He had cause to be sure. The Giants devastated the world-champion Redskins 36-0, with Bull Karcis, Danowski, Howell, Leemans, and the line playing their best game of the season.

"I'm not sure I should pick any Redskins for this year's All-Star team either," Owen barbed. "I didn't see anybody good today."

Satisfied with their victory, the Giants prepared to meet the 8-3 Green Bay Packers for the NFL championship. Green Bay, with Cecil Isbell, Don Hutson, Clarke Hinkle, and Arnie Herber, had one of the most electrifying offenses in league history. The Packers had scored 223 points during the regular season and were counted on to score against any team, even the Giants, who owned the most miserly defense in the league.

The Giants, on the other hand, had been injured all season, and at one time or another any six starters might be expected to miss a game or play at much less than full strength. As the day of the championship game dawned, there was much pessimism on the part of the fans. The Packers were 3-2 favorites, and the Giants were acting like losers.

But the team knew that, with all hands healthy, they could stop the Packers, and by Sunday morning they were sure of it. "I spent so much time taping and bandaging them before the game," said the long-time team doctor, Francis Sweeny, "that they looked like mummies when they got ready to put on their uniforms. I don't think I ever saw so tough a team. They were all determined to play, and if some of them had been private patients, I would have sent them to bed or to the hospital."

The Giants, concerned with Green Bay's penchant for springing sudden long gainers, had devised a waiting defense.

Hein, the defensive center, was the key to its success. He did not charge into the Packer backfield but stayed on the line, waiting to see where the play was going. Then he would pursue and make the tackle.

As the game progressed, Green Bay made much yardage, but only on short gains. Owen was concerned, but Hein reassured him. "It's working, coach. I give them short stuff, and Hutson doesn't beat us."

Hutson, the Hall of Fame receiver, had drawn double coverage from the Giant backs plus the attention of Hein. Gradually the strategy began to work. After a blocked punt, the Giants took over on the Green Bay 7. The Packers held, but Cuff kicked a field goal for a 3-0 lead. Then Leemans used a special play put in by Owen, a sliding, against-the-grain slant run, and sliced over for a touchdown. The conversion was missed, but the score was 9-0 for New York.

The teams then traded touchdown passes, Herber hitting Carl Mulleneaux with a 55-yard pass and Danowski finding Hap Barnard, a little-used receiver, for a Giant touchdown. The score was 16-7. Shortly before the end of the half Isbell threw a 66-yard pass to Wayland Becker, and Hinkle pounded over for another Green Bay score to make it 16-14 at the intermission.

Hein had suffered a concussion after being kicked in the head, and Shaffer had broken his leg. Without them, the New Yorkers weakened, and when Green Bay cashed in on a field goal in the third quarter, the Giants trailed for the first time in the game, 17-16.

John Gildea was practically in tears. He had missed the conversion following Leemans' touchdown, and as he recalled, "All I could think of was that my missed kick was going to cost us the title."

But the setback was only temporary. The Giants, forced to pick their best available 11 men and abandon any thoughts of a 2-platoon day, took the ball on their own 34 and began the final drive of the game late in the fourth quarter.

Soar did the bulk of the ball carrying, gaining 13 and 8 yards in his first two carries. But then Danowski was thrown for a loss, and on the next play he made just a single yard. Now it was fourth down and 1 to go on the Green Bay 44.

Danowski called for a line buck by Soar, and the powerful runner came through. He made the first down, and 5 plays later Soar caught the winning touchdown pass from Danowski, a 23-yard play that made Soar, later to become an American League baseball umpire, the hero of New York.

The game was far from over despite New York's 23-17 lead, but the Giants were able to hold the Packers without further scoring. On the last play of the game Herber overshot Hutson, his last-ditch hope to even the score, and the Giants won.

Even the usually phlegmatic Owen was moved to emotional praise. "This is the greatest team I've ever seen," he said. "They were up against it all year, but they wouldn't quit. I'll never forget a single one of them."

The Giants' success was not limited to football heroics. The team realized a then-staggering $200,000 profit, the first real indication that Tim Mara's 1925 gamble was going to pay itself back thousands of times in dividends.

The season had been magnificent, but 1938 ended in tragedy. Tackle Len Grant was killed when struck by lightning on a golf course, and his uniform—number 3—was permanently retired; permanently, that is, until soccer-style place-kicker Pete Gogolak joined the Giants in 1966 and requested the number since he had worn it in Buffalo when he played for the Bills. He was given the uniform only to draw cries of outrage from fans who remembered the 1938 championship team and courageous tackle Len Grant.

When it was time for the Giants to begin summer training in 1939, they were a haughty bunch who felt that no team in the league could challenge their superiority. Surprisingly, they proved to be correct.

Key rookies had been added from the annual player draft, one of them coming equipped with an intriguing story. Wellington Mara, then just a year out of Fordham, had impressed the team owners with his knowledge of the college players worthy of drafting. He impressed them so much that he was put in charge of compiling the master list of 300 names from which all teams would pick.

"The success of the Giants," said Bert Bell, then coach of the Philadelphia Eagles and later the NFL Commissioner, "is in their organization. Tim Mara is a smart businessman, Jack Mara is a great executive, Steve Owen coaches the hell out of them, and then there is that damn little Wellington. Nobody ever beats him on some unknown player who can be a star, and he won't take a well-known player if he feels the man won't produce. The little son-of-a-gun is never wrong."

Few men were as shrewd, either. When Wellington made up that list of 300, a fullback from the University of Arizona named Walt Nielsen was not mentioned. When the teams gathered to conduct the draft the Giants' first selection was Walt Nielsen. "I didn't think I had to put every name on that list," Wellington said.

So Nielsen was one of a handful of prize rookies who reported to the Giants in the summer of 1939, some others being Eddie Miller, a runner from New Mexico A&M, and guard Doug Oldershaw of Santa Barbara. There was a surprise return, too, that of Ken Strong, who had jumped to an unsuccessful American League three years earlier.

Owen had pointed to 1939 as the year the Giants "would again be on top of the league," and he wasn't far wrong. His team burned the Eastern Division and ran off to a 9-1-1 record, with only the rival Redskins offering any sort of pursuit. Washington finished with an 8-2-1 record, one of the losses and the tie coming in their two games with the Giants, including the 9-7 defeat in the final game of the season that cemented the Giants' third straight division championship.

In the West it was Green Bay again with a 9-2 record that

barely bested the Bears' 8-3. The two had hoped for a rematch, Green Bay because it felt the Giants had been lucky in the championship game the previous year, New York because it resented some of the Packers' statements and innuendoes.

But instead of the game being played in Green Bay, the Packers chose to entertain New York in the larger Milwaukee Fair Grounds Stadium (a practice, incidentally, that the Packers still adhere to, playing 3 home games in Milwaukee and 4 in Green Bay each year). It was a cold and windy day, and the rickety stadium was filled to more than capacity. More than 100 sportswriters were perched in a small wooden press box high atop the stadium, a press box that shook and shivered with each gust of wind. The teams had insured the sportswriters for $300,000, just in case.

Unhappily, the Giants collapsed before the onslaught of the fired-up Packers and absorbed the worst defeat in NFL championship game history, losing 27-0. It was a miserable day, and it did not improve even after the Packers had their victory and the record winners' shares of $850 (the Giants, too, earned record losers' shares of $650).

The ill-equipped Milwaukee Stadium did not have facilities for showering or changing, and the Giants, still bloodied and sweaty, had to leave for the airport on a chartered bus. Many were crying on the bus; others sat in numbed silence, and several moaned with the pain of agonizing injuries.

Then a brick flew through a window, tossed by some overzealous Packer backer, and the Giants were sprayed and cut by shards of glass.

"The only thing I regret," said Tim Mara, "is that we didn't lose last week to Washington. Then Marshall and his team would have had to take this beating and this indignity, not us."

The championship game notwithstanding, it had been another banner year at the box office for not only the Giants but the league. Money was beginning to mushroom, the interest in professional football was increasing at a record pace, and as the third decade of the twentieth century came to an end, the Giants were in the most enviable of positions.

They still had most of their championship team members, and even the impending retirements of Danowski, Karcis, Richards, Bill Walls, and Art White would not seriously deplete their strength.

New York had enjoyed its most successful and satisfying decade in professional football. Tim Mara and his two sons were celebrities in the world of sports. Never again would they have to hand out free tickets and plead with friends to come to games. They had the New York Giants, and the New York Giants had a bright and lucrative future.

GIANTS OF THE THIRTIES

Anderson, Winston	End	Colgate	1936
Artman, Corwan	Tackle	Stanford	1931
Badgro, Morris (Red)	End	Southern California	1927-35
Barnard, Charles	End	Edmond State	1938
Barnum, Len	Quarterback	West Virginia Wesleyan	1938-40
Bellinger, Bob	Tackle	Gonzaga	1934-35
Borden, Les	End	Fordham	1935
Bowdoin, Jim	Guard	Alabama	1932
Boyle, Bill	Tackle	No College	1934
Broadstone, Marion	Tackle	Nebraska	1931
Bucklin, Tom	Back	Idaho	1931
Burnett, Dale	Back	Kansas Teachers	1930-39
Cagle, Chris	Back	Army	1930-32
Campbell, Glen	End	Kansas Teachers	1929-33
Cannella, John	Tackle	Fordham	1933-34
Clancy, Stuart	Back	Holy Cross	1933-35
Cole, Pete	Guard	Trinity (Texas)	1937-40

Comstock, Rudy	Guard	Georgetown	1930
Cope, Frank	Tackle	Santa Clara	1938-47
Corzine, Lester	Back	Davis-Elkins	1934-37
Cuff, Ward	Back	Marquette	1937-45
Danowski, Ed	Back	Fordham	1934-41
Davis, Gaines	Guard	Texas Tech	1936
Dell Isola, John	Center	Fordham	1934-40
Dennerlien, Gerry	Tackle	St. Mary's	1937-40
Dubifsky, Maurice	Guard	Georgetown	1932
Dugan, Leonard	Center	Wichita	1936
Dunlap, Bob	Back	Oklahoma	1936
Falaschi, Nello	Back	Santa Clara	1938-41
Feather, Elwin	Back	Kansas State	1929-30, 1932-33
Flaherty, Ray	End	Gonzaga	1928-35
Flenniken, Max	Back	Geneva	1930-31
Frankian, Mal	End	St. Mary's	1934-35
Friedman, Benny	Quarterback	Michigan	1929-31
Galazian, Stan	Center	Villanova	1937-39
Gelatka, Charles	End	Mississippi State	1937-40
Gibson, Denver (Butch)	Guard	Grove City	1930-34
Gildea, John	Back	St. Bonaventure	1938
Goodwin, Tod	End	West Virginia	1935-36
Grant, Len	Tackle	NYU	1930-37
Gutowsky, Leroy	Back	Oklahoma City	1931
Haden, John	Tackle	Arkansas	1936-38
Haggerty, John	Back	Georgetown	1926-30
Hanken, Ray	End	George Washington	1937-38
Hein, Mel	Center	Washington State	1931-45
Hilert, Hal	Back	Oklahoma City	1930
Howard, Bob	Guard	Marietta	1929-30

Howell, Jim Lee	End	Arkansas	1937-42, 1946-48
Hubbard, Cal	Tackle	Geneva	1927-29, 1936
Irvin, Cecil	Tackle	Davis-Elkins	1932-35
Johnson, Larry	Center	Haskell	1936-39
Jones, Tom	Guard	Bucknell	1932-36
Kaplan, Bernie	Guard	W. Maryland	1935-36
Karcis, John	Back	Carnegie Tech	1938-39, 1943
Kelly, John S.	Back	Kentucky	1932
Kerrigan, Tom	Guard	Columbia	1930
Kitzmiller, John	Back	Oregon	1931
Kline, Harry	End	Kansas Teachers	1939-41
Kobrosky, Milt	Back	Trinity (Connecticut)	1937
Leemans, Tuffy	Back	George Washington	1936-43
Lewis, Art	Tackle	Ohio	1936
Lunday, Ken	Center	Arkansas	1937-41, 1946-47
McBride, John	Back	Syracuse	1925-28, 1932-33
Mackerell, John	Back	Davidson	1935
Manton, Taldon	Back	TCU	1936-38
Marsh, Dick	Guard	Oklahoma	1933
Mellus, John	Tackle	Villanova	1938-41
Mielznier, Saul	Center	Carnegie Tech	1929-30
Miller, Ed	Back	New Mexico	1939-40
Mitchell, Grandville	End	Davis-Elkins	1935
Molenda, John	Back	Michigan	1932-35
Moran, Dale (Hap)	Back	Carnegie Tech	1928-34
Morgan, Bill	Tackle	Oregon	1933-36

Mullenaux, Lee	Back	Arizona	1932
Munday, George	Tackle	Kansas Teachers	1931-32
Murtaugh, George	Center	Georgetown	1926-32
Neill, Jim	Back	Texas Tech	1937
Newman, Harry	Quarterback	Michigan	1933-35
Norby, John	Back	Idaho	1934
Oldershaw, Doug	Guard	Santa Barbara	1939-41
Owen, Alton	Back	Mercer	1939-41
Owen, Steve	Tackle	Phillips	1926-36
Owen, William	Tackle	Oklahoma A&M	1929-37
Parry, Owen	Tackle	Baylor	1937-39
Phillips, Ewell	Guard	Oklahoma Baptist	1936-37
Poole, Jim	End	Mississippi	1937-41, 1946
Powell, Dick	End	Davis-Elkins	1931
Quatse, Jess	Tackle	Pittsburgh	1935
Reese, Henry	Center	Temple	1933-34
Rhenquist, Milt	Center	Bethany	1931
Richards, Elvin	Back	Simpson	1933-39
Rose, Ray	End	Tennessee	1936
Rossell, Fay	Back	Lafayette	1933
Rovinski, Tony	Back	Holy Cross	1933
Sarausky, Tony	Back	Fordham	1935-37
Sark, Harvey	Guard	Phillips	1931
Satenstein, Bernie	Guard	NYU	1933
Schwab, Ray	Back	Oklahoma City	1931
Sedbrook, Len	Back	Oklahoma City	1929-31
Shaffer, Leland	Quarterback	Kansas State	1935-43, 1945
Singer, Walter	End	Syracuse	1935-37
Smith, Richard	Guard	Notre Dame	1930-31

Smith, Willis	Back	Idaho	1934-35
Soar, Hank	Back	Providence	1937-44, 1946
Stafford, Harrison	Back	Texas	1934
Stein, Sam	End	No College	1931
Strong, Ken	Back	NYU	1933-35, 1939-47
Tarrant, Bob	End	Kansas State	1936
Tuttle, Orville	Guard	Oklahoma City	1937-41
Tyler, Pete	Back	Hardin-Simmons	1938
Vokaty, Otto	Back	Heidelberg	1932
Walls, Bill	End	TCU	1937-43
Westoupal, Joe	Center	Nebraska	1929-30
White, Art	Guard	Alabama	1937-39, 1945
Widseth, Ed	Tackle	Minnesota	1937-40
Wilberg, Oscar	Back	Nebraska Wesleyan	1930
Wilson, Fay	Back	Texas A&M	1927-32
Wolfe, Hugh	Back	Texas	1938
Wycoff, Doug	Back	Georgia Tech	1927-31
Zapustas, Joe	End	Fordham	1933
Zyntell, Jim	Guard	Holy Cross	1933

6

Jack and Well

On June 29, 1965, the New York Giants were in the midst of conducting a three-day tryout camp for rookies at Fordham University in the Bronx. It was a warm, almost sultry afternoon, feeling more like late August than late June. Allie Sherman, the head coach, was on the field putting the hopeful youngsters through basic drills, agility tests, and simple calisthenics. It was a wondrous day to be outdoors, and the warm sun baked deep into the glistening bodies of the athletes and the somewhat less aesthetic forms of the coaches, sportswriters, and fans.

Then the word came, and a chill changed the day of pleasant diversion into a night of sorrow. Jack Mara had died at the age of 57 in New York's Memorial Hospital.

In several ways it was the end of an era for the Giants.

Jack Mara, born in 1908, was 17 when his father took that wild gamble and purchased a National Football League franchise for New York City in 1925. He attended Fordham

University and graduated in 1930. Shortly thereafter he earned a law degree, also through Fordham, but he never practiced law. Instead, he plunged into the operation of the family business, the Giants.

"Jack was always the businessman in the family," his father used to say. "He was very good with columns of numbers, he had a good business head, and he seemed much more interested in the team's financial dealings than with the players. But he was a great fan, too."

In 1930, afraid that increasing debts, losses suffered in the stock market, and pending law suits and legal actions would result in his loss of the team, Tim Mara signed over ownership of the club to his sons. Jack was 22, Wellington 14. In 1936 Tim made Jack president of the team and reserved a spot for himself as chairman of the board.

Even as a youth Jack never involved himself in the acquisition of players and the on-the-field efforts of the Giants, preferring to leave that to his father and younger brother, both of whom showed a flair for team management. He contented himself with the role of executive, a position he handled admirably. As T.J. once remarked, "Well was much more interested in the team than Jack. Jack wanted to see the ledgers, the balance sheets. He hated to spend money, just as I did."

Jack became the quiet man who intentionally shied away from publicity or exposure. "I'm just a businessman," he said. "I let Well run the team and talk to the sportswriters. I'm only doing what I feel I can do best. If I tried to mix in elsewhere, I might hurt the team. And the team is the family. I'm just doing my job."

Jack, however, became enamored of several players. He took pleasure in watching them arrive as fresh-faced college boys and leave years later as mature and accomplished men. He once admitted that his favorite Giants included quarterback Charley Conerly, running back Frank Gifford, and safety Emlen Tunnell. When Gifford retired from football to begin a television career, Jack was moved to comment, "Our loss is CBS's gain. There is no finer young man in this field than Frank."

When word of Jack's death was announced on the field at Fordham, Emlen Tunnell sat down on the grass and sobbed. He had been the Giants' first black player, and just that year he had become the league's first black coach, joining the team's staff as an assistant under Sherman in charge of the defensive backfield.

Charley Conerly made the trip up from his native Mississippi to attend the funeral, and even this grizzled old Marine, who became famous as the first "Marlboro man" on posters and television commercials, found himself in tears at the St. Ignatius Loyola Church on Park Avenue in New York City.

Jack's contributions to the team transcended the Giants and became services to the entire league. He was instrumental, for instance, in establishing the first really lucrative television contract, which provided for equal payment to each team. Prior to that, teams were free to negotiate on their own, and some of the less desirable or successful franchise cities found themselves shut out or forced to sign minimal contracts. Through the efforts of the committee of which Jack was a member, the first league contract provided for a guaranteed one million dollars for each team.

Jack, who befriended sportswriters and players alike, was a fun-loving man. Unlike Wellington, he found no difficulty at all in separating his football life from his social life, perhaps for the simple reason that Well was so obsessed with the Giants that Jack knew the team was in capable hands.

Jack spent his summers at the family resort in Spring Lake, New Jersey, a seaside community, and was as devoted to golf as he was to the Giants. "I'm not a football player, so I play golf instead," he joked. "I wish I was as good at it as the Giants are at football."

Golf for Jack Mara was an almost year-round avocation. He was a member of the exclusive Winged Foot Country Club

in Mamaroneck, New York, and each year he eagerly anticipated the arrival of the spring thaw so that he could be back
on the fairways slamming away at the little white ball. "Golf
relaxes me," he said. "When I go to the office, I get all
wound up in the business. Even if we're making money, I
find myself worrying. So I get out. Mostly, I get out to the
golf course. But sometimes I get myself to the race track.
Either way, I can relax away from the office."

In the 1930s Jack was part of a three-man group (the other
two being George Halas of the Chicago Bears and George
Preston Marshall of the Washington Redskins) that persuaded
the other owners to stick with the league. Many had wanted
to disband because of huge losses over a succession of lean
years. During World War II, there was a motion to suspend
operations for the duration of hostilities, but Jack again
urged that the teams continue to play their schedules, finding whatever players "or civilians" were available.

A strong sense of humor motivated much of what Jack
did. I can remember writing a particularly controversial story
in 1961 when the Giants first obtained quarterback Y.A.
Tittle and then were faced with the sticky dilemma of
deciding whether to play him or Conerly.

It was my contention that Tittle moved the team more
effectively, that Conerly's years of service did not require any
further allegiance in the face of a more efficient performer,
and that it might be time to sit Charley on the bench.

The article raised the hackles of the Giants, and since it
appeared on a Tuesday, it brought me face-to-face with the
team. Tuesdays were, and still are, press luncheon days during the football season.

When I arrived at Yankee Stadium a few of the other men
covering the team took me aside and told me, "Well is really
ticked off, and Allie is ready to strangle you." I was understandably upset, being 21 and still a bit awed of such men.

Well refused to speak to me; he turned his back abruptly
when I appeared, but not before offering me a stare that

NEW YORK FOOTBALL GIANTS
vs.
PHILADELPHIA EAGLES

HARRY NEWMAN

OLO GROUNDS   OCTOBER 15, 1933

Red Grange, the Galloping Ghost, helped bring pro football to New York and proved that Timothy Mara's franchise could be successful. Fans jammed the Polo Grounds to see the Giants try to stop Grange.

University of Illinois

The early Giants sometimes couldn't even give their tickets away. The addition of Jim Thorpe to the roster eased their troubles for a while. While at Carlisle, Thorpe had gained 1,869 yards rushing in 10 games.

(Left) Mel Hein came to the Giants from Washington State and became a star at center. (*Below*) Stout Steve Owen (55), his brother Bill, and Len Grant of the 1930 Giants. Steve believed that football is played down in the dirt, and his training method was simple—hit them harder than they hit you.

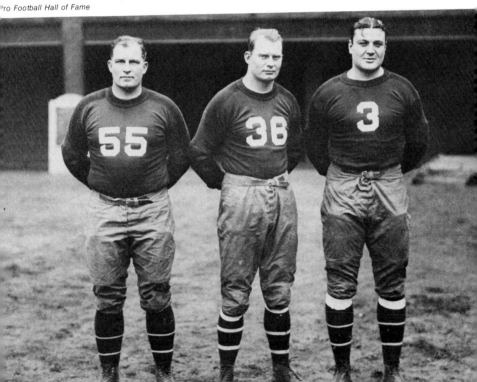

Cliff Montgomery (with football) and Benny Friedman in 1934.

Pro Football Hall of Fame

(Left) Trainer Gus Mauch pours Eddie Danowski a cup of pineapple juice—a forerunner of Gatorade? (Below) The Giants faced a severe crisis when Frank Filchock, shown here in action, became involved in a gambling scandal.

Pro Football Hall of Fame

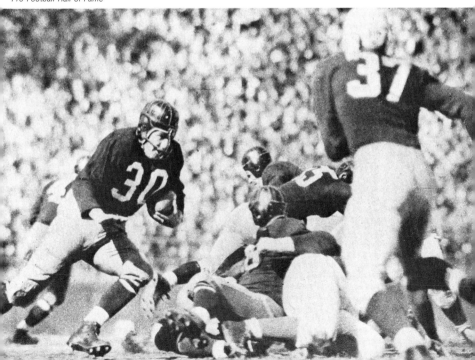

Steve Owen, Giants' coach for 23 years and inventor of the Umbrella Defense.

(Above) Jim Lee Howell and Vince Lombardi, two superb managers of men, chalk up their strategy in 1958. (Left) Allie Sherman, the genius of the T-formation, beams at club president Jack Mara's news of his new 5-year contract as head coach in 1963.

(Above) NFL All-Star quarterback Y. A. Tittle (left) in conference with NFL Coach of the Year Allie Sherman. (Below) Head coach Alex Webster (left) and team owner Wellington Mara become two of the first interviewees of Sam Huff, making the transition from linebacker to broadcaster in 1972.

Timothy J. Mara, the founder.

(Opposite page) Bob McChesney (88) and two Washington defenders chase the ball in a 1950 Giants-Redskins encounter. (Above) Tittle goes to the air against Washington in 1964. (Below) Frank Gifford, pursued by Cleveland tacklers, slips out of bounds in a 1956 contest.

(Right) Pat Summerall boots a field goal through the blizzard for an upset against Cleveland in 1958. (Below) The awesome Giants defense—Huff (70), Grier (76), and Modzelewski (77)— maul Pittsburgh's Tom Tracy.

Opposing linemen found this a rare sight—
a Rosy Grier smile.

The League-leading Giants trot out for a practice in 1961. Left to right: end Kyle Rote, quarterback Y.A. Tittle, halfback Alex Webster, and end Del Shofner.

Charley Conerly and Y.A. Tittle, gentlemanly competitors for first-string quarterback, strike an action pose shortly before the 1961 championship game with Green Bay.

Frank Gifford puts on one of the uncanny moves that made him a star.

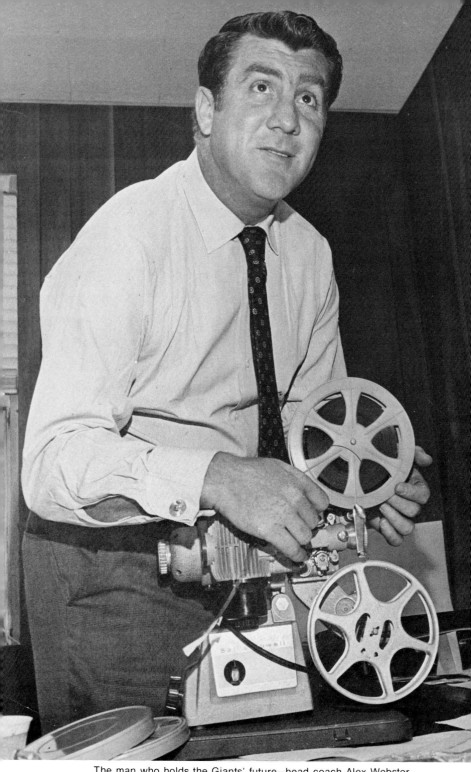

The man who holds the Giants' future—head coach Alex Webster

would have melted rock. Sherman, his face red and his extremities visibly trembling, told me in no uncertain terms what a cad I was, how I had irreparably damaged the morale of the team, and what an ignorant theme I had pursued in my story.

Then I bumped into Jack. He smiled at me, chuckled deep in his chest, and said, "Kid, you've really done it, haven't you? Well wouldn't even talk to me this morning. But keep fighting. I don't think you're right, either, but I've learned not to feud with writers."

Once, at the Pro Football Hall of Fame in Canton, Ohio, a man found Jack standing before the bust of his father. "Just think," Jack said. "My son and all of Well's kids will be able to come out here and know their grandfather was so famous. I hope they'll be able to remember me with the same respect. I never felt myself equal to dad."

Jack Mara, along with the late Dan Reeves of the Los Angeles Rams, was prominent in pushing the young and relatively unknown Pete Rozelle for the position of NFL Commissioner when Bert Bell died in 1959.

"He's young, but he's a good man," Jack said. "Rozelle is my man, and if you are with me, he's your man, too."

Upon Jack's death Rozelle delivered the following message to the Giants: "Like his father Tim before him, Jack represented the fine family tradition and spirit that carried the league through its difficult, formative years. . . . I feel a deep personal loss, but all of sports has lost one whose extremely high principles and ethics gave it immeasurable dignity."

As a man possessed by the ideals of tradition, loyalty, and friendship, Jack often admitted that his most difficult act as president of the Giants was the day in 1953 when he had to fire Steve Owen as coach. Owen had been the team's head coach since Jack was a teenager. Owen had been a close family friend, perhaps old Tim's closest friend in the game, and Jack stuck with Steve long after most men would have made the change.

A few days before he would dismiss Owen, Jack told a friend the news and begged him to keep it confidential. "My God, Jack," said the friend, "I feel terrible."

Jack nodded. "But how do you think I feel?" he countered. "Steve Owen is my friend, almost a part of the family." It was his lifelong regret that Owen left the team bitter and disappointed; but shortly before Steve's death, when Owen was in financial difficulties, Jack hired him back as a scout. Owen died before he could begin to fill the position, and later, when Jack exposed his emotions to a friend, he said, "I'm glad Steve was back where he belonged before the end. He was never meant to leave the Giants."

During his career with the Giants, Jack saw their value increase from the paltry $500 investment to considerably more than $10 million, and in his mind this was the monument he admired most. "We've made it work," he once said. "My father and Well and myself have devoted our lives to this team, and it is very satisfying to see that it has been all worthwhile."

A group that Jack never really believed in but that gave him boundless satisfaction anyway was the large "Giant family." In the finest tradition of the Notre Dame Subway Alumni, hundreds of thousands of people were able to relate to the Giants, were able to find release and enjoyment and identification with Jack's team.

The pews were filled with the famous at Jack's funeral. Rozelle and Halas and Bishop Sheen and hundreds of former players were in seats of honor. But a man remembers glancing at the back of the church and being surprised at the throng of shirtsleeved citizens who had walked in and stood, alone and anonymous, because they felt they owed something to Jack Mara.

Jack's charity, as with so many other genuine philanthropists, was conducted quietly. He wished for anonymity as much as he wished to help. At Christmas he would send money to the Angel Guardian Home and the Sisters of Mercy for gifts to be distributed among the homeless orphans of the city. Hundreds of former players who had failed to make it when their careers had finished received money from Jack Mara. Several were given jobs, though Jack never cared if they worked at the job; he simply wanted to spare them the humiliation of charity.

What got Jack was quick-spreading cancer, mercifully fast in its dreadful work. It was just a matter of months from the time he found out until the day he died, but his religion and his strength of character prevented even such a horror from changing him.

While visiting a friend two months before his death, Jack quietly revealed that his doctor had found a tumor in his abdomen and that he would have to undergo surgery. "I have straightened out my financial affairs," he said, "and I am at peace with my God. There's nothing more I can do but resign myself to whatever God wishes."

Jack apparently kept the condition to himself longer than he should have, withholding the information from his family and his most trusted employees. But eventually it had to come out. Don Smith, who was hired by Jack as the team's publicity man in 1959 and stayed through 1971, when he was fired by Jack's puzzling son, Timmy, remembers clearly the day he first realized his boss was seriously ill:

> We had our offices on the sixteenth floor of the Coliseum building, and they were no longer satisfactory. We needed more room, and there was a suite available on the eighteenth floor. Jack arranged for the rental lease and then put me in charge of laying out the offices and designing the rooms. This was, I guess, in March of 1965. By April or May we were ready, and we decided to furnish the new office only after visiting other offices and getting ideas. So this day in May four of us started making the rounds—Jack, Timmy, [general manager] Ray Walsh, and myself. Each place we went, Jack had to excuse himself and go to the men's room. Each time he came out, he

looked pale and concerned. I had never seen him that way.

Eventually, when we were alone for a minute, he said, "This thing has me really worried. I don't know if I'm going to beat it." It was the first inkling I had that something was really wrong, but the man never quit. He forced himself to keep going until the day he had to go to the hospital. Even then, when he knew he wouldn't be coming back, he insisted on telling everyone he'd see them in a couple of weeks.

Jack had married in 1934 to Helen Phelan, the daughter of Brigadier General John J. Phelan, former chairman of the New York State Athletic Commission. That same year, on August 6, a son was born, Timothy J. Timmy became a source of worry for Jack in later years. A headstrong youth, he found himself in numerous scrapes and difficulties, some of which might have become even more serious had he not had the reputation of the Giants and the Mara family to fall back on.

Jack was overjoyed when Timmy married, feeling that marriage would be a settling influence on his tempestuous lifestyle. But as the marriage began to break up, Jack's concern returned and his anxiety deepened, though he would never speak of such things publicly. Timmy was divorced after his father's death and was remarried in 1972. That marriage is still holding together, and perhaps now, at the age of 39, Timmy will begin to assume his obligations. He is obviously second in line as head of the Mara sports family since he is older than any of Wellington's children, of which there are 10.

Today Timmy is vice-president and treasurer of the team, and he has begun to realize that he inherited responsibilities as well as financial freedom and the opportunity to enjoy luxuries and privileges few men have been fortunate enough to experience.

Timmy is not a particularly warm man, choosing to

remain somewhat cool and aloof. At first impression he is close to the image of a young eighteenth-century aristocrat, free to wander about and partake of anything that might strike his fancy. But the older members of the official family, many of whom have had to bear the burden of Timmy's earlier escapades, now insist that he has "come around" and has evidenced flashes of his father's administrative abilities. A complete assumption of his rightful duties, in addition, would remove a great amount of stress from the mind of his uncle, who, approaching 60, might begin to consider a slowing-down should there be a member of the family ready to take on additional authority.

The passing of Jack Mara brought great sadness and a large measure of confusion to the team's front office. Wellington, who had avoided a total immersion in the business end of the team, was faced with doing it all. One of his first acts, shortly after his brother's burial, was to extend Sherman's contract for an unprecedented ten years, explaining that "what I wanted to establish most of all was permanence, in an attempt to lessen the confusion and sense of loss we all felt."

It proved to be a costly error in judgment, for 4 years later, when Sherman was abruptly and somewhat callously fired, Wellington was forced to continue to pay the $50,000 annual salary for 6 more years even though Sherman was no longer a part of the team.

Less than a year after Jack's death, the John V. Mara Memorial Cancer Research Unit was dedicated at St. Vincent's Hospital in New York by Francis Cardinal Spellman. All funds raised since then have been allocated to cancer research, and the New York Giants have been by far the most generous and consistent contributors.

Wellington Mara, then 50 years old, was suddenly the only Mara left to run the Giants. It was a traumatic experience.

Little Well, who as a boy was dubbed "The Duke of Mara" by his father and other owners in the league and who had the honor of seeing the official NFL football named "The Duke," had never been far from the Giants since they became family property in 1925. He was then nine years old.

His experiences with the team blended into the act of the boss's son "working his way up the ladder." He was a ballboy for the team during its summer training camps, and one day he was inadvertently given a crushing body block by Mel Hein, which resulted in a black eye and several painfully sore bruises and sprains. "I got too close to him when he was snapping the ball," Well remembers, smiling at the thought. "I would get the loose balls on the field and bring them to him, and each time he snapped he'd run through a fake blocking drill. Well, he didn't see me and just charged off the line with his elbows and fists churning. Boy, did he catch me. It might have been the first time Mel blind-sided anybody."

From the beginning Well was dedicated to an extreme. He quickly developed his talent for scouting and finding players, and he has continued to involve himself in the workings of the team today, going so far as to take part in drills, clad in a gray sweatsuit, and to make decisions normally reserved for the coaching staff such as trades, draft selections, and game strategy.

To this day Well Mara stations himself in a private booth high atop the stadium and, equipped with a long-lens Polaroid camera and a supply of weighted white socks, snaps pictures of formations as they develop during a game. Placing the photos in the socks, he drops them to the Giants' bench area for the coaches to study.

Wellington attended Fordham University, though he did not continue his education as did Jack; Well was content with a B.A. earned in 1937. He was interested only in joining the Giants, and a law degree or any other postgraduate project would have stood in his way.

Incidentally, one of Well's classmates at Fordham was Vince Lombardi, who later became an assistant coach for the Giants prior to starting his storied career as head coach and general manager of the Green Bay Packers. Mara often tried to lure Lombardi back to New York as the Giants' head coach, but contracts stood in the way of these two friends, and their careers would never again merge after 1958.

Wellington Mara was born on August 14, 1916, and attended Loyola High School in New York City before he went on to Fordham. But long before Fordham—indeed, while he was still a prepper—he had started compiling scouting reports, player draft lists, and football strategies. There was some thought in the middle 1950s that after Steve Owen was fired Well himself might assume the coaching position. That, however, would not have been in keeping with the family image, and as much as he might have wanted to take the step, his sense of propriety prevented it.

Well is an enigma. He is at once friendly and secretive, affable and cool, cooperative and closed. Football is his life, and anything that interferes with football has no place in his day's work. He has often insisted that he knows how to relax, but his occasional forays to a race track or a golf course never last very long, nor does his attitude during such periods away from the team convince anyone that he is really enjoying himself.

Well has built a reputation throughout the world of professional football as an expert. "He knows more about football than anyone would think," says Jim Trimble, the team's director of pro personnel and the man Well hired to "relieve some of the burden from my duties and to give the team some professional guidance." Trimble has not been given any significant authority, though, and he must confer daily with Wellington on matters of player contracts, waiver claims, and potential trades. Well is still the boss.

Through the years Mara has made several notable trades. Among the heroes he brought to New York for comparatively nothing are Y.A. Tittle, Andy Robustelli, Dick Modzelewski, Joe Walton, Alex Webster, Ron Johnson, Del Shofner, Pete Case, Homer Jones, and Dick Lynch. Team draft selections greatly influenced by his "gut feelings" have resulted in the acquisition of Frank Gifford, Kyle Rote, Charley Conerly, Tucker Frederickson, Jim Files, and Rosey Grier.

Well has made errors. For a long period, through most of the 1960s, his high draft choices bore names such as Joe Don Looney, Glynn Griffing, Bob Timberlake, Chuck Mercein, Bobby Gaiters, Rocky Thompson, Dick Skelly, Rich Buzin, Wayne Walton, Bruce Tarbox, Bob Mischak, Joe Biscaha, Lou Cordileone, Lee Grosscup, Jerry Hillebrand, Frank Lasky, Francis Peay, Lou Thompson, and Don Davis. Most of them were flops. Many never played again after taking much Giant money and failing on the field. A few drifted to other teams but never performed anywhere near the level necessary to justify such a high draft status. These men were clearly mistakes, and their presence kept the Giants from escaping their dreadful slide to obscurity and ridicule through most of the 1960s.

Were they all choices made by Well Mara? Perhaps not, but in cases when others were asked to submit an opinion, those men were employees of Well Mara, and too much heated disagreement, in their minds, might have affected their future with the Giants. If others made the choices, insisted on making the choices, they still had to win Mara's tacit approval.

Perhaps Well's most successful trade was the one in which the Giants obtained Tittle, already a veteran of 13 years, the last 10 of which had been spent with the San Francisco 49ers. He was a favorite in the Bay City, but gradually, as the 49ers continued to chase an ever more elusive championship, the fans cooled to him. Spectacular, yes, but not a winner, they groused.

The critical move that made Tittle available was a decision on the part of the coach of the 49ers, Red Hickey, to install a single-wing offense, one in which the quarterback would have to do as much running as passing. Tittle, a classic

T-formation, drop-back passer, took great care to explain that he never preferred to run and that when he did, it was simply to escape the clutches of a would-be tackler.

Tittle's age, too, seemed to work against him in San Francisco. He was 35 years old, far too ancient to handle a new offense that demanded agility and mobility from its quarterback. San Francisco had John Brodie and Bill Kilmer. Clearly, they would fight for the job.

So Y.A. became expendable. The Giants were interested.

They were, at the time, spending a three-week hiatus in Salem, Oregon, having broken summer camp at Fairfield, Connecticut, in order to play two preseason games on the West Coast against the 49ers and the Los Angeles Rams.

Working with Allie Sherman, then a rookie head coach, Mara determined that, although Conerly was still the starter and seemed to have at least one more season left in his 40-year-old arm, a passer of Tittle's proven talents would be hard to reject if the cost were not prohibitive.

Hickey and Vic Spadia, the 49ers' general manager, welcomed the contact made by Mara and Sherman. They knew Tittle would not be playing regularly, and they were aware that the Giants had a number of young athletes at several positions, any one of which might be of help in rebuilding the 49ers.

Several names were bandied back and forth until Mara offered Lou Cordileone, who had been the Giants' number-one draft pick in 1960. A bulky, squat guard from Clemson, Cordileone was a picture player. He did everything right—in practice. Other coaches used films of him as coaching aids. He was able to instruct the veteran New York linemen in the intricacies of line movement. But he never played well in a real game, a flaw fatal to both his career and the 49ers' decision.

"Well, I want Cordileone," said Spadia. "I'll take him and give you Tittle."

Barely able to contain themselves, Mara and Sherman

readily agreed. When they informed Cordileone that he had been traded to San Francisco for Y.A. Tittle, he uttered a now-famous, two-word question: "Just me?"

Indeed, it was just Cordileone, even up for Y.A. Tittle, and that one trade created a new three-year dynasty of championships in New York City.

At that time Mara had completed a series of equally brilliant trades. First he secured a wide receiver named Del Shofner from the Los Angeles Rams for the Giants' number-one draft choice. Then he acquired tight end Joe Walton from the Washington Redskins. In a deal with the Chicago Bears, New York came up with cornerback Erich Barnes.

Sherman had been concerned with the offense and the offense only. The defense was nearly invulnerable, including the front four of Andy Robustelli, Jim Katcavage, Rosey Grier, and Dick Modzelewski, linebackers Sam Huff, Cliff Livingston, and Tom Scott, and a secondary that boasted Jimmy Patton, Dick Lynch, and now Barnes.

"We needed firepower," Sherman said. "With Tittle, Shofner, Walton, and the return of Alex Webster, we suddenly had more of it than I would have dared hope."

Tittle played for the Giants for four seasons. The first three, which also were Sherman's first three as coach, resulted in Eastern Division championships. Tittle's final season, 1964, marked not only his personal end of the line but a severe crumbling of the Giants that would not be healed until the start of the 1970s.

With the 1964 season Mara's magic touch faded. He approved a disastrous trade of Sam Huff to Washington for two faceless defensive players named Andy Stynchula and Dick James, and the reaction of the public was unique in its fury. Huff had captured their loyalty and their imagination, and when the Columbia Broadcasting System filmed a special entitled "The Violent World of Sam Huff," he became a household word. His passage, as well as the trading of Grier and Modzelewski and the retirement of several others, including Robustelli, Conerly, Livingston, Scott, Rosey Brown, and Jack Stroud, turned the fans against the Giants as they had never been before. They did not stop coming to the games, nor did they cease purchasing season tickets, but now they came to hoot and jeer, to boo lustily, to ridicule, and finally to sing a humiliating *a cappella* rendition of "Goodbye, Allie" to the tune of "Good Night, Ladies." The fans had turned against Sherman and Mara.

What kind of a man is Wellington Mara? First, he is a man who knows what he wants. Late in 1935, with the college football season already concluded, Well Mara, then a stripling of 19, walked into his father's office and said, "I'm on my way to Washington, dad. I've got some business there."

Tim chuckled. "What kind of business could you have?" he wondered.

"I'm going to sign Tuffy Leemans."

"Who?"

"Tuffy Leemans. He's a runner for George Washington. You might not have heard of him, but you will ... you will."

Having sent a telegram to Leemans signed with his father's name, Well arranged to meet the runner on campus. When he arrived, a tall, athletic type was lounging on the steps of a building. "Excuse me," said Well Mara, "do you know where I can find Tuffy Leemans?"

"I'm Leemans," the man said, expecting to be asked for an autograph.

"I'm Well Mara, secretary of the Giants. I want you to sign a contract."

By the end of the day Leemans not only stopped questioning the identity of this skinny kid but agreed to play for his dad's team. The following February, the Giants drafted Leemans. He signed a $3,000 contract and went on to become one of the team's all-time stars.

Well has never changed. He is forthright and direct, often single-minded, sometimes narrow-minded, but always working for the improvement and glory of the Giants, the family heirloom. To this day he keeps a master list of all available college seniors, and at a time when the scouting and drafting process has become so complicated that computers have to keep track of the players, Mara still knows more than any other man in the business.

"Sure, he could have been a coach," said Lombardi, his close friend. "That little brat knew everything about the game when we were in Fordham together. He was quiet and shy, he never spoke much about how important his father was, but he knew what he was talking about. We had many wonderful times sitting at dinner and boring our wives with football talk."

Well became the Giants' first team photographer in 1936 after receiving a movie camera from his parents for Christmas. The Giants had tried game films for a year or two, but the quality was so poor that the films never were used as a coaching aid.

"I knew all our plays," Well remembers, "so I knew where the ball was going. The other cameraman knew little about football and nothing about our team. I knew what the coach [Steve Owen] wanted."

Indeed, the films were so helpful that Owen and his staff took to studying them each week, and soon Owen began asking Well for his opinion of personnel switches and proposed new plays.

The Duke was by then fully immersed in the fortunes of the Giants, so much so that he began to devote his time year-round, studying other rosters and scouting for unknown players during the off-seasons. Perhaps one-dimensional in his fanaticism, Mara nevertheless proved to be the most able junior executive the league had ever known, and he acquired a working knowledge of every phase of the game. Most owners worried about gate receipts and little else. Well had

Jack to worry about that. He chose to concern himself with winning games.

Mara is a fantastically loyal man, and he has surrounded himself with members of the Old Guard of the Mara family. Father Benedict Dudley, who was befriended by Tim Mara and who soon became the team's "official" chaplain, is still part of the Giants' entourage today and leads the team in pregame prayer services each Sunday morning. Ray Walsh, the team's general manager (in reality more of a business manager), was a schoolmate of Mara's. Ticket manager Harry Bachrach has been with the team since shortly after its inception. The late Dr. Francis X. Sweeny, one-time Broadway doctor to stars and celebrities, was retained by Tim Mara and continued in the same position until his death in 1968. Sweeny, a likable elf with a sharp tongue and a limitless capacity for firewater, was the source of many colorful tales by virtue of his temperament and the condition in which he often found himself—or in which others often found him.

The stubbornness of Well Mara was never more obvious than during the last war of leagues, when the established NFL had more trouble than it ever expected from a rival American League. Formed in 1959, the AFL quickly made serious inroads, and when it landed a multimillion-dollar television contract from the National Broadcasting System, it suddenly had the cash and recognition necessary to wage a spirited battle for players.

Mara was steadfast in his refusal to recognize the "other" league and spent more than his father or his brother would have dreamed of not only to sign the players drafted by the Giants but to insure the downfall of the AFL. Yet the practicality of his nature showed itself, too, for when he saw that a merger and realignment were unavoidable, he held it up until he was able to extract a staggering $10 million in "indemnity money" from the other New York team, the Jets.

When the rival AFL was absorbed by the NFL in 1966, Mara cooperated with the committee that arranged the dramatic and historic amalgamation. But when the total of 26 teams met in 1969 to "realign" into conferences, Mara absorbed a major disappointment.

Not content to continue as a separate but equal grouping, the militant ten owners of AFL teams insisted on the transference of three NFL teams to the American Conference. Mara fought that one long and hard, but in the end he lost two of his dearest friends to the AFC—Modell and the Browns and Rooney and the Steelers, along with the Baltimore Colts. "Those two teams had come to be identified as the Giants' most traditional rivals," he explained, "and it bothered me deeply that we would not be allowed to continue those rivalries during each season. I admit I was against the switching of those teams, but I finally went along with it in the best interests of the league."

One condition that Mara insisted on, however, was an annual preseason game with each team, terms the Browns and Steelers were glad to accept. "And when we got around to setting up three divisions in our conference," he adds, "I insisted on being grouped with at least Washington and Philadelphia. I had given up a great deal, and I was not about to lose the chance to play those teams twice each season. They represented our next two oldest rivals." Mara got what he sought, and the Giants now play in a division containing Philadelphia, Washington, St. Louis (another long-time rival, if the team's years as the Chicago Cardinals are included), and Dallas.

There are stories and more stories that point to Mara's devotion and dedication to the Giants. In the summer of 1971, for example, four years after he had engineered a major and costly trade to secure quarterback Fran Tarkenton from the Minnesota Vikings, Well locked horns with the abrasive but intelligent quarterback.

Tarkenton wanted not a salary but an "interest-free loan" in the neighborhood of $400,000, with which he would shore up several of his outside business interests. Mara refused; Tarkenton balked. The two were soon debating points of principle and honor, and neither would budge.

Finally, when the team flew to Houston to open its preseason schedule, a final meeting was held. With no settlement in sight, Tarkenton said he would not play the Oilers without a contract. Mara suggested that if those were his feelings, he would not be allowed to play at all until he signed.

Tarkenton, near midnight the night before the game, packed his bags, took a cab to the airport, and flew home to Atlanta, Georgia.

The next day, after the accompanying sportswriters had ferreted out the information of Tarkenton's departure from his roommate, Bob Tucker, and from the head coach, Alex Webster, Mara hastily called a press conference.

The team's two publicity men, Don Smith and Ed Croke, had the colossal bad luck to have planned a golf date, so neither was present. Indeed, neither was aware of what had transpired the night before.

Still visibly fuming, Mara strode into the Roughrider Room of a Marriott Hotel near the Houston Astrodome and informed the press that Tarkenton "had quit professional football."

He chose not to comment on the details of the contract negotiations, skirting that issue by insisting that it would infringe not only on his privacy and business dealings but on those of Tarkenton as well.

Then he pointed to the Giant emblem on his golf shirt. "This," he said, "is the only important thing. The Giants will survive. With or without Fran Tarkenton, there will always be the New York Giants."

If he meant it to be a touching moment, he came up short. But he did indicate, perhaps more clearly than ever before, his feelings about the team and those who dared to defy him.

That night, during the game, I pried loose Tarkenton's

home telephone number from one of the publicity men and, from a booth in the Astrodome, placed a call to Atlanta. Fran answered. He admitted he and Well had "experienced great difficulty" in settling the terms of his new contract. But when told that Mara had announced his retirement, Tarkenton became angry. "I want to play football," he said. "If I cannot play for the Giants, all right. But I have not retired, and he has no right to say that I have."

Three days later, looking more like a whipped puppy than a masterful quarterback, Tarkenton returned to the team's summer training base in Brookville, Long Island, having signed a contract at a midnight meeting under Mara's terms.

"It's over and done with," he said. "I'm here to play football."

But for Mara it was hardly over, and it would not be done with until Tarkenton was removed. The following January, less than 6 weeks after the conclusion of a dismal 4-10 season, Tarkenton was traded back to the Vikings for a handful of players and draft choices. To those who knew Wellington Mara, that trade had become inevitable 6 months earlier when Tarkenton besmirched the honor of the Giants.

Another incident must be noted, though Mara denies that it holds any significance. In 1971 defensive end Bob Lurtsema was asked by Mara to canvass the players and "find out what they think of me." Lurtsema, a big, friendly bear of a man, complied. Some time later, he called on Mara with the findings.

"You won't like this," he said.

"Go ahead," Mara answered. "I want the truth."

Lurtsema proceeded to read a lengthy list of complaints, which ranged from Mara's interference with the players' private lives to his insistence on being a part of team meetings to the presence of his children—"like a bunch of little blond bats"—at training camp and during in-season practices.

Mara, according to Lurtsema, was shaken but thanked him for the report. Later that day, Bob Lurtsema's name appeared on the waiver list of the New York Giants. He had been cut loose.

Mara insists he had nothing to do with the waiver, that he had no knowledge of the coach's decision to cut Lurtsema. Understandably, Lurtsema, who went to the Vikings and played well, feels differently. "I just wonder what would have happened if I hadn't turned in that report, or if I had lied to him and told him the players loved him. I just can't accept such a coincidence. Yeah, I feel I was used."

Several other players in the past decade have insisted that their sudden departure from the Giants had more to do with their private lives than with any shortcomings on the field. Among them are Ernie Wheelwright, Steve Thurlow, Erich Barnes, Fred Dryer, Steve Wright, Pete Gent, and Jimmy Holifield.

Thurlow frequented night spots in New York and had a problem keeping his weight consistent during the season. Wright was outspoken, a freethinker and a man with a ready barb to jab at the coaches or the team management. Wheelwright collected debts the way some men collect stamps, and Barnes made a habit, before, during, and after his years with New York, of collecting advances on his salary. Dryer spoke his mind, wore his hair to his shoulders, resented Mara's interference with the team, and preferred the "beach boy" life he lived in his native San Diego. His lifestyle was one that Mara simply could not understand.

They were players who did not fit the "Giant mold" or, more correctly, the "Mara mold."

But considerably more players, both former and current, swear by Well Mara and liken him to a saintly father-figure who helps them as if they were sons rather than mercenaries. Like his father and his brother before him, Well has had his favorites, some of whom included Y.A. Tittle, Tucker Frederickson, Greg Larson, Joe Morrison, and Jim Katcavage.

The best conclusion, however, is to take the disenchanted athletes for what they are, men whose egos have been bruised by rejection, and discount much of what they charge. If Mara has done half the good that has been attributed to him, those unhappy players must be wrong.

Some sportswriters have accused Mara of being distant, and with some of them he is. He has the privilege, as do others, of picking and choosing those he decides to befriend. In the case of sportswriters, though, he might have more data to weigh.

In the past the Mara family has come to the aid of several sportswriters. One found himself in difficulty and needed an urgent loan of $1,500. It was granted. Another needed a down payment for a home. That, too, was granted. During the newspaper strikes that have frequently plagued New York City, it was not unusual for the Maras to hire some out-of-work journalists as "consultants" until hostilities ended. Veteran sports columnist Arthur Daley of the *New York Times* has been a family friend, and perhaps the Maras' closest confidant, for nearly 40 years. Another aging sportswriter, when his newspaper went out of business, was hired as a publicity assistant.

Having done so much for the sportswriting fraternity, Mara is also one of the few remaining team owners in any professional sport to carry the regular writers for free on road trips, at least those whose newspapers care to accept the opportunity. Many of them do, not because of a need for cash but because in the newspaper business today any saving is a bonanza.

The danger in this is that Mara feels those who have availed themselves of such an offer should owe some loyalty to the team, and when a particularly acid story appears under the by-line of one of those writers, Mara feels betrayed.

For the first six Super Bowls the Giants paid the full fare for their regular writers to Los Angeles, Miami, New Orleans, and so forth, going so far as to provide first-class air transportation, hotel rooms, and unlimited signing privileges in the hotel dining rooms. It was, as Well often said, "just a way of saying thanks for being with us all season," even though the Giants have yet to appear in a Super Bowl as participants. But many reporters abused the opportunity, came to take it for granted, and, as one member of the front office once complained, "Well was upset because almost no one even thought to send a simple note of thanks."

So, prior to Super Bowl VII, Timmy Mara sent a note to all the writers explaining that the honeymoon was over.

"As you know," the letter read, "since the Super Bowl was started, it has been our pleasure to have the press who normally cover the Giants as our guests for Super Bowl week. Beginning this year, we regretfully will discontinue this practice. I am advising our friends of the press of this change of policy at this time so that you may be aware of the situation this far in advance and make your plans accordingly." The letter was dated August 9, 1972.

Well Mara never once mentioned it, and he was genuinely uncomfortable when the subject was once brought up. Despite his appearance of writing off the expense of hosting the writers, he considers them, especially those who have put in several years with the team, as "part of the family." Perhaps he was not in total agreement with the suspension of the Super Bowl safari, but perhaps he had taken enough abuse from those he had tried to befriend. There, perhaps, is the answer. Those who anger the lord of the manor ultimately will feel the sting of retribution, and in 1971 and 1972 the press had been particularly sharp in its criticism of the team and its management.

It might be added that only one of the regular writers who are part of the Giants' "family" was forced to miss the 1973 Super Bowl. As for the other newspapers involved, they simply had accepted what was offered, and when the offer was no longer extended they were ready and able to pay their own way. It is doubtful that any of the newspaper executives ever expected such a windfall, but they were quick to accept it.

Unfortunately, newspapers are not in the business of making friends. If a story demands to be published, however damaging or critical it might be, it will be published. This, clearly, does not agree with Well Mara's "old family friendship" theories, and the practice has several times caused him to be disillusioned.

Well Mara is a private person. His friends among the NFL hierarchy include Art Modell, owner of the Cleveland Browns; Art Rooney, owner of the Pittsburgh Steelers; George Halas, owner of the Chicago Bears; Bill Bidwill, owner of the St. Louis Cardinals; Lou Spadia, one of the owners of the San Francisco 49ers; NFL Commissioner Pete Rozelle; and a few other executives of other teams. He has not shown many deep friendships with any of the former AFL teams' owners, being a man who does not easily surrender past grudges.

He has admitted he no longer reads the city newspaper that in 1971 carried a five-part series entitled "Maranoia," a brutal attack on the Mara family tradition that represented the first overt, public ridicule Mara had ever experienced. The columnist's name was Merchant, and in a subsequent speech Mara grouped all those writers who had taken up the battle as "Merchants of venom."

As to tradition, even the smallest earns Mara's loyalty. Years ago at a summer training camp the team started its Five-Thirty Club ritual, an hour at the end of the day's work when the coaches and writers gather for a bit of harmless socializing. Unwritten rules preclude any work on the part of the writers; it is just a way to include them in a bit of informal camaraderie.

Well Mara, of course, is a daily participant in the Club during summer camp and at every hotel the evening before a road game. But he spends much of his time whispering to the coaches, excluding the writers and the ever-burgeoning number of invited guests. Not that Well wants to ignore the writers; he simply cannot stop working.

Mara's chief regret in all his years with the team was his failure to bring Vince Lombardi back as head coach.

Lombardi was perhaps his closest friend, a friendship that transcended football. When Jim Lee Howell was named to replace Steve Owen as coach in 1954, Well insisted on the inclusion of the young Lombardi, then an aide at West Point, on the coaching staff—with Howell's approval, of course. Lombardi stayed through the 1958 season, at which time he was offered the head coaching job in Green Bay. He had received another offer a year earlier, but Well had counseled him against taking it. Mara was of the opinion that "it wasn't the right spot." This time, however, Well agreed that the Packers carried the potential to become winners, hence making the job a worthwhile opportunity. But he added a promise, one which, as it later developed, he was not able to keep: "If the job here opens up, if Jim Lee decides to step down, I will bring you back as head coach. You will be my only choice."

Ironically, Howell retired just one year later, telling Mara he was tired of coaching and of the extensive travel it demanded. When Mara offered him the position of director of personnel and head of the network of scouts, Howell accepted quickly.

Then Mara contacted Lombardi, told him the job was open, and officially offered it to him. Lombardi was ecstatic. He and his wife, Marie, native New Yorkers, deeply yearned to return. But the answer was to be no.

The Green Bay board of directors refused to allow Lombardi to break his contract, though they did offer him a significant raise. Sadly, Mara had to look elsewhere. The man he selected was Allie Sherman — "the second-choice coach" — who was to capture three consecutive championships. But Mara still regretted the conditions that prevented him from championing Lombardi's triumphant return.

Eight years later, when Mara had to dismiss Sherman, there was a report that he had once again offered the job to Lombardi, by then a nationally famous coach and general manager who had led Green Bay to six championships and victories in the first two Super Bowls. But Vince wanted more than just another job now; he asked for part ownership in the team. For the first time in the Mara family history, an outsider was almost brought in. But, according to the story, Helen Mara, Jack's widow, refused to part with a portion of her stock holdings. Hence, Lombardi could not return. He was made part owner-general manager-head coach of the Washington Redskins instead, and a year later he was dead, another victim of the virulent cancer that also had claimed Well Mara's brother.

Another facet of the Mara personality is his deep commitment to his religion. Well attends eight o'clock Mass every morning, and he has been seen crossing himself in the press boxes of various stadiums as the Giants were lining up for a critical play. Several of his friends are priests, that in addition to the constant presence of Father Dudley, a regular member of the Giants' official traveling party. Mara is not a church-goer for any other reason than because he believes in such a way of life. Clearly, the ten children he and his wife Ann have had point to his devotion to other aspects of the teachings of the Catholic Church.

Mara's penchant for unbecoming petty acts of anger have clouded his greater image. He has been known to telephone sports editors and demand that a particularly annoying writer be removed from the assignment. At one point he wrote a scathing letter to the sports editor of the *New York Times* asking that its representative, Bill Wallace, be switched to another beat. The letter was pinned to an office bulletin board—bad press, indeed, for Well Mara—but Mr. Wallace found that he was no longer covering the Giants.

Players of less than superstar quality who allow foul language to assail the ears of Mara may find themselves shipped out. Once Well's anger passes, though, he often tries to set things right. Mara was instrumental in 1972 in the addition of former star Sam Huff to the radio team that broadcasts each Giant game, perhaps trying to indicate his repentance for having traded Sam in 1964.

Others, too, have been rewarded for long and faithful service. Jim Lee Howell, of course, still handles all personnel for the college draft. The coaching staff is almost exclusively a club of former players, from head man Alex Webster to aides Emlen Tunnell, Ray Wietecha, Jim Katcavage, Joe Walton, and Y.A. Tittle. Even Jim Garrett, the defensive coach and architect of the radical "rover defense," which bore immediate fruit in 1972, was a would-be Giant who made it to the team's inactive roster—"taxi squad"—but never played in a regulation game for New York. Chief scouts include Pop Ivy, a former assistant coach, and Harry Buffington, a one-time guard for the Giants. Joe Sulaitis, who holds the title of Assistant Director of Personnel, was a former fullback who put in ten years of service as a Giant and who then fell upon harsh financial times.

Well Mara sits with them all, taking obvious pleasure in seeing "his boys" share the job of running "his team" according to "his methods." They owe him much, and he feels that he, as well, owes them a great deal. They spent a good portion of their lives as devoted employees. The least he can do is make the rest of their lives secure.

Thus Well Mara is a complex man at the same time as he is a singularly motivated man. He is difficult to read, but his own image of himself must surely be that of a benevolent and wealthy man who has rewarded his friends, spurned his adversaries, and strived each day to uphold the honor and tradition of his family.

What wrong he does he cannot see. On the other hand, his many brilliant moves have never been recounted by him. There are those he likes, and he likes them a great deal; there are those he dislikes, and whatever they may do cannot cause him to stop disliking them.

He is an astute football man, perhaps an anachronism in this day of computers and coldly calculating businessmen. He cannot compete with the ruthless intensity of Al Davis of the Oakland Raiders, George Allen of the Washington Redskins, or Gil Brandt of the Dallas Cowboys. But he would not want to compete with such men.

His firmly held belief that pro football can be blended with a personal touch and a family effort will not be diminished. Whatever the future of the New York Giants, this man will direct it, and more important, he will do so in the manner in which he has always operated.

Mara bridles at the suggestion that his way of administering the team is outdated and ineffectual in today's game. "I don't have a general manager the way most people picture one," he says. "But there is Ray Walsh, and I prefer him to be a financial man. Jim Trimble [the director of pro personnel] handles some of the functions one would normally associate with a general manager. I perform some of the others. What's wrong with that?"

As long as the team is successful, nothing. But during the extended run of disastrous seasons, many blamed this closed-shop operation for the collapse and futility of a team that once ruled the league.

Many men love Wellington Mara. Many others do not. A few harbor deep feelings of hatred and distrust for the man.

To his way of thinking, that is all part of the life and times of a closely knit family unit. The important word is family. Blood ties are impossible to break, and those with different blood find breaking in to the family impossible.

"The Giants are my family," he says, and he means it. In 1962, during the playing of a critically important game late in the season, one of his sons slipped on the steps in Yankee Stadium, suffered a bad fall, and broke his shoulder. When they found Well in his Polaroid booth and told him the news, he was understandably upset.

"But it could have been worse," he said. "It could have been Tittle."

7

The Third Decade — 1940 - 1949

Not only for the New York Giants but for the National Football League and the country itself, the 1940s proved to be more significant than anyone could have imagined. The United States would be thrust into a grisly, bloody, and fearful war; the NFL would be subjected to its strongest challenge yet from an aspiring rival league; and the New York Giants would be rocked by a gambling-bribery scandal that would threaten the very fabric of the league and the sport of professional football.

For the first and only time since he was nine years old, Wellington Mara would be taken away from his beloved Giants. He would spend more than three years in the Atlantic and Pacific theaters serving on aircraft carriers as a lieutenant commander in the United States Navy.

The Giants would add such fabled heroes to their roster as

Emlen Tunnell, Charley Conerly, Ward Cuff, Bill Paschal, and Gene "Choo Choo" Roberts. Moreover, they would be among the first teams to bring in a revolutionary formation called the T.

The team would find its first consistent success at the gate, a success that peaked in 1946 when the average home attendance for 8 games was 50,000.

But the third decade of the Giants' history started quietly. In 1940 the New York Giants managed just a 6-4-1 record, bringing to an end their run of three consecutive division championships that had closed out the 1930s. The Giants skidded to third place behind the 9-2 Washington Redskins and the 8-3 Brooklyn Dodgers.

Steve Owen could find humor and relief even in that because the Western Division champions, the 8-3 Chicago Bears, shredded the Redskins in the championship game 73-0. "It's a good thing the Redskins beat us out," Stout Steve cracked. "We might have won the division and then had to play the Bears. I'm even glad we didn't come in second. Second would have been too close."

Never before had a team absorbed such a frightful beating in a championship game. It was so ludicrous, so inexplicable, as to bear more humor than tragedy for the whipped Redskins, who 3 weeks earlier had beaten the Bears 7-3.

Early in the championship game, with Chicago ahead 7-0, a Washington end dropped a pass from Sammy Baugh in the end zone; the pass would have earned a 7-7 tie for the Redskins. After the game somebody asked Baugh if the early score would have had an effect on the final outrage.

"Yeah," he drawled wearily. "It would have been 73-7."

Andy Farkas, a great running back with the Redskins, once remembered in detail the surrounding atmosphere of the game. "They came out screaming like a pack of wild Indians. They took off and ran the length of the field shouting and bellowing. They circled the goal posts and started back and still they were screaming. I've never seen anything like that. It was really frightening."

So the Giants considered themselves fortunate to have escaped the brutalizing of the Chicago team, already dubbed the Monsters of the Midway. They were confident that 1941 would be their year. It was, but by the time it became official too many other dramatic developments had occurred, rendering a mere football championship nearly meaningless.

The 1941 Giants won the Eastern Division in a tight race with Brooklyn. They had added a banner crop of rookies—a group that Owen called "the best we have ever had"—including backs Len Eshmont of Fordham, Frank Reagan of Penn, Marion Pugh of Texas A&M, Andy Marefos of St. Mary's, Red McLain of SMU, Howie Yeager of Santa Barbara State, and George Franck, an All-American from Minnesota and a 9.6 sprinter, which in 1941 placed him in world class.

Linemen new to the team that year included Vince Dennery of Fordham, Len Younce of Oregon State, Lou DeFilippo of Fordham, Ben Sohn of Southern California, and Don Vosberg of Marquette.

Danowski decided to come out of retirement, providing what Owen described as "the last piece of the puzzle we needed. Now everything fits right in place. We have the makings of a championship team."

And so they did. The Giants won their first 5 games of the season, 3 of them shutouts, and then hit a slump. They lost 2 in a row, 16-13 to the Dodgers and 10-7 to the Chicago Cardinals. Reagan, the promising rookie, already had been called up by the Marine Corps, but even his loss, plus a broken ankle suffered by Ed Widseth, the All-Pro lineman, could not stop the Giants permanently. They snapped out of their slide with 2 victories, 20-13 over Detroit and 49-14 over Cleveland. Now it was Washington coming up, the one game the Giants needed to sew up the division championship.

They came back from a 13-10 deficit in the fourth quarter to beat the Redskins 20-13, and in so doing they became Eastern Division champs for the fourth time in the last 5 years.

The one remaining game on the schedule was to be played in the Polo Grounds against the cross-town Brooklyn Dodgers. As far as the Giants were concerned, it was a meaningless exercise. They had already clinched, as had the Bears, who had beaten Green Bay in a final-game showdown 33-14 after finishing their season a week earlier at 10-1.

The date of the Giants-Dodgers game was December 7, 1941. By no stretch of the imagination would that day be meaningless.

In the first quarter the public address announcer issued a message to the crowd: "Attention, please. Here is an urgent message. Will Colonel William J. Donovan call Operator 19 in Washington immediately?"

Well, what of it? A birth perhaps, or a bit of business. Army men were always being disturbed.

Moments later, at 2:18 P.M., a Western Union telegrapher turned to a sportswriter in the press box and said, "Hey, look at this. The Cards are beating the Bears."

Soon after, he bent to his ticker to copy another message.

"My God," he said. "It can't be."

"What, the Cards score again?" asked the preoccupied sportswriter, busily charting the play-by-play of the game.

"No, the Japanese have attacked Pearl Harbor."

Soon, in a sequence of world-changing phrases, more news issued forth: ". . . war imminent . . . U.S. Fleet destroyed . . . thousands dead . . . President Roosevelt in emergency meeting . . ."

At halftime the full impact of the tragedy hit home. The Dodgers, leading 14-7, wanted to suspend the game. Their star, Ace Parker, remembers sitting in the locker room asking, "What does it matter? Let's get the hell out of here and see what we can do to help."

But the game continued. The Dodgers won 21-7, with both teams simply going through the motions. Another public address announcement near the end told the full, awful story: "All officers and men of the Army and Navy are to report to their stations immediately. We repeat. All armed forces personnel will report to their stations immediately."

In two weeks the Giants would meet the Bears for the NFL championship in Chicago's Wrigley Field. But who could care? What did a game matter now?

There was a move to cancel the championship game, but it was played nonetheless. The Bears, burly and brutal, were virtually unchanged from the cast that had buried the Redskins a year earlier. The addition of a monstrous fullback, Norm Standlee of Stanford, seemed to make them all the more potent.

The adding machine offense was in perfect condition, and after an early trading of advantages, Chicago simply pulled away. The Giants drew even at 9-9 on a Cuff field goal. It was their last gasp.

Quarterback Sid Luckman, teaming with Standlee, George McAfee, Hugh Gallerneau, Ken Kavanaugh, and Ed Kolman, scored 4 touchdowns in the final quarter and won the game easily 37-9.

That game was to mark the end of one of the most powerful dynasties in football history, for soon the events that had taken place in Europe and the Pacific would drain the talented athletes and put them in a different sort of uniform. The first Bear to go would be Lieutenant Commander George Halas.

By the summer of 1942, when the Giants gathered for the first day of training camp, their roster already had been sapped by the war. There were 20 rookies present, but only 2 were legitimate players—fullback Merle Hapes of Mississippi and tackle Al Blozis of Georgetown.

Eighteen other Giants, as well as Wellington Mara, were in service, and four others had retired. Most of the new players on the scene were, in Owen's words, "dog meat."

Leemans, the great running back who had given so much, took one look at the aspiring Giants and almost cried. "I wanted to go home," he said. "The Giants I loved never had such a miserable group as we saw there."

It was not to change, and the Giants of '42 were fortunate

to play at .500, finishing with a 5-5-1 record. Al Blozis, who was to lose his life in France in 1944, was the only bright spot, earning a starting position as a rookie and, a year later, being named to the All-Pro team.

The league, however, was in far more perilous straits. Attendance had understandably shriveled, and interest in games was at an all-time low. Owners such as Halas, Dan Reeves, and Fred Levy were away fighting, and most of the others insisted on suspending operations for the duration of the war as not only the easiest but the most practical move that could be made.

But Tim and Jack Mara and George Preston Marshall were against it. Their reasoning was sound: major league baseball was not planning to go under, and they felt that pro football had worked too hard and too long to quit now. Calling off an undetermined number of seasons might have been enough to finish the league forever.

They persevered in their arguments but agreed that a drastic set of changes had to be made. Schedules were cut to 10 games, travel arrangements were shortened, player limits were reduced to 28, and training sites were moved to nearby areas. The Cleveland Rams dropped out for the 1943 season, and the Philadelphia Eagles and Pittsburgh Steelers merged into a team called the Steagles.

Players were scarce. The Giants alone had 45 men in the service. The remaining athletes were older men long since retired, 4-F rejects, youngsters waiting to be drafted, high school dropouts, sandlot pretenders, and visiting servicemen on weekend passes.

Three rookies made it to the Giants and proved they were not simply "wartime athletes"—Bill Paschal of Georgia Tech, Emory Nix of TCU, and Carl Kinscherf of Colgate. A linebacker named Bill Piccollo enjoyed a few good games, but he had been forced to start and was not able to handle those responsibilities. As a result the proud Giant defense weakened.

Nevertheless, the 1943 Giants were able to compile a 6-3-1 record, enough to earn a tie with Washington for the division championship. But in a play-off game the Redskins waltzed by 28-0 and went on to meet the Bears once more for the championship. The Bears, weakened by the war and without several of their stars, nevertheless routed the Redskins 41-21.

The play-off game marked one of the Giants' more heroic efforts. Because of the reduced and travel-eased schedule, New York and Washington were to finish the season with back-to-back meetings. Prior to their first game, Washington was 6-1-1, New York 4-3-1. Obviously, the Giants would have to win both those games just to force a tie-breaking play-off.

They accomplished two-thirds of their improbable task, winning those final games 14-10 and 31-7. But they could not do it a third time, and Washington went on to the championship.

As the Giants prepared for 1944, they had every reason to be pessimism champions and no reason to be football champions. Blozis, Cuff, Nix, Paschal, and halfback Dave Brown had all been drafted, and Leemans had retired. The first week of summer practice brought yet another blow—star Leland Shaffer had splintered his kneecap and would not be able to play for the rest of the season.

Training at Bear Mountain State Park in New York, Owen was disconsolate. He confided in an assistant coach, Red Smith, that "we'll be lucky to win one game," and Smith later admitted, "I had no choice but to agree with him. It looked just terrible."

Arnie Herber, the one-time Green Bay quarterbacking great, was lured to New York and brought with him, as Jack Mara once recalled, "an extra 25 pounds of lard attached to various parts of his body." Herber, then 34, had not played in 3 seasons. The rookies, for the most part, were hapless.

Then the luck turned. Cuff was discharged, and Paschal received permission to play on weekends if the Giants were nearby. To top it off, Jack Mara talked Ken Strong out of retirement at the age of 37 to handle the placekicking.

Meanwhile, other changes had taken place around the league. The Brooklyn team had given itself a new name, the Tigers. Pittsburgh merged with the Chicago Cardinals to make up a team with the unlikely name of the Carpitts. Their talent was equally unlikely, and the Carpitts stumbled through an 0-10 season. A new franchise called the Yankees popped up in Boston.

The greatest surprise of all was to be the Giants' record. They lost one game to Philadelphia, 24-17, and they tied another one with the Eagles. Those turned out to be the only games the Giants did not win. Their final record was 8-1-1, and they took the Eastern Division championship from the 7-1-2 Eagles. New York's defense had been spectacular, allowing just 75 points in the 10 games. Rookie back Howie Livingston was another unexpected source of pleasure, finding his niche on defense and, among other accomplishments, stifling the pass-receiving talents of Green Bay's Don Hutson in a 24-0 regular-season victory.

But when the Giants played the Packers for the NFL championship, the strategy of stopping Hutson backfired. While New York shackled the great receiver, fullback Ted Fritsch carried out Green Bay's surprisingly effective ground game and scored both touchdowns as the Packers won 14-7.

Still, New York newspapers had every reason to call their team the "Miracle Men of Mara Tech." It had been a spectacularly successful season, one in which the Maras' experiment with "season tickets" began to pay dividends. More than 4,000 such packages were sold, a harbinger of the 60,000 they now sell annually to insure capacity crowds all season.

Tragedy and stiff competition hit the Giants as well as the league in 1945. New York received the news that end John Lummus had been killed by a land mine on Iwo Jima, months after Al Blozis, one of the most likable and promising young Giants, had given his life on a search patrol mission in the Vosges Mountains of France. Blozis, 6-feet-6 and 245 pounds, had been one of Owen's favorites. Steve had discovered him as a shot-putter in Madison Square Garden one night. Owen's grief was profound, and the Giants promptly retired Blozis's jersey number.

On the league level, there was financial trouble. A rival league, the All-America Conference, had banded together and made an attempt to seek a peaceful agreement with the older NFL. Having already signed a few top players—Notre Dame's Angelo Bertelli, for one—they met with fury.

"Go buy a football and play a game," snapped NFL Commissioner Elmer Layden, the former All-American halfback at Notre Dame. "Then come around and see us again in a few years."

The representatives, angry and confident of their undertaking, retaliated by signing more players, offering huge sums of money to NFL stars, and fielding teams that were, if not the equal of NFL teams, most certainly strong and representative. Their efforts were to result in a mini-merger in 1950 in which three teams—Cleveland, San Francisco, and Baltimore—were given entrance into the NFL while the others disbanded.

But the Giants had problems on the field in '45, too. Owen, disturbed at first and then absolutely depressed, told a writer that "things have never been this bad for the Giants. Besides Paschal, we don't have another back who could make an NFL team. I've never had a worse line, and these morons don't know the first thing about defense."

Owen's opinion was upheld. The Giants of 1945 were 3-6-1, their worst showing since 1932 and only the fourth sub-.500 season in their history.

Tim and Jack Mara were determined to change the face of disaster in a hurry, and they set out to find, sign, or purchase as many quality athletes as they could over the winter and spring months.

They acquired Notre Dame tackle Jim "Superman" White,

and when DeWitt "Tex" Coulter was flunked out of West Point he, too, signed on with the Giants. White and Coulter were both 225-pound linemen with sprinter's speed, and they promised to give a new look to the tired old Giant lines.

With Paschal and Hapes to run the ball, Owen felt he was close to fielding the ideal backfield for his A-formation. But he still needed one player, a hard-running back who could pass with superior talent. He studied rosters of the other nine clubs and then told the Maras who he wanted.

"If you get me Frankie Filchock," he said, "I'll win you a championship."

Tim Mara tried, but Filchock, who had sat as Sammy Baugh's understudy in Washington, was not easily available. T.J. finally convinced the Redskins to trade him but then found he had to break a long-standing policy to sign the 5-feet-11, 195-pounder. Filchock wanted more than one year's security, and Mara had never offered any of his players or coaches—including Benny Friedman, Ken Strong, Ward Cuff, Tuffy Leemans, Mel Hein, or Steve Owen—anything more than 1-year terms.

But T.J. wanted Filchock badly. To get him, he had to agree to a 3-year, $35,000 contract, the first multiple-year agreement in the history of the team.

Filchock was worth it. He could run and he could pass, and he did both with a superstar's flair. The mere presence of this performer on the field rejuvenated the team, and after Filchock won the home opener 28-24 against the Chicago Cardinals on a 55-yard pass to Frank Liebel, Owen was jubilant. "I never thought one man could make such a difference to a team," he said, "but Frankie is amazing."

In a later game against the Bears, Filchock so dominated the result—a 31-0 Giant victory—that Tim Mara compared him to Friedman for his spectacular effect on the club.

The 1946 season ended with the Giants on top of the East with a 7-3-1 record, and Filchock's statistics were startling. He had established team records for completions, yardage gained passing, and touchdowns passing, as well as leading the team in rushing. At the age of 30, his career was still mostly ahead of him.

The Bears had won the West with an 8-2-1 mark, and the championship game, which would be played in the Polo Grounds, saw the Giants installed as surprising but solid 5-1 favorites.

Such success clearly came because Filchock was so extraordinary. But on the morning of the championship game, stunned fans found out something else about this product of Crucible, Pennsylvania. He was also dishonest.

The afternoon before the game, Tim Mara had been summoned to the office of New York City Mayor William O'Dwyer. "I cannot discuss this on the phone," he said, "but something is wrong. Get over here right away. You have to be told immediately."

What Mara learned was that, less than twenty-four hours before the most important game of their careers, Filchock and Hapes were being questioned as to their part in attempting to fix games through a known gambler named Alvin Paris.

As it developed, both had been offered bribes to fix the championship game, to let Chicago win. Hapes admitted his part in not reporting Paris's offer—$2,500 in cash and a $1,000 bet in his name on the 5-1 underdog Bears. But Filchock denied knowledge of any bribe or fix attempt, admitting only that he knew Paris and had had dinner with him on occasion.

The police, determining that the two players had done nothing criminal, released them. Then NFL Commissioner Bert Bell, the one-time owner and coach of both the Philadelphia and Pittsburgh franchises who had replaced Elmer Layden a year earlier, had to act. The integrity of the game had been damaged, and the fans were questioning the teams' honesty.

Mara offered to bench both players. Bell, believing the

players' stories, ruled that Hapes, who admitted receiving a bribe offer, could not play. Filchock, who denied receiving one, would be allowed to play. The loss of Hapes would be all but fatal; he had been an All-Pro runner, and his value to the team was great. But at least Filchock would play. Perhaps the Giants had a chance.

Father Benedict Dudley, a permanent member of the Mara entourage, was given the task of telling the players. "I didn't know what to say," he recalls. "Nothing like this had ever happened. I was bitterly disappointed myself, and I could only imagine how the team felt. This was their chance to become champions, and now their chance had been greatly reduced."

Walking quietly into the dressing room, Father Dudley told the players what had transpired in the past 24 hours. Then he exhorted them to act as men. "This game of yours has always been played in the sunlight. Because of this incident, today's game will be played in the shadows of doubt. It is up to you to restore the faith of the fans in professional football and in the New York Giants."

Filchock was there, and he knelt with the rest of the team to pray. Only Filchock knew that he, too, had been offered a bribe. He had lied when he denied the accusation, lied to play in this championship game. He was the Giants' most valuable player, yet when he trotted onto the field the crowd cascaded him with jeers. He had no way to hide. He had no choice but to play as well as he could, to try to drown his guilt in the glory of victory.

He tried. After the Giants fell behind 14-0 in the first quarter, after his nose had been broken and the blood was streaming down his face, Filchock still refused to give up. He passed for 2 touchdowns to Liebel and Steve Filipowicz to tie the game, but that was the Giants' best effort. The Bears, with Sid Luckman directing a potent offense, tore New York up after that, winning the championship 24-14.

It was to be Filchock's final game as a Giant. Some months

later, testifying under oath at Paris's trial, he admitted that he had lied and had received a bribe offer from Paris.

Paris was convicted, and so was Filchock—by Bert Bell. Realizing that he made a mistake in allowing Filchock to play in the championship game, Bell corrected his error with an official statement: "As commissioner of the National Football League," he said, "I find Merle Allison Hapes and Frank Filchock guilty of actions detrimental to the welfare of the National Football League and of professional football, and I hereby suspend each of them indefinitely. This suspension prevents the employment of Hapes or Filchock by any club in the National Football League as player, coach, or in any capacity whatsoever."

Owen, perhaps as much as the Maras themselves, was crushed. "It just makes you sick when you think of how hard so many people have worked to build this game up, and then think of how those lice tried to wreck it. They went to work on those kids in a dirty, shameful way and got them into a spot where they didn't dare try to get out. They ruined their lives."

The damage had been done, and now that damage had to be corrected and forgotten. Although the Giants were not to win another championship in the 1940s, they were to play an integral part in the costly and tenacious battle against the All-America Conference.

Lightly regarded and often ridiculed by the NFL, the AAC nevertheless had made an astonishing impact on the country, and when it became clear that the league had one powerhouse team that was being compared to the old Chicago, Green Bay, and New York juggernauts, the NFL knew at last that it was in a fight for its very life.

The first season of the AAC was 1946, when eight teams formed two divisions. The East had New York, Brooklyn, Buffalo, and Miami; in the West were Cleveland, San Francisco, Los Angeles, and Chicago. The Browns of Cleveland were 10-3-1 and won the league title.

In 1947 Miami was replaced by Baltimore. The Browns were 12-1-1 and won the league title. In 1948 the teams remained static. The Browns were 14-0-0 and won the league title. In 1949 the AAC departed from its 2-division setup because only 7 teams were left to play, the New York and Brooklyn teams having merged to form one franchise. The Browns were 9-1-2 and, in a complicated play-off system, won the league title.

Meanwhile, the NFL had become increasingly concerned at the success of the AAC. Despite the fact that many of its teams were financially ailing, they had attracted a fan following. And they had the Browns, a team said to be capable of beating any NFL team handily.

There was merit to this statement. Cleveland, coached by Paul Brown, who loaned his name to the team, had collected an array of stars perhaps unmatched in pro football's history. He had quarterback Otto Graham, runners such as Dub Jones and Marion Motley, receivers such as Mac Speedie (aptly named, for he had fire in his feet) and Dante Lavelli, and linemen Lou Groza, Tony Adamle, Lou Rymkus, Bill Willis, and Lou Saban.

The offense was fearsome. In 1949 the Browns beat Los Angeles 61-14 and 42-7; in 1948 they took Buffalo 42-13; in 1947 they registered such scores as 55-7 over Brooklyn, 42-0 over Baltimore, and 28-0 over the Colts in a rematch; in 1946, the first year of AAC operation, they scored a record 423 points in 14 games, including such exercises as 66-14 over Brooklyn, 44-0 over Miami, 51-14 over Chicago, and 42-17 over Buffalo.

Financial miseries compelled the AAC owners to seek peace in 1948, and although many of the NFL owners were ready to call off the costly war, Tim Mara and George Preston Marshall refused.

The 1948 peace proposal brought by the hard-pressed AAC asked that Cleveland, Baltimore, and San Francisco be given NFL franchises. Mara and Marshall refused, saying that would be too great a concession. Privately they speculated that by forcing the AAC to go it alone for one more year, they might water down the league sufficiently to walk in and claim what players they wanted.

The AAC, though on its final legs, refused to crumble. In 1949 Cleveland once again dominated the young league, finally causing fan boredom, and a peace was made. Ironically, it was made under the same conditions that Mara and Marshall had rejected a year earlier—San Francisco, Baltimore, and Cleveland were granted NFL status, and the rest of the teams were disbanded, their players to be chosen by the NFL teams.

When the AAC died the Giants were given their choice of any five players from the New York Yankees. They selected All-Pro tackle Arnie Weinmeister, defensive backs Tom Landry, Otto Schnellbacher, and Harmon Rowe, and guard John Mastrangelo. In addition to this impressive group, the Giants drafted well in 1949 and came up with fullback Eddie Price, quarterback Travis Tidwell, ends Bob McChesney, Kelly Mote, and Jim Duncan, guard Jon Baker, and running backs Forrest Griffith and Randy Clay.

Two key men had been added the year before—quarterback Charley Conerly from the University of Mississippi and safety Emlen Tunnell of Iowa. The Giants did not find Tunnell—he found them. Undrafted after his class had graduated, he simply traveled to New York, showed up at the Giants' offices, and asked for a tryout.

"Never heard of you," growled Owen. But general manager Ray Walsh, having worked with Well Mara on so many scouting lists, had. "Didn't you play at Iowa?" he asked. When Tunnell said he had, Walsh suggested that Owen give him a chance.

Tunnell was black, and the Giants had never before had a black player. "Heck, there wasn't any problem," Tunnell said. "I just came to play football, not make speeches. Besides, it was New York, not somewhere in the deep South.

Once I showed I could play, the guys all treated me fine."

Tunnell, in turn, treated the Giants just fine. Before he ended his career he was to intercept a league record of 79 passes, a standard that stands today despite the challenges of such superstars as Night Train Lane, Bob Boyd, and Dick LeBeau. Tunnell, a 7-time All-Pro, still holds team records for interceptions, most yards gained with interceptions, most yards gained in a season with interceptions, most touchdowns scored in a career as the result of interceptions, most punt returns in a season, career, and game, most yards returning punts in a season, career, and game, highest punt return average for a career and a game, most touchdowns returning punts in a season, career, and game, longest kick-off return, and most touchdowns by kick-off return in a game. In addition he holds the team record for most fumble recoveries in a season.

In 1967 Tunnell was inducted into the Hall of Fame to become the first black member of that honored group of men.

"Emlen," remembered Jim Lee Howell, who coached him in the later part of his career, "changed the theory of defensive safeties. He would have been too big for the job earlier [Tunnell was 6-feet-3 and 210 pounds], and they'd have made him a lineman. But he had such strength, such speed, and such quickness I'm convinced he was the best safety ever to play."

The acquisition of Charley Conerly was a bit more organized, even if the quarterback himself wasn't particularly impressed by news that the Washington Redskins had drafted him in 1945.

Conerly had spent just two years at Ole Miss before enlisting in the Marines. He spent three years in the South Pacific, and when he returned he decided to continue his education. The Redskins chose not to wait for him to graduate, relinquished their claim to him, and promptly saw both the Giants and the Brooklyn team of the AAC begin a bidding war.

Charley turned down the AAC money—a reported $80,000, four-year contract—to accept $62,500 from the Giants, saying he preferred to play in the more-established league. Well Mara and Steve Owen had seen Conerly play in a long-defunct postseason affair called the Delta Bowl, and both were impressed. Indeed, they were intrigued by his striking resemblance, facially and on the football field, to Washington's Sammy Baugh.

The young Conerly had several lean years with New York, showing great promise but exhibiting an equal flair for errors and dull play, and he became the target of an increasing number of fans who came as much to plague Charley as to see the Giants play.

The Giants of 1948 were terrible, finishing with a 4-8 record and surrendering a then-league record of 388 points defensively. But Conerly showed enough potential to give the Mara family cause for hope, and the addition of a receiver named Bill Swiacki gave Charley the target he so badly needed.

In 1949 the record was identical— 4-8—but Owen was confident that he was building yet another power. Tunnell had shaken some rookie problems and become a star, intercepting 10 passes for 251 yards and 2 touchdowns, running back 26 punts for 315 yards, and showing great improvement in both his tackling and on-the-field awareness.

Moreover, Owen had installed the T-formation with the help of a one-time Brooklyn College quarterback named Allie Sherman, and Conerly quickly took to the alignment designed for the passer. Another young player, Gene "Choo Choo" Roberts, served nobly, gaining 634 yards and scoring 17 touchdowns from his backfield positions. In addition Roberts became another Conerly target and added 711 yards with receptions, once beating the Bears by catching a Conerly pass and sprinting 85 yards in the closing minutes. Roberts, no bigger than 5-feet-11 and 185 pounds, still holds the team record for the 218 yards he gained rushing in one game in 1950, and in 1949 he went over the 100-yard mark in 3 games.

The 1940s had not been kind to the Giants or to the NFL, but as they passed into history, a new dynasty was struggling through its infancy in the Polo Grounds. All the ingredients were either there or on the way—Conerly, Roberts, Swiacki, Tunnell, Weinmeister, Landry, Schnellbacher, DeRogatis, and Coulter were members of the team. Others, such as Frank Gifford, Kyle Rote, Ray Krouse, Roosevelt Brown, Jack Stroud, Bill Stribling, and Ray Beck would soon be signed.

The war with the AAC was over, and so was the drop in attendance, which was attributable to World War II and the sinking Giant fortunes on the field.

The development of Conerly, Gifford, and Rote would take the bulk of the headlines in the 1950s, but before they, too, passed into the next decade, scores of football players would earn praise for their performances in New York.

The Golden Age of the New York Giants was dawning.

GIANTS OF THE FORTIES

Adams, O'Neal	End	Arkansas	1941-45
Adams, Verlin	Tackle	Morris Harvey	1942-45
Agajanian, Ben	Kicker	New Mexico	1949, 1954-57
Atwood, John	Back	Wisconsin	1948
Austin, Bill	Guard	Oregon State	1949-50, 1953-57
Avedisian, Charles	Guard	Providence	1942-44
Baker, Jon	Guard	California	1949-52
Barbor, Ernie	Center	San Francisco	1945
Barbour, Wes	Quarterback	Wake Forest	1945
Barker, Hubert	Back	Arkansas	1942-45
Barrett, Emmet	Center	Portland	1942-44
Beeble, Keith	Back	Occidental	1944
Beil, Kay	Tackle	Washington State	1942
Beil, Lawrence	Tackle	Portland	1948

Blazine, Anthony	Tackle	Illinois Wesleyan	1940-41
Blozis, Al	Tackle	Georgetown	1942-44
Blumenstock, Jim	Back	Fordham	1947
Brahm, Larry	Guard	Temple	1943
Brovarney, Casimir	Tackle	Detroit	1941
Brown, Dave	Back	Alabama	1943, 1946-47
Browning, Greg	End	Denver	1947
Buffington, Harry	Guard	Oklahoma A&M	1942
Butkus, Carl	Tackle	George Washington	1949
Byler, Joe	Tackle	Nebraska	1946
Cantor, Les	Back	UCLA	1942
Caranci, Roland	Tackle	Colorado	1944
Carroll, Vic	Tackle	Nevada	1943-47
Cheverko, George	Back	Fordham	1947-48
Chickerneo, John	Back	Pittsburgh	1942
Clay, Roy	Back	Colorado	1944
Coates, Ray	Back	LSU	1948-49
Cole, Pete	Guard	Trinity (Texas)	1937-40
Colhouer, Jake	Guard	Oklahoma	1949
Conerly, Charley	Quarterback	Mississippi	1948-61
Cope, Frank	Tackle	Santa Clara	1938-47
Coulter, Dewitt (Tex)	Tackle	Army	1946-52
Cuff, Ward	Back	Marquette	1937-45
Culwell, Val	Guard	Oregon	1942
Damiani, Francis	Tackle	Manhattan	1944
Danowski, Ed	Back	Fordham	1934-41
DeFillippo, Lou	Center	Fordham	1941, 1945-48
Dell Isola, John	Center	Fordham	1934-40
Dennerlien, Gerry	Tackle	St. Mary's	1937-40
Dennery, Vince	End	Fordham	1941
DeRogatis, Al	Tackle	Duke	1949-52

Dobelstein, Bob	Guard	Tennessee	1946-48
Doggert, Keith	Tackle	Wichita	1942
Doolan, John	Back	Georgetown	1945-46
Dubzinski, Walt	Guard	Boston College	1943
Duden, Dick	End	Navy	1949
Duggan, Gil	Tackle	Oklahoma	1940
Eakin, Kay	Back	Arkansas	1940-41
Eaton, Lou	Tackle	California	1945
Edwards, Bill	Guard	Baylor	1941-42, 1946
Erickson, Bill	Guard	Mississippi	1948
Eshmont, Len	Back	Fordham	1940-41
Ettinger, Don	Guard	Kansas	1948-50
Faircloth, Art	Back	North Carolina	1947-48
Falaschi, Nello	Back	Santa Clara	1938-41
Fennema, Carl	Center	Washington	1948-49
Filchock, Frank	Quarterback	Indiana	1946
Filipowicz, Steve	Back	Fordham	1945-46
Fischer, Cletus	Back	Nebraska	1949
Fox, Samuel	End	Ohio State	1945-46
Franck, George	Back	Minnesota	1941, 1945-48
Garner, Bob	Guard	No College	1945
Garzoni, Mike	Guard	Southern California	1948
Gehrke, Bruce	End	Columbia	1948
Gehrke, Fred	Back	Utah	1948
Gelatka, Charles	End	Mississippi State	1937-40
Gladchuck, Chet	Center	Boston College	1941, 1946-47
Gorgone, Pete	Back	Nuhlenberg	1946
Governali, Paul	Quarterback	Columbia	1947-48
Grate, Carl	Center	Georgia	1943
Greenhalgh, Bob	Back	San Francisco	1949
Hachten, Bill	Guard	Stanford	1947
Hall, H.	Center	No College	1942

Hapes, Merle	Back	Mississippi	1942-46
Hare, Cecil	Back	Gonzaga	1946
Harrison, Granville	End	Mississippi State	1941
Harrison, Max	End	Auburn	1940
Hein, Mel	Center	Washington State	1931-45
Hensley, Dick	End	Kentucky	1949
Herber, Arnie	Quarterback	Regis	1944-45
Hienstra, Ed	Center	Sterling	1942
Horne, Richard	Guard	Oregon	1941
Hovious, John	Back	Mississippi	1945
Howell, Jim Lee	End	Arkansas	1937-42, 1946-48
Hutchinson, Bill	Back	Dartmouth	1942
Hutchinson, R.	Tackle	Chattanooga	1949
Iverson, Chris	Back	Oregon	1947
Johnson, Jon	Back	Mississippi	1948
Kane, Herb	Tackle	Oklahoma Teachers	1944-45
Karcis, John	Back	Carnegie Tech	1938-39 1943
Keahy, Eulis	Guard	George Washington	1942
Kearns, Tom	Tackle	Miami	1945
Kershaw, George	End	Colgate	1949
Kerzko, Alex	Tackle	Michigan State	1942
Keuper, Ken	Back	Georgia	1948
Kinscherf, Carl	Back	Colgate	1943-44
Klasoskus, Al	Tackle	Holy Cross	1941-42
Kline, Harry	End	Kansas Teachers	1939-41
Klotovich, Mike	Guard	St. Mary's	1945
Kolman, Ed	Tackle	Temple	1949
Landsholl, Granville	Back	Southern California	1940
Lasri, John	End	Georgetown	1942

Lechner, Edgar	Tackle	Minnesota	1942
Leemans, Tuffy	Back	George Washington	1936-43
Lieberum, Don	Back	Manchester	1942
Lieble, Frank	End	Norwich	1942-47
Lindahl, Virgil	Guard	Nebraska State	1945
Little, Jim	Tackle	Kentucky	1945
Livingston, Howard	Back	No College	1944-47
Lovuolo, Frank	End	St. Bona-venture	1949
Lummus, John	End	Bayler	1941
Lunday, Ken	Center	Arkansas	1937-41 1946-47
McCafferty, Don	End	Ohio State	1946
McClain, Clint	Back	SMU	1941
McGee, Ed	Tackle	Temple	1940
McLaughry, John	Back	Brown	1940
Maikkula, Ken	End	Connecticut	1942
Mallouf, Ray	Quarterback	SMU	1949
Marefos, Andy	Back	St. Mary's	1941-42
Marone, John	Guard	Manhattan	1943
Martin, Frank	Back	Alabama	1945
Mead, John	End	Wisconsin	1946-47
Mellus, John	Tackle	Villanova	1938-41
Mercer, Jim	Quarterback	Oregon State	1942-43
Mertes, Bernie	Back	Iowa	1949
Miklich, Bill	Back	Idaho	1947-48
Miller, Ed	Back	New Mexico	1939-40
Minisi, Tony	Back	Penn	1948
Moore, Ken	Center	W. Virginia Wesleyan	1940
Morrow, Bob	Back	Illinois Wesleyan	1945
Mullins, Noah	Back	Kentucky	1949
Nielsen, Walter	Back	Arizona	1940
Niles, Gary	Back	Iowa	1946-47
Nix, Emery	Quarterback	TCU	1943-46

Nutt, Richard	Back	Texas State	1949
Oldershaw, Doug	Guard	Santa Barbara	1939-41
Owen, Alton	Back	Mercer	1939-41
Owen, Vilas	Quarterback	Wisconsin Teachers	1942
Palazzi, Lou	Center	Penn State	1946-47
Paschal, Bill	Back	George Washington	1943-47
Paschka, Gordon	Guard	Minnesota	1947
Pederson, Winifield	Tackle	Minnesota	1941-45
Perdue, Willard	End	Duke	1944
Petrilas, William	End	No College	1944-45
Piccolo, Bill	Center	Canisius	1943-45
Pipkin, Joyce	End	Arkansas	1948
Poole, Jim	End	Mississippi	1937-41, 1946
Poole, Ray	End	Mississippi	1947-52
Principe, Dominic	Back	Fordham	1940-42
Pritko, Steve	End	Villanova	1943
Pugh, Marion	Quarterback	Texas A&M	1941-45
Ragazzo, Phil	Tackle	Western Reserve	1945-47
Reagan, Frank	Back	Penn	1941, 1946-48
Roberts, Gene	Back	Chattanooga	1947-50
Roberts, Tom	Tackle	DePaul	1943
Royston, Ed	Guard	Wake Forest	1948-49
Salschieder, John	Back	St. Thomas	1949
Sanchez, John	Tackle	San Francisco	1949-50
Schmeelk, Gary	Tackle	Manhattan	1942
Schuler, Bill	Tackle	Yale	1947-48
Scott, Joe	Back	San Francisco	1948-53
Seick, Earl	Guard	Manhattan	1942-43
Shaffer, Leland	Quarterback	Kansas State	1935-42, 1945
Shediosky, Ed	Back	Tulsa	1945
Siegel, Jules	Back	Northwestern	1948

Sivell, Ralph	Guard	Auburn	1944-45
Soar, Hank	Back	Providence	1937-44, 1946
Sohn, Ben	Guard	Southern California	1941
Springer, Harold	End	Oklahoma State	1945
Stenn, Paul	Tackle	Villanova	1942
Strong, Ken	Back	NYU	1933-35, 1939-47
Sulaitis, Joe	Back	No College	1943-53
Swiacki, Bill	End	Columbia	1948-50
Tobin, George	Guard	Notre Dame	1947
Tomaini, Army	Tackle	Catawba	1945
Treadway, John	Tackle	Hardin-Simmons	1947-48
Trocolor, Bob	Back	Alabama	1942-44
Tunnell, Emlen	Back	Iowa	1948-58
Turbert, Francis	Back	Morris Harvey	1943
Tuttle, Orville	Guard	Oklahoma City	1937-41
Umont, Frank	Tackle	No College	1943-45
Visnic, Larry	Guard	St. Benedict	1943-45
Vosberg, Don	End	Marquette	1941
Walker, Paul	End	Yale	1948
Walls, Bill	End	TCU	1937-43
Weiss, John	End	No College	1944-47
White, Art	Guard	Alabama	1937-39, 1945
White, Jim	Tackle	Notre Dame	1945-50
Widseth, Ed	Tackle	Minnesota	1937-40
Williams, Frank	Back	Utah State	1948
Williamson, Ernie	Tackle	North Carolina	1948
Wynne, Harry	End	Arkansas	1945
Yeager, Howard	Back	Santa Barbara	1940-41
Younce, Len	Guard	Oregon State	1941-48

8

Jim Lee Howell

It was time to fire Steve Owen.

Nothing like that had ever happened to the New York Giants before, mainly because Owen's 23-year tenure had precluded the hiring, or firing, of many head coaches. The four who served only briefly at the start of the team's history—Bob Folwell, Joe Alexander, Earl Potteiger, and Leroy Andrews—had all retired or resigned.

But Stout Steve was permanent. He had become as closely aligned with the Mara Family as any man could or would. He had taken the team to championships and glory and had supervised its growth from a period of financial insecurity to one of flowering affluence.

Then in 1953 it became obvious to the three Maras that their old friend had been caught and passed by the more imaginative coaches all over the National Football League.

The 1953 Giants were terrible. Their record was 3-9, and

even that was not indicative of the sort of calamity that had befallen the House of Mara. Their football was outdated and sluggish. The team had suffered from within; the organization and coaching techniques were no longer adequate for modern players in the modern NFL.

"It was," Jack Mara recalled, "the toughest thing I ever had to do with the Giants. Steve was like family."

Nevertheless, it had to be done, and just days after the final game of the season—a humiliating 42-14 loss to Cleveland—Steve was asked to pay a visit to the Giants' offices.

He was totally unaware of what was to transpire, and when he strode casually into T.J.'s office, he flopped into a chair, looked around at three troubled faces, and asked, "What's up, men?"

It was Steve's job that was up, and Jack Mara, who acted as family spokesman, broke the news. He softened it with explanations—the search would be for a younger man, a healthier man, a man with the "new football" in his head. He told Steve there would always be a job for him in the Giants' scouting department.

Steve refused the job. He was bitter and hurt, astonished that his old friend T.J., with whom he had worked for so long without even the formality of a signed contract, would tolerate his sons' actions.

It was sticky, but it had been done. Now the Maras set out to find a new coach, for there was an opening in New York for the first time in more than two decades.

"We tried for Red Blaik," admits Well Mara, "but he said he wouldn't care to leave West Point. He had been working with us as a sort of adviser, and he said he'd continue to do that if we wanted it, and he'd help us find a new coach. But he didn't want the job."

Other men's names were considered, men in both the collegiate and professional ranks.

Then Jack and Well surprised everyone.

"When we fired Steve," Well says, "we had three assistant coaches on the team: Allie Sherman, Jim Lee Howell, and Ed Kolman. We did not consider Kolman for the job, but I sat down with the other two men and told them I was going to ask for Blaik. But, if he turned me down, I would consider them. I also had to tell them that I couldn't guarantee their jobs if Blaik accepted because head coaches should have the right to choose their own assistants.

"Jim Lee said he could accept those terms. Allie could not and made plans to accept a job in the Canadian League."

As Jim Lee recalls the weeks of doubt after Owen's firing, the last thing in his mind was getting the head coaching job. "Heck, I figured Well was just being nice to me. So right after the season we packed our bags and were about to start for home when I got a telegram from Well asking me to stop by the office before we left. I never thought about the coaching job. I figured it was some minor detail that I was supposed to take care of during the off-season."

Jim Lee walked into the team's 17th-floor office on West 42nd Street and found the Maras waiting for him.

"Better take a seat," said Jack. "How would you like to coach the Giants?"

Howell would, indeed, like to coach the Giants, and in less than an hour details were arranged and a contract was signed.

Jim Lee then went back downstairs, joined his wife, and began the drive to Lonoke, Arkansas, where the winter would be spent on the Howells' 700-acre farm.

But Jim Lee left the Maras to the outrage of New York's press. Howell was virtually unknown. He certainly had no name with which to sell tickets or assure fans of success. His coaching duties, in the main, had consisted of schooling the receivers. Most of the criticism included the charge that the thrifty Maras had hired Jim Lee because he would work cheaply, whereas a big-name coach would have demanded much more money. Such criticism did not faze the Maras.

"I was impressed with his character and strength," Well says. "In a lot of ways he reminded me of Steve Owen."

Well had another surprise for Howell. The surprise was named Vince Lombardi.

"I had wanted Vince to join us as an assistant coach," Well says. "He had been working under Red Blaik at West Point, and he had impressed everyone with his dedication and knowledge of the game. I can remember one summer when we invited the Army coaching staff to our training camp at Bear Mountain, when I knew I wanted Lombardi.

"We were sitting in the dining room up there. It was crowded. Vince had gotten fascinated by a new way of snapping the ball from center—with a little twist, so that the quarterback would get the ball crosswise, ready to grip the laces and throw or hand off. He wanted to convince us that the extra turn of the hand wouldn't slow up the snap. 'Look,' he bellowed, slapping his forehead excitedly. 'I can hit myself with the side of my hand as fast as with the palm. Look!' And there he was, while all the other diners in the room watched dumbfounded, slapping himself repeatedly on the head."

Well Mara informed Jim Lee that he had invited the West Point aide to join the Giants' staff, but only if Lombardi met with Howell's approval. "Tell him to come on down to Arkansas and see me," Jim Lee said. "We'll talk."

A week later, Lombardi flew to Arkansas. A week after that, he returned to New York. "I don't think I made a very good impression," he told Well Mara. "I called his town Lonesome Oaks, and when I got there he was out plowing the fields or something and I had to walk through the mud with my city shoes. I must have looked silly."

But Howell already had called Mara. "I think that young man is going to be a hell of a coach. I'm delighted to have him."

Lombardi would be Howell's offensive backfield coach. Ed Kolman would be retained as offensive line coach. Bill

Swiacki was persuaded to leave the insurance field and sign on as coach of the receivers. Tom Landry, the All-Pro defensive back, would act as a player-coach. That staff, which later would include Allie Sherman, Bill Austin, and Harland Svare, would revolutionize professional football.

Indeed, the staff was the hallmark of Howell's success. Unlike Sherman, his successor, Jim Lee felt entirely comfortable delegating most of the authority to his assistants once he was convinced that they had the ability to coach. He often joked that "All I do for this team is run the curfew checks and blow up the footballs." But Jim Lee also gave the team leadership, direction, and strength.

"There was a lot more to Jim Lee than anyone thought," said Alex Webster, who played for him and later accepted the head coaching job when Sherman was dismissed in 1969. "He was a tough man, but fair, and you always knew exactly how he felt. If you did your job, he'd leave you alone. If you didn't, he'd tell you and he wouldn't waste words."

Jim Lee Howell knew where he stood and what he had to do. "Yep," he drawled once, "one fellow is responsible for the ground attack here, another for the defense, another for the passing. But when it's fourth-and-one, that's mine."

The new coach was an example of the rewards of the Mara family. He had played well and long for the Giants, from 1937 through 1942, and then from 1946 through 1948 when he returned from a tour of duty with the Marines in World War II.

The Marines had toughened him, but only externally. The toughness from within was an inherent trait. "I only saw him angry, really angry, once," recalled safety Jimmy Patton, who was killed in an automobile crash in December 1972. "We were playing an important game with the Browns, and somebody on the field had missed a block or a pass or something. I wasn't sure because we were conferring with the defensive coaches at the time. But all of a sudden I saw this gigantic man [Howell is 6-feet-4 and 250 pounds] racing up the sideline. The look on his face was pure anger. He knew he couldn't hit the player, but he had to do something, so he reached down and punched the bench. You know something? A part of it splintered. He knew what he wanted, and what he wanted was perfection."

Howell was a native of Arkansas, and even today, in his role as director of personnel for the Giants, he has lost neither the pleasant drawl nor the gentlemanly hospitality of the South. His sports involvement was not limited to football as a collegian, for he was a member of the United States Olympic basketball team in 1936. The following year he joined the Giants as a two-platoon end.

"He was really tough," Well Mara says. "He was a big, fast, strong, and smart football player. I don't think he ever made All-Pro, but he could have. He was a fine player."

During his playing career, Jim Lee was a member of four championship teams in New York, always one of the quiet, unnoticed players but one integral to the success of the team.

"I just loved football," he says. "It was what I wanted to do, and I had always thought about coaching, too."

In fact Howell realized his coaching ambitions before he finished his career as an active Giant. He assumed the role of head coach at Wagner College on Staten Island, and he commuted between the Giants and the college not only as a player but later when he was an assistant coach under Owen.

"I would leave home each morning at 7:30 to be at the Polo Grounds in uniform at 9:30," he remembers. "Then I turned around in the afternoon and made the trip back to Wagner. I'd take a train to the ferry, the ferry across New York Bay, and then the subway up to the Polo Grounds."

During Jim Lee's tenure as head coach, which lasted for 7 years, the Giants won 3 conference championships—1956, 1958, and 1959—and 1 league title, in 1956, on a 47-7 rubout of the Chicago Bears.

Howell was the coach when the Giants and the Baltimore

Colts played "the greatest game in the history of professional football," the 1958 sudden-death, overtime championship game, won by Baltimore 23-17 after 8:15 of the extra period.

"I guess that was my greatest thrill, despite losing the game," he says. "I don't think two teams ever played a better game. We couldn't find more than two or three mistakes, total, when we studied those films."

Several other notable events occurred during Howell's seven years at the helm of the Giants. The emergence of Charley Conerly as a quarterback of consummate skills gave the team a weapon more potent than it had had in decades. The addition of such defensive players as Sam Huff, Rosey Grier, Andy Robustelli, Dick Modzelewski, Jimmy Patton, and Tom Scott created the league's most frightening defensive unit.

Offensive players such as Frank Gifford, Kyle Rote, Alex Webster, Mel Triplett, Bob Schnelker, Don Heinrich, Joe Morrison, and Phil King, who either joined the team or blossomed under Howell, made points and yards easier and easier to accumulate.

Linemen came by the droves, the best of them being tackle Rosey Brown, a twenty-seventh round draft choice from Morgan State; Darrell Dess, a bulky, squat guard from North Carolina State; Jack Stroud, a muscular, weight-lifting giant from Tennessee; center Ray Wietecha, a clever, tough, one-time baseball professional out of Indiana; and tackle Frank Youso, another hulking brute from Minnesota.

It was a period of plenty, and Howell knew his staff would put the pieces together. That fact, perhaps more than any other, stands out as the best tribute to Jim Lee's teaching skills. No head coach in the history of this game has had as many apprentices achieve success than those men who worked under the towering, prematurely gray, cackling-with-laughter Howell.

A list of those men includes Lombardi, who became one of pro football's Hall of Fame members in 1971; Tom Landry, the only coach the Dallas Cowboys have ever had; Allie Sherman, who took over the Giants in 1961 and won three consecutive championships; Harland Svare, who went on to coach both the Rams and the Chargers; and such players-turned-head coaches as Alex Webster, Bill Austin, Dick Nolan, and Ed Hughes.

No other head coach has been able to produce so many men who achieved success on their own. Lombardi, for example, who built powerhouses in Green Bay, realized that the Packers' success was mostly his own doing since none of his assistants who left for teams of their own made it.

Jim Lee maintained a warm and friendly atmosphere, and perhaps because he was vulnerable to the "Mara way" he treated his players and assistant coaches more as a doting father than as a boss. He speaks highly of all those who worked for him; indeed, few men can recall a time when Jim Lee did not speak kindly of anyone. It is simply not in his nature.

The closest Howell ever came to criticism was in reference to Landry when Tom assumed the Dallas job and began showing his now-obvious talents. "Tom is a warm person," Howell says, "but not with his players. He gets impatient with them. He doesn't pat them on the back. He expects them to go out there and do their jobs. One thing is that he's so much smarter than most of the players. Maybe he should be more of a dope, like me. He's a cold type, like Paul Brown. He's a perfectionist, too, like Brown. And he's smarter than anyone."

Howell enjoys telling a story on Landry about the time they were preparing a defensive setup for a Sunday game. "Every defense has a weakness if you can spot it," Howell says, "and one of our players pointed out the weakness in this defense and asked Tom what would happen if the offense did a certain thing.

"'They won't do it,' Tom said. 'They won't be able to see

it. It's too complicated.' Well, they didn't do it. Tom was right, and the defense worked."

Howell had equal praise for Lombardi and Sherman, even after the latter was dismissed amid signs of tension within the team administration. Jim Lee always speaks his mind. "Allie Sherman, I guess, was the smartest offensive football person I ever knew. With a blackboard and a piece of chalk, the man was a genuine genius."

What finally convinced Howell to resign?

"I didn't have a home life," he said. "I married late [1952], and that was my mistake because I see I've missed a lot of good livin'. Coaching the Giants takes too much time, requires too much travel, and because of our late start, our kids were growing up without me being around too much. I didn't like that, but I didn't know what to do because I couldn't afford to just quit."

Howell was changing. "I'd spend all day at practice, travel all weekend, argue with the coaches and yell at the players, and when I got home I found I was still irritable with my wife. I couldn't even sleep any more, and I stopped getting any pleasure at all from football. I couldn't stand losing, but I didn't really enjoy winning."

He was, clearly, in a quandary. But Well Mara was aware of the situation even before Jim Lee mentioned it:

I can remember being with him on the field during a practice. We were talking about the next season, about the draft coming up and all the scouting that still had to be done, and I said something about the job getting too big for me to handle by myself. His eyes kind of lit up, and he said he understood that and would be interested in doing that sort of work some day.

Later on, when we won the Division again [it was 1959], I spoke with Jim Lee again. He said his attitude hadn't changed, and I told him I had decided to create a new position for a personnel director. I made it a joke. I said the man I wanted had to have a great deal of football background, had to know our needs, and might even have to be a former Giant coach. Then I asked if he knew anyone with those qualifications.

He looked up at me and asked if I was kidding. I said I was serious. Then he said he'd be thrilled to take the job if his salary would be the same and if he didn't have to travel very much. We agreed to that.

But there was still a championship game to play [a rematch with the Colts]. He said he would retire if we won, but that he would coach for the 1960 season if we didn't. He wanted to go out as a winner.

Either way, Howell wanted to make the announcement as soon as possible. The championship game was played, and the Giants lost 31-16 on a Colt explosion in the fourth quarter.

Then, on February 24, 1960, Jim Lee told the public of his decision and forthcoming new position.

"I'm not sick, not mad at anybody, and my wife didn't tell me to quit," he said, quickly erasing all three stock excuses used when a coach or manager resigns. "If we had beaten Baltimore I would have wound up my coaching then and there. The pressures which I had built up within myself became too difficult to bear."

Well Mara added that he had gently pushed Howell into the decision. "I've been in the field and away from the business end of the organization too long," he said. "If something happened to my brother we'd be up a creek without a paddle, so Jim Lee goes into my job and I go into the front office."

That statement, of course, proved to be misleading. Well hasn't left the team end of the business to this day, but he did have Howell handle much of the telephone and desk work.

"I know I'm going to like my new job," Jim Lee said.

"Although we lost only two games last fall, the best record compiled by any NFL club in years, each one became un-bearable. I couldn't forget the defeats. I'd study films after practice, then take them home with me, not even pausing to say hello to my wife and kids. My eyes began to twitch, and I'm going to have to get glasses. I told Well I'd quit in a minute if I could afford to, and that's the way this started."

Howell also pointed out what he felt were flaws in his own make-up and approach to the game. "I'm just lazy, I guess. I'm not as dedicated a man as I should be. Writers would call me up at dinner time and ask if I was eating. When I said that I was, they would say it would only take a minute. Well, my dinner always got cold. My wife got to resent my attitude. If I got too cantankerous, she'd say, 'Don't you get nasty to me, and go take out the garbage.' It would bring me back to reality, and when I saw reality I saw that coaching wasn't as important to me as it once was. I'm happy to get out of it now, and I look on this new job as a tremendous challenge."

After Howell's final game as the coach of the Giants, a 34-28 loss to the Cleveland Browns, the players gave him a silver football with their names engraved on it. They also presented him with a statue of a runner. He always ran them hard in training camp, and that was their way of kidding him about it. He was pleased and laughed about it. It meant a lot to him that after so many years his players would rib him on a sentimental occasion.

The players said he was tough if you tried to get out of working hard, but they agreed he was fair. He did what he had to do for no other reason than because he had to do it. Jim Lee never carried a grudge, and he often said that one player was just like another "except some are better at football; but they're all men, and they all matter to me."

9

The Fourth Decade — 1950 - 1959

The 1950s were the decade when professional football first swept across the country, a harbinger of the multi million-dollar industry that today has captivated a nation, reduced baseball to second-fiddle status, and influenced the economics of network television.

The New York Giants, as usual, were at the forefront of this renaissance, and many of their deeds and decisions were to alter not only their future but that of the NFL as well.

It was a decade of change. Jim Lee Howell replaced Steve Owen, and the team moved its home from the Polo Grounds, where it had played since its inception in 1925, to Yankee Stadium, just across the Harlem River.

The final death throes of the All-America Conference had unleashed upon the NFL one of the most powerful teams ever assembled, the Cleveland Browns, and their battles with the Giants over a period of ten years were woven in the threads of drama and legend.

A new galaxy of superstars, more than most teams see in a

160

decade, hit the Giants' roster with shattering impact. The names of Charley Conerly, Frank Gifford, Kyle Rote, Sam Huff, Andy Robustelli, Rosey Grier, Pat Summerall, Rosey Brown, Jimmy Patton, Alex Webster, and Don Chandler became household words to millions of fans.

The Giants were to win three conference championships and a world championship in the 1950s; they also were to finish second four times. In 1958 they would take part in a breath-taking, mind-boggling, sudden-death championship game, a game that, according to most sports historians, pushed pro football to the forefront.

The juggernaut built in New York would make defense a brutal art form and would turn their fans into chanting mobs that would cheer a goal-line stand rather than an 80-yard touchdown pass.

The 1950s also would mark the death of Timothy J. Mara, founder of the team, who had seen his nickel-and-dime gamble become a success gone out of control, a money-maker beyond even the wildest dreams of this plunger and promoter to whom the unreal was a goal.

The team would watch as Vince Lombardi, an assistant coach, built a legend in Green Bay, Wisconsin, and would try mightily to lure him back to the Giants, only to be defeated by a contract and a stubborn board of directors.

And it all started with failure.

The Giants of 1950 were solid. It was a veteran team, one only beginning to show the promise of the next few years, and without the presence of the Cleveland Browns these Giants surely would have been champions of the Eastern Division, which was called the American Conference after the realignment that brought in Baltimore, San Francisco, and Cleveland as survivors of the defunct All-America Conference.

Cleveland had won 4 AAC championships in 4 years. It had the coach with the brains, Paul Brown. It had a gifted, nearly magical quarterback, Otto Graham. It had a bruising, hammering fullback, Marion Motley. It had lost just 4 games in 58 AAC tests. It was fearsome and awesome and then some, and the Giants, a team schooled in and committed to defense, seemed to have no chance.

The Browns, who were ridiculed by many as champions of a nothing league, proved their greatness in their very first NFL game. They were pitted against the NFL-champion Philadelphia Eagles in the league opener, a macabre joke on the part of the schedule-maker. Cleveland won 35-10. It wasn't even close.

In the American Conference the Browns were grouped with the Giants, Philadelphia, Pittsburgh, Washington, and the Chicago Cardinals. Nobody had a chance. It was Cleveland all the way, destined to go on to a championship game with either Los Angeles or the Chicago Bears from the National Conference.

But the Giants had profited from the collapse of the AAC. The Yankees of that league were made Giant property, and the Maras had their choice of any five players. They chose wisely and selected tackle Arnie Weinmeister, guard John Mastrangelo, and defensive backs Tom Landry, Otto Schnellbacher, and Harmon Rowe.

For the Giants' second game of the season, against the invincible Browns, Owen was ready. He sprang his Umbrella Defense on the Browns' feared passing game and initiated what has since become a common practice—keying the star runner with a defender who has no responsibilities except to dog the star's steps and be wherever the runner goes. The key for the Giants was John Cannady, and he kept Marion Motley at bay.

Graham did not complete a pass in the first half, and the Giants intercepted three. The Browns did not make a first down in that first half. The Giants could not score, either, and it was 0-0 at halftime. Even so, 0-0 against Cleveland was a marvelous situation in which to be. The Browns were confused and on the run.

"We did such a job that afternoon that I never again wanted to play offense," said Emlen Tunnell, whose judgment was never better—he became the NFL's finest strong safety.

Cleveland came out with strategy changes in the second half, but nothing worked. Owen and his staff had anticipated it all. Then Eddie Price finally crashed over for a New York touchdown, and the Giants had all the points they were to get. It was 6 more than Cleveland would earn, and the Giants registered a stunning 6-0 upset.

Two weeks later, after a 17-6 loss to Pittsburgh, the Giants hosted the Browns in the Polo Grounds. At halftime Cleveland led 13-3, and even Giant fans were talking about the first win as a fluke. "Bull," said Weinmeister. "There was nothing lucky about beating Cleveland. We were smarter and better, and we proved that defense was more important than offense."

They proved it in the second half, too, holding the Browns scoreless. One touchdown cut the Browns' lead to 13-10, and then, with 5 minutes to go in the game, the conservative Owen went for the big one. It was fourth down and 2, and the Giants were close enough for an almost-certain field goal and a 13-13 tie. Steve wanted to win it, though, and he ordered a trick play.

To achieve the first down, the Browns knew, the Giants had to give the ball to Price, the powerful inside churner. So Conerly faked to Price, and most of the Browns tackled him. Price did not have the ball. It was in the hands of halfback Joe Scott, who had taken a behind-the-back hand-off from Conerly and raced around end. Scott raced until he ran out of field. The Giants had a touchdown, a 17-13 victory over Cleveland, and 2 victories in as many meetings with the team no one should have been able to beat.

The remainder of the season saw Cleveland reassert its dominance, while the Giants lost another game that should have been won. The teams finished the season with identical 10-2 records; the Browns would have been 12-0 but for their 2 meetings with New York.

A play-off game was needed, and it was played in Cleveland's cavernous Municipal Stadium on an icy, wind-blown day. The Giants, buoyed by the confidence gained in beating the Browns twice, were just as tough as before, and they held Cleveland without a touchdown. With the score tied at 3-3, an apparent touchdown pass from Conerly to end Bob McChesney gave New York a 10-3 lead. But the other end, Kelley Mote, was whistled for being offside, negating the play. Lou Groza put Cleveland ahead with his second field goal, and a safety in the final minutes put the lid on the Giants' hopes—an 8-3 defeat.

The Rams had finished in a tie with the Bears in the West and then had won a 24-14 play-off game. The Browns, seemingly impotent only against the Giants, took the NFL championship in their first try, beating Los Angeles 30-28.

The frustrated Giants thus made plans for 1951, and the most important event was blind luck—Owen drew a slip out of the hat of commissioner Bert Bell at the draft meeting to earn the NFL's bonus pick, and the Giants landed SMU All-American Kyle Rote, a snake-hipped, swivel-jointed halfback.

Injuries, including knee damage suffered by Rote, kept the Giants from realizing their full potential, though. The 1951 season ended with a fine 9-2-1 record, but it was not enough to beat Cleveland, which had defeated the Giants twice en route to an 11-1 mark.

Conerly had been injured, and he resorted to secret medical attention so as to keep his status as the Giants' starting quarterback. Half a dozen other regulars sat out much of the year, and the wonder of the 9-2-1 record was that it was carved out on the efforts of almost one man, Eddie Price, the 5-feet-11, 190-pound second-year player who gained 971 yards and set a league record with 271 carries.

The injuries, however, worried the Maras and Owen. Rote and Conerly had them especially concerned, and when drafttime came around again they decided to draft another quality back. His name was Frank Gifford, a tall, handsome, articulate son of southern California, a multithreat performer who could run with the ball, throw it, catch it, and kick it. Many teams had Gifford rated as the country's best defensive halfback as well.

"I wanted to play for the Rams," said Gifford, today a nationally known sportscaster. "It took me a long time to make up my mind. I remember a local newspaper guy calling me and asking me how I felt about being drafted by the New York Giants. I didn't have the faintest idea of what he was saying. I guess I had heard of them, but I wasn't sure. I thought maybe the guy meant the baseball team, and that puzzled me."

Gifford eventually signed with the Giants, passing up a $10,000 offer from the Edmonton Eskimos of the Canadian League. The Giants had offered Giff only $5,000, but, as he now laughs, "At least I knew where New York was, and I knew it was big."

The addition of this man, who was to become one of the team's all-time greats, did nothing for the 1952 Giants. Rote had recovered and enjoyed a fine season, but Conerly went into a dismal slump and heard a chorus of boos in the Polo Grounds for the first time in his career. Gifford? He was an enigma. The team felt he wasn't trying hard enough. Owen thought he was loafing. There was some resentment, too, for this handsome Californian who had the All-American image, who had acted in Hollywood films, and who did not immediately become an All-Pro.

Owen was so distressed, he later said, that "I would have cut the good-looking son-of-a-bitch if he hadn't been our top draft pick." As it was, Stout Steve took this triple-threat runner-passer-receiver and put him on the defensive team.

The rest of the team suffered through a horrid season, reaching a low in the next-to-last game when Pittsburgh routed the once-proud Giant defensive unit and won 63-7. Conerly, who felt miserable, was replaced by young Fred Benners and then by Tom Landry, who had played a bit of quarterback at the University of Texas.

"I was knocked out in the third quarter," Rote cracked,

"but unfortunately I came to and had to go back in the game."

The team's final record, 7-5, was its last gasp, its last chance at respectability. The 1953 Giants skidded to 3-9 and would have been last in the Eastern Conference but for a 1-10-1 disaster suffered by the Chicago Cards.

Fans picked Conerly as the recipient of their fury. He was the villain, it was his fault, and the jeering became vicious. Signs hung from the Polo Grounds rafters—CHARLEY MUST GO, BACK TO MISSISSIPPI, YOU CREEP, CONERLY CAN'T CUT IT, WHO NEEDS CHARLEY? The grizzled Marine veteran even found boos and threats being hurled at him in the off-season while eating dinner or viewing basketball games in Madison Square Garden. Charley was 32 then, and he decided that he and his wife Perian had had enough. He said he would retire and return to his native Mississippi.

Meanwhile, Owen was in deep trouble. He was a man whose roots were too deeply entrenched in the past. He could not break away from his A-formation backfield, for instance, while all around him new minds were tapping the potential of the T-formation.

Steve refused to change. He ridiculed the new ideas, bristled at criticism, and refused to revamp the Umbrella Defense even after Paul Brown, the human computer, showed other coaches how to poke holes in it.

The next-to-last game of the 1953 season was a 62-14 loss to Cleveland. The final game was a 27-16 loss to Detroit.

The next loss was Owen's. He lost the job he had held since 1931. Steve had become a dinosaur, a symbol of the past unable, or unwilling, to adapt to the new ways.

"We needed something different, and Steve wasn't giving it to us," Gifford remembers. "I hated to see him get fired— hell, I don't like to see anybody get fired—but I sure wasn't surprised when he got it. What surprised me was who we got, Jim Lee Howell."

Although sportswriters and outsiders criticized the selection of Howell, the players applauded it. "If anything, he was a fair man, and he knew a hell of a lot about football," Gifford said. "We were sure there would be new things, a new concept. I, for one, almost fell over when I heard it was Jim Lee, but then I couldn't wait for training camp to start in 1954. I was really excited."

Perhaps Howell's first major contribution was to accept Well Mara's candidate for the offensive backfield coaching job, Vince Lombardi. An intense, totally dedicated man, Lombardi welcomed the runners in the 1954 summer camp with detailed camp schedules, clear-cut rules and regulations, and plans for a physically demanding conditioning program. "We're through fooling around," he said. "We're going to win with you people, or you people won't be around to see us lose."

Lombardi had Howell's backing, as did the other assistants, and the Giants soon realized the new regime brought with it punishment.

"We worked," said Landry, "and then we worked some more. And when we couldn't stand up any longer, we went to work all over again."

Tunnell, another superstar who had grown accustomed to the easy-going ways of the Owen administration, felt the sting of harsh practices but appreciated their value. "It was time to get the fires lit," he said. "Lots of guys needed a boot in the butt. Jim Lee and Vinnie and the others provided it. Lord, did we work."

Jim Lee had talked Conerly out of retirement, guaranteeing that he would secure the guards and tackles Charley needed for his protection. "If you do that," Conerly said, "I'll try it."

Howell succeeded wildly. Stroud and Dess, Wietecha and Brown, Schnelker and Barney Poole, Dick Nolan and Bobby Epps, Bill Svoboda, Cliff Livingston, Ken MacAfee, Herb Rich, and Don Heinrich were all brought in, either through the draft or via the trade route.

There were budding stars and former stars and current stars, and the Giants of 1954, though no better statistically (they were 7-5 and third in the East), could feel what was happening. Jim Lee discarded the outdated A-formation and put in the T-formation regularly. He delegated authority and was rewarded by the imaginative Landry, who devised the beginnings of today's 4-3-4 defense. Howell installed automatics for Conerly, enabling the quarterback to change plays at the line of scrimmage by use of code words and numbers. He put the pass back into the Giants' offense, and though the receivers caught only 3 touchdown passes in 1953, they hauled in 20 scoring passes in 1954. Schnelker and MacAfee had 8 each.

With protection, a well-devised offense, receivers who could catch, and runners who could take the pressure off, Conerly became a polished quarterback. No longer did signs wave at him. No longer was his name answered by a crescendo of boos. Toward the end of the 1954 season he threw the 100th touchdown pass of his career; only Sammy Baugh and Sid Luckman had thrown more than that.

By 1955 the Giants were moving. "We were the best damned 6-5-1 team you ever saw," said Conerly. "We lost games we should never have lost. We tied the Browns [35-35], and we should have killed them. The damned Cardinals even beat us, and that was my fault. But we were coming strong. We all felt it. The next season was going to be ours."

The 1955 season had brought Jimmy Patton to the Giants, as well as Mel Triplett, Rosey Grier, Ray Beck, Walt Yowarsky, and Harland Svare. But perhaps the most important addition was motivated by revenge. The Canadian League had raided the Giants and had come up with Arnie Weinmeister, the All-Pro defensive tackle. Well Mara was incensed. "Here we go," he said. "Let's get the best they have."

Enter Alex Webster. The 225-pound fullback was clearly the best player in the Canadian League. He was the league's Most Valuable Player in 1954, a success story in its own right.

Alex, who was a high-school All-American at Kearny, New Jersey, earned a scholarship to North Carolina State. There he acquired a well-deserved reputation as the toughest of men, once playing a full game with two broken ankles.

Gino Marchetti, the Hall of Fame defensive end from the Baltimore Colts and the man generally recognized as the toughest and strongest in the NFL throughout the 1950s, once spoke about Alex. "Tell you what," he growled. "If me and Alex are in a bar and get jumped by a dozen guys, we'll walk out without a scratch, and he'll be the one who got ten of them."

Webster was drafted by the Washington Redskins, but he was placed on defense and then cut when Don Doll, cut by Detroit, became a waiver pickup.

Disconsolate, without work or plans, Alex returned to Kearny and began to resign himself to a job with the local industry, an elevator-car factory. But one night, sitting in a bar with a newspaperman and high school friend named Paul Durkin, the pair decided to give football one more shot.

"Paul wrote a telegram to the Montreal Alouettes," Webster said, "and I sent it that night, a night letter, I think they called it. All I know is I had to borrow money to pay for it."

The next morning Alex was awakened by his mother, who told him he had a long-distance telephone call from "some man with a funny name who doesn't talk very clearly."

The man was Peahead Walker, head coach at Montreal, and he was characteristically blunt. "You must be some moron," he yelled at Webster. "You send me a telegram and you don't put in your telephone number. I had to call a dozen people to get it. Can you be up here by tonight? We have practice, and I want to see you."

Alex made it. He borrowed $100 from the grocer across the street, flew up to Montreal, and showed up in time for practice.

"I didn't know the players or the plays," he said, "but I told Peahead I was a fullback. So they put me at fullback and on the first play some great big tackle hit me a shot and put me on my ass. I was embarrassed, and in the huddle I told the quarterback to call the same play. He did. Here came the tackle, big grin on his face, and I planted my left foot and threw a right at him that cold-conked him right there on the field. Peahead thought that was funnier than hell, and he kept me over a few veterans. I guess he liked tough guys."

Webster made it big. He became a hero in Montreal and a celebrity throughout Canada, but when the Giants contacted him, he thought he was hallucinating. "The Giants? All my life I had rooted for them. I grew up just over the river, and the Giants were my team. I had hoped they would draft me out of college. Now they were asking me if I wanted to play for them. I would have given them my right arm if they had asked."

All they asked was that Webster, a solid blocker, fine receiver, and uncanny runner—he had no real speed but possessed the ability to cut and veer on a dime—perform up to the standards he had set as an Alouette. He didn't. He exceeded them. Howell stopped worrying when Big Red scored three touchdowns in the team's first two exhibition games. He had a fullback.

The team won 4 of its final 5 games and closed with a 6-5-1 record, and the league knew the truth—the Giants were on the way back, bigger and faster and smarter than ever before. The 1956 season was just around the corner.

First, the college draft produced a guard from West Virginia who turned out to be the most respected middle linebacker in the history of the league—Sam Huff. Then the Giants claimed such rookies as defensive end Jim Katcavage, receiver-punter Don Chandler, and defensive back Ed Hughes.

Huff, who was overshadowed at West Virginia by All-American tackle Bruce Bosley, was a third-round selection. The scouts raved at his strength, violence, and tenacity. He was 6-feet-2 and weighed 235 pounds, but once he arrived at the Giants' training camp he discovered he was a man without a position. He was too small for the defensive line, too slow for offensive guard, and not heavy enough for offensive tackle.

Even the coaches wondered if he would make the team, and one day Huff heard them talking about him. "I don't know what the hell to do with him," said offensive line coach Ed Kolman. "I just don't know where he can play."

Huff was depressed. He and his roommate, Don Chandler, decided they had no future in professional football. Indeed, a seriously injured shoulder had left Chandler as a punter only, and in those days roster spots were too valuable to give up for a specialist.

So the two decided to pack up and leave. They drove to Burlington Airport near the camp site in Winooski, Vermont, and waited for a scheduled flight to arrive. It was an hour late, perhaps the most fortuitous hour in the Giants' history.

While they were waiting Lombardi came speeding up, ran from the car, and found the two defectors.

"Chandler," he shouted, "you may not make this team, but I'll be damned if you run out on me. Get back to camp. And you, too, Huff. Make it fast."

They returned and became superstars in New York City.

Well Mara was busy at the same time making trades. And what trades! First, he acquired from the Rams a rookie defensive end who had played at Arnold College (now part of Bridgeport University) in Connecticut named Andy Robustelli. Robustelli had asked for permission to report two weeks late to Los Angeles since his wife was due to give birth. The Rams said they could not wait, so Andy said he would not report at all.

Then Mara called him, found out he wanted to play in New York, and one day later managed to talk the Rams into making a "minor" trade. Robustelli, of course, became part of the Giants' "Fearsome Foursome" defensive line, and in 1971 he was inducted into the Pro Football Hall of Fame.

Another trade brought the man who would play alongside Robustelli, tackle Dick Modzelewski, a rookie pried loose from the Pittsburgh Steelers.

Finally, the Giants found a new home for this new team. During the winter of 1955, a syndicate approached the Maras with an offer of $1 million to purchase the franchise and move it to Yankee Stadium. The Maras, of course, refused to sell, but they did like the idea of Yankee Stadium. It was the largest of New York City's stadiums and was more modern than the Polo Grounds. Besides, with the best of the stadiums secured, they would be in a more desirable position in the event of another challenge from a new league. The decision proved to be frighteningly accurate.

The Giants were set: new confidence, new stadium, new stars. The offense set up with Conerly at quarterback, Gifford and Webster at halfbacks, and Triplett at fullback. The offensive line was a collection of massive and mobile men. Rosey Brown (6-feet-5, 260) and Dick Yelvington (6-feet-2, 230) were the tackles; Bill Austin (6-feet-1, 225) and Jack Stroud (6-feet-2, 245) were the guards. Rote and Schnelker were the receivers.

Defensively, the front four was made up of Robustelli and Jim Katcavage (alternating with the veteran Walt Yowarsky) at ends, Modzelewski and the gargantuan Grier (6-feet-5, 285) at tackles. Ray Beck, Harland Svare, and Bill Svoboda were the linebackers. Landry had retired as a player to work full-time as the defensive coach, but the secondary still had Tunnell, Herb Rich, Dick Nolan, and Jimmy Patton. Soon Huff replaced Beck as the middle linebacker, and the team took off.

The Giants split their first 2 games of the season and then headed for yet another grudge match in Cleveland. They won it 21-19, and the offense was in high gear. Gifford came into his own as the top back in the league. Webster and Triplett were brutish, punishing runners. Don Heinrich, the reserve quarterback with a rapier mind, started every game and played just long enough to learn what the defenses were doing. Then he'd come out and confer with Conerly, and the master passer would come in and make Heinrich's analysis stand up.

The home opener was a 38-10 thrashing of Pittsburgh, followed by a 20-3 whipping of Philadelphia, and 2 more victories were added to the streak before a loss to Washington and a tie with the Bears put an end to the Giants' fantastic climb.

Then a second meeting with the Redskins produced a 28-14 victory. Even a 24-7 loss to the Browns could not prevent New York from clinching the Eastern Conference the following week with a 21-7 decision over the Eagles.

Another streak had ended, too, with the Giants' clinching. For the first time since they joined the NFL in 1950, the Cleveland Browns had failed to win their conference championship. The Giants, at 8-3-1, had easily outdistanced the 5-7 Browns, who had suffered through the first losing season in the history of the franchise. Now, for the first time in 10 years, the Giants were preparing for a championship game. The Chicago Bears, 9-2-1 in the West and a fearsome team that had scored 363 points, provided the opposition.

It couldn't really be called *opposition*. Playing in New York before a crowd of 56,836, the Giants borrowed a page from their 1934 predecessors and wore sneakers on a frozen, concrete-hard field. They were magnificent, and the Bears never even challenged them. The score was 47-7, and as Gifford remembers, "We could probably have scored a few more, but I think we had proved our point."

Huff stuck it to the Bears' All-Pro fullback, burly Rick Casares. Webster, Gifford, and Triplett ran with power and abandon. Rote used every one of his fakes and feints, operating with the skill of a surgeon on the Bears' defensive backs. Robustelli and Grier squashed whatever Huff missed. It was devastating.

"I can remember the team in the dressing room right

before the game," Howell said, "and I don't think I had ever seen a team that way. All we did was open the door and get the hell out of the way. I don't think anybody could have beaten the Giants that day. It was by far my best team to that point in my career, and that was its best game."

The Giants were on the verge of creating a dynasty, but in 1957 they were side-tracked. The reason was a rookie full-back out of Syracuse University drafted by the Cleveland Browns. His name was Jim Brown, and before his nine-year career ended he became acknowledged as the greatest full-back in the history of professional football.

Brown, 6-feet-2 and 232 pounds, hurt the Giants badly and led the Browns to a pair of regular-season victories over New York, 6-3 and 34-28. More important, he led the Browns to a 9-2-1 record, he led the league in rushing with 942 yards, and he led a Cleveland charge that took the Eastern Conference by storm. The 1957 season was 1 of only 2 in which Brown would not gain more than 1,000 yards—the other was 1962, when he amassed 996. In 1963 Brown gained 1,863 yards, an NFL record that still stands and that might in time become the one unreachable goal for future superstars.

The Giants were second to Cleveland with a disappointing 7-5 record, and all they could do was point to 1958 and mark it as a year of revenge.

It turned out to be that and much more.

Key additions were the first order of business, and Well Mara saw to that. Rosey Grier had returned from a brief stint with the Army, and such draftees as fullback Phil King, tackle Frank Youso, and guard Bob Mischak were to become solid performers. The Giants acquired defensive back Carl Karilivacz and guard Al Barry in trades, but the most impor-tant trade was the acquisition of defensive back Linden Crow from the Chicago Cards, along with placekicker Pat Summerall for rookie Bobby Joe Conrad and defensive back Dick Nolan. Nolan, incidentally, was to return in trade the following season and become part of several more championship teams in Yankee Stadium.

The early season gave no indication of the glory to follow. The Giants lost five of their six exhibition games, dropped two of their first four regular-season encounters, and then lost Gifford for a while thanks to torn ligaments in his knee.

Gifford returned to the team though not to the field, and in their next two games the Giants showed their quality. First was a meeting with the Browns, a game in which the key figure became the moody Triplett, who had to be prodded into a supereffort by defensive coach Tom Landry. "Jimmy Brown makes more yardage in a game than you do all year," Landry said, baiting Triplett. "How is that? Is he that much better than you?"

Triplett responded with a 116-yard game. Brown gained 113, and the Giants won 21-17. Conerly, who threw 3 touchdown passes, brought his career total to 140, surpassing Luckman's figure and standing second only to Sammy Baugh.

The next game was against the Baltimore Colts, who at the mid-point of the season were still undefeated. The names of the stars ring with the familiarity of all-time heroes—Johnny Unitas, Alan Ameche, Lenny Moore, Gino Marchetti, Don Pellington, and Raymond Berry.

The New York defense, rising to undreamed-of heights, stifled almost everything the Colts tried, and the Giants came away with a 24-21 victory earned on a 28-yard Summerall field goal with less than 2 minutes to be played in the final quarter.

There were now 5 games to play, and the Giants were 5-2; a 31-10 upset in Pittsburgh sorely hurt their chances. With 4 games to go, the Giants had to win them all. They beat Washington 28-14 and Philadelphia 24-10, then engineered another stunning defensive victory in Detroit, winning 19-17 when Svare blocked a 25-yard field goal attempt with 1:03 remaining.

The final game was with Cleveland, and the best the Giants could do was to finish the season in a tie with the Browns, thus necessitating a play-off the following week. In order to qualify for the NFL championship game, New York had to defeat the mighty Browns twice in two weeks. It was hardly a likely situation, and even the New York fans were pessimistic.

The game was tied at 10-10 with 4:30 to play when Summerall came on for a 38-yard field goal try. He lined up the ball, squinted through the snowstorm raging in Yankee Stadium—and missed.

But the Giants' defense did it again. The ball came back to New York, and when it was fourth down it all fell to Summerall again. This would be the final chance, and the chance was dismal since the ball was on the Cleveland 42-yard line. Pat's kick would be from the 49, a field goal of heroic proportions.

"The one I missed had not been affected by the wind," he explained. "I had figured it would be, and I had tried to kick it accordingly. This time I just tried to get it straight, but I needed a real good hit. It was a terribly long try, and with all the snow blowing around I wasn't sure I could see the goal posts."

Summerall swung his right leg, and the ball soared just past the reach of the frantic Brown defenders. It gained altitude, began to arc, and then dipped triumphantly to the ground behind the goal posts, cleanly through.

"You know something? It surprised the hell out of me," Summerall laughed much later. "I never thought I'd make it."

He had made it, and so had the Giants. Their 9-3 record matched Cleveland's, and a play-off was needed to decide the Eastern Conference winner. The game would be played the following Sunday in Yankee Stadium, and it was win or go home for both teams.

Aside from the questionable home-field advantage (which does not seem to be very strong in football), all the odds, including those of the bookmakers, favored Cleveland. The Giants already had beaten the Browns twice in 1958, and a third win seemed unlikely. The Giants had reached several peaks of emotion, each one higher than the next, and it was equally unlikely that they could achieve still another pinnacle. And Cleveland had Jim Brown waiting, ominous and threatening.

The Giants won 10-0. Huff was never better, keying on Brown so adroitly and tackling him so viciously that the fabled fullback was limited to a net gain of 18 yards by the game's end. The rest of the defense took away the passing, and it was inconceivably easy.

New York was in the championship game, and the championship game was in New York. The opposition? The Baltimore Colts, a team the Giants already had beaten during their season 24-21.

The Giants started the game badly. Gifford fumbled twice, and the Colts' offense, led by the incomparable Johnny Unitas, converted each bobble into a touchdown. New York only had Summerall's 36-yard field goal, and at halftime it was 14-3.

Early in the third quarter the Colts drove again and made it to the New York 3-yard line with a first down. But the defense, down to its last chance, came through. The next four plays cost the Colts 2 yards, and the Giants took over, battered but not beaten, with an incredibly difficult task ahead of them and the clock already working in Baltimore's favor.

Then, suddenly, it was Conerly, Rote, and Webster, and on one play the complexion of the game and its momentum swung to the Giants' side. From their 5, the Giants had managed to gain just 8 yards in 2 plays. Conerly had to pass.

The Colts knew that, but stopping him was another matter. Conerly called for Rote on a long pattern known as the Giant Special, and while the offensive linemen blocked with the fanaticism of assassins, Rote beat his man. The ball spiraled out, dropped into Rote's hands, and he raced all the way to the Baltimore 25.

Then he fumbled.

The fans sat in stunned silence. Rote seemed to be frozen by fear and crushed by the weight of what he had done. The Colts began to celebrate this act of providence before they had made sure that the ball was theirs. Only Alex Webster kept his head, and as the ball bounced crazily on the field he chased it, fielded it, cradled it in his huge hands, and was dragged down on the Baltimore 1-yard line by an army of repentant, avenging tacklers.

On the next play Triplett crashed into the end zone. It was 14-10. The Giants were moving, and the Colts suddenly were no more than decorative statuary.

Baltimore had the ball, but the New York defense got Unitas twice, spilling him for punishing losses, and the Colts had to punt. Then Conerly went to work and completed 2 passes to his deceptively fast tight end, the 6-feet-4, 220-pound Schnelker, for gains of 46 and 17 yards. Conerly faded to pass again, faked to his right, drew the Baltimore defenders in that direction, and then pivoted with the assurance of a magician whose sleight-of-hand is flawless. Conerly found Gifford all alone on the left sideline. He threw, Frank caught it—pandemonium. The Giants had taken the lead 17-14.

After that the game degenerated into a jungle war of fists and knees and elbows. Oaths and screams and splintered teeth gave a captivated television audience a glimpse of a kind of football that had not been played in decades. It was crude, cruel, wild-eyed football played by men possessed. Its fury gripped fans across the nation and instilled in them a respect, and a fear, for the game and the two extraordinary teams fighting their war.

On one play Huff chased Raymond Berry out of bounds and enraged the Colts' head coach, Weeb Ewbank, who felt that Sam had taken a cheap shot at his star receiver. Although normally a placid man, as befits an older fellow who stands 5-feet-6 and weighs perilously more than 200 pounds, Weeb went berserk. He waded into Huff cursing and swinging and landed a fist on Sam's neck. Huff exploded, long since having parted with his reason, and attacked the older man. One of his punches tagged Weeb on the chin. The two antagonists were forcibly separated by members of both teams, and they all remember Sam's eyes—wild, glassy, protruding from their sockets.

"I might have killed that man if they didn't pull us apart," Huff admitted. "I was wild. I couldn't control myself."

The Giants still had their lead, and the game dwindled down to a precious few moments. New York had the ball, and the crazed crowd kept up a steady cacophony that poured down on the field in ever-increasing waves. It was third and 4 on the Giants' 39, and 2 minutes remained. A first down would give the team ample time to run out the clock. It was nearly won, nearly over.

Conerly handed off to Gifford, who cut wide to the right and swept the end. Marchetti, pursuing with the determination of a tracking missile, nailed Golden Boy at the sideline. It was Gino's final play of the game, for in the collision he snapped his ankle and screamed in agony. The referee, who should immediately have spotted the ball, went instead to Marchetti's aid. In the ensuing confusion, the Giants insisted the ball was moved.

"By the time they got Gino off the field," Gifford claims, "the ball had been moved around, and we came up inches short. To this day I'm convinced I made that first down. It was a rotten call."

New York now had the ball and a fourth down. Chandler came in to punt since Howell played the percentages, and the prematurely balding Oklahoman boomed one to the Baltimore 14, where the Colts took over.

Could Unitas move the team quickly enough for a shot at the tie? Could he find holes in the armor-clad New York defense? Does Monday follow Sunday? No quarterback in history could make more of a single minute than Unitas when he was at the top of his form, and in this game he was at the peak of his career. He was a rapier, a scalpel. The Giants dropped back extra men to guard against the pass—and Unitas completed 4 passes in a row, 3 to Berry, the last one to the New York 13.

No huddle now, no time for that. Only 7 seconds stood on the scoreboard. Kicker Steve Myhra raced onto the field and, from the New York 20, broke the Giants' hearts. His field goal was good. The game was tied 17-17, and for the first time in the annals of the NFL, an overtime, sudden-death period was needed to find a champion.

After a brief rest-period on the sidelines, the team captains met at midfield for the coin flip. The flip was vital since the winners would have the ball, and if they scored even a field goal they would have the championship.

Unitas called tails. It was heads. The ball belonged to the Giants; the Colts had to kick off.

But New York could not move. On third down Conerly kept the ball and ran, and he was tripped a foot short of a first down. Chandler came in to punt, and the Colts started from their 20.

Now Unitas wove the thread of legend. He mixed his plays with the cunning of a lynx and the genius of a Leonardo. When the Giants expected him to pass he went to his bullish fullback, Ameche, who ground out yards through the belly of the defense. When the Giants keyed for Ameche, Unitas threw, finding Berry, a wizard in his own right, and in a dozen plays the Colts were there . . . almost.

They had the ball on the Giants' 1-yard line. Ameche, who already had 23 yards in 6 carries in the drive, was Unitas's choice to end this longest game. He crashed over left tackle, scored, and at 8:15 of the NFL's historic sudden-death overtime, the Colts became 1958 champions.

Marchetti, whose broken ankle caused him to drift in and out of consciousness, refused to be carried off the field until the game ended. He ordered the stretcher-bearers to place him in the end zone, and he watched as his team made history. Then he agreed to go to the hospital.

Never had a team lost a game played under so much pressure, and the impact of that overtime game seems to have diminished the fact that the Giants did, after all, lose. The Giants who played in it, to a man, claim it as their most unforgettable moment in football.

But at the time, when the experience was still fresh and raw, all they could promise was retribution. They devoted the 1959 season to the single ambition of gaining the championship again, and many of the players openly cheered for Baltimore to win once more in the West. "Even when they beat us during the season," Phil King once recalled, "we were upset because we lost, but we knew the Colts had come closer to their division. We just had to get 'em again."

They did. The Giants finished 1959 with a 10-2 record, easily the best in the league. Baltimore, hard-pressed by the Bears, nevertheless came in first in the West at 9-3. There would be another confrontation.

But Timothy J. Mara would not see that game. On February 16, 1959, at the age of 71, the founder of the team passed away, felled by a heart attack in his apartment on Park Avenue. An era had ended.

Lombardi left to take the head coaching job in Green Bay, and he was replaced by the brilliant Allie Sherman as backfield coach. "I had to get the same ground rules that Vinnie had," Sherman recalls. "I told Jim Lee I had to be in charge, just me, of the offense. He agreed to it."

And it was a masterful offense, one that scored 284 points, second in the league to Baltimore's 373. Sherman, who had converted Conerly into a T-formation quarterback in the late 1940s, knew the personnel well.

He changed and adjusted, fussed and fumed, and worked the offense into dazzling shape. He used the talents of the superstars perfectly, blending the grace of Gifford with the muscle of Webster, the passing of Conerly with the receiving acrobatics of Rote.

"It was getting to be an old team," Allie says, "but not in years. The guys had just played together for a long time. They were easy to coach. It's always easier to work with veterans." They were ready.

They seemed to have their revenge; going into the fourth quarter in Baltimore, the Giants held a 9-7 lead on 3 Summerall field goals. Then it all crumbled. Patton was knocked out of the game, Crow suffered a concussion, and the Colts began taking advantage of the Giants' greener replacements.

A Unitas keeper in the final period gave Baltimore a 14-9 lead. An interception by Baltimore's Andy Nelson put the Colts on the New York 14, and Unitas threw a TD pass to rookie Jerry Richardson. It was 21-9, and the Giants were fading. Johnny Sample intercepted another Conerly pass, and it became a 42-yard TD return, making the score 28-9. Myhra finished it with a field goal, and the Giants scored a meaningless touchdown with just seconds to play on a Conerly-to-Schnelker pass good for 32 yards.

The final score was 31-16, but for the Colts, 2-time NFL champions, it would be a far longer wait until the next title game. They were about to enter a 5-year slump.

The Giants? They were about to enter their most glorious period of all, the decade of the 1960s. And by a cruel twist of fate, the second part of that decade would bring them to their lowest point in more than 40 years.

GIANTS OF THE FIFTIES

Agajanian, Ben	Kicker	New Mexico	1949, 1954-57
Albright, Bill	Guard	Wisconsin	1951-54
Amberg, John	Back	Kansas	1951-52
Anderson, Cliff	End	Indiana	1953

Austin, Bill	Guard	Oregon	1949-50, 1953-57
Averno, Sisto	Guard	Muhlenberg	1951
Avinger, Clarence	Back	Alabama	1953
Baker, Jon	Guard	California	1949-52
Barry, Al	Guard	Southern California	1958-59
Barzilauskas, F.	Guard	Yale	1951
Baur, John	Guard	Illinois	1954
Beck, Ray	Guard	Georgia Tech	1952, 1955-57
Benners, Fred	Quarterback	SMU	1952
Berry, Wayne	Back	Washington State	1954
Biscaha, Joe	End	Richmond	1959
Boggan, Rex	Tackle	Mississippi	1955
Bookman, John	Back	Miami	1957
Brackett, M.L.	Guard	Auburn	1958
Brossard, Fred	Center	N. W. Louisiana	1955
Brown, Roosevelt	Tackle	Morgan State	1953-65
Burnin, Hal	End	Missouri	1956
Cannady, John	Back	Indiana	1947-54
Carrocio, Russ	Guard	Virginia	1954-55
Chandler, Don	Kicker	Florida	1956-64
Clatterbuck, Bob	Quarterback	Houston	1954-57
Clay, Randy	Back	Texas	1950-53
Collins, Ray	Tackle	LSU	1954
Conerly, Charley	Quarterback	Mississippi	1948-61
Coulter, Dewitt (Tex)	Tackle	Army	1946-52
Crawford, Ed	Back	Mississippi	1957
Crow, Linden	Back	Southern California	1958-60
DeRogatis, Al	Tackle	Duke	1949-52
Dess, Darrell	Guard	North Carolina State	1959-64, 1966-69

Douglas, Everett	Tackle	Florida	1953
Dublinski, Tom	Quarterback	Utah	1958
Duncan, Jim	End	Wake Forest	1950-53
Epps, Bobby	Guard	Pittsburgh	1954-55, 1957
Ettinger, Don	Guard	Kansas	1948-50
Filipski, Gene	Back	Villanova	1956-57
Galiffa, Arnold	Quarterback	Army	1953
Gifford, Frank	Back-End	Southern California	1952-60, 1962-64
Grandelius, Ev	Back	Michigan State	1953
Grier, Roosevelt	Tackle	Penn State	1955-56, 1958-62
Griffith, Forrest	Back	Kansas	1950-51
Guy, Melwood	Tackle	Duke	1958
Hall, John	End	Iowa	1955
Hannah, Herb	Tackle	Alabama	1951
Hauser, Art	Tackle	Xavier	1959
Heap, Joe	Back	Notre Dame	1955
Heinrich, Don	Quarterback	Washington	1954-59
Herman, John	Back	UCLA	1956
Hodel, Merwin	Back	Colorado	1953
Hudson, Bob	End	Clemson	1951-52
Huff, Sam	Linebacker	West Virginia	1956-63
Hughes, Ed	Back	Tulsa	1956-58
Huth, Gerry	Guard	Wake Forest	1956
Jackson, Bob	Back	North Carolina A&T	1950-51
Jelacic, Jon	End	Minnesota	1958
Johnson, Herb	Back	No College	1954
Karilivacz, Carl	Back	Syracuse	1958
Kelly, Ellison	Guard	Michigan State	1959
Kemp, Jack	Quarterback	Occidental	1958
Kennard, George	Guard	Kansas	1952-55
Kimber, Bill	End	Florida State	1959-60
King, Phil	Back	Vanderbilt	1958-63

Knight, Pat	Back	SMU	1952, 1954-55
Krause, Ray	Tackle	Maryland	1951-55
Lagood, Chester	Guard	Chattanooga	1953
Landry, Tom	Back	Texas	1950-55
Livingston, Cliff	Linebacker	UCLA	1954-61
Long, Buford	Back	Florida	1953-55
Lott, Billy	Back	Mississippi	1958
Lynch, Dick	Back	Notre Dame	1959-66
MacAfee, Ken	End	Alabama	1954-55
McChesney, Bob	End	Hardin-Simmons	1950
Mackrides, Bill	Quarterback	Nevada	1953
Mangrum, Pete	Linebacker	Mississippi	1954
Maronic, Dusan	Guard	No College	1951
Martinkovich, J.	End	Xavier	1957
Mastrangelo, John	Guard	Notre Dame	1950
Maynard, Don	End	Texas Western	1958
Menasco, Don	Back	Texas	1952-53
Miles, Leo	Back	Virginia State	1953
Milner, Bill	Guard	Duke	1950
Mischak, Bob	Guard	Army	1958
Mitchell, Harold	Tackle	UCLA	1952
Modzelewski, Dick	Tackle	Maryland	1956-63
Moore, Henry	Back	Arkansas	1956
Morrison, Joe	Back-End	Cincinnati	1959-72
Mote, Kelly	End	Duke	1950-52
Murray, Earl	Guard	Purdue	1951
Nolan, Dick	Back	Maryland	1954-57, 1959-61
Ostendarp, Jim	Back	Bucknell	1950-51
Patton, Jim	Back	Mississippi	1955-66
Patton, Robert	Tackle	Clemson	1952
Pelfrey, Ray	Back	Kentucky State	1953
Peviani, Bob	Guard	Southern California	1953

Poole, Barney	End	Mississippi	1954-55
Poole, Ray	End	Mississippi	1947-52
Price, Ed	Back	Tulane	1950-55
Pritchard, Bosh	Back	VMI	1951
Ramona, Joe	Guard	Santa Clara	1953
Rapacz, John	Center	Oklahoma	1950-54
Rich, Herb	Back	Vanderbilt	1954-56
Roberts, Gene	Back	Chattanooga	1947-50
Robustelli, Andy	End	Arnold	1956-66
Roman, George	Tackle	Western Reserve	1950
Rote, Kyle	Back-End	SMU	1951-61
Rowe, Harmon	Back	San Francisco	1950-52
Sanchez, John	Tackle	San Francisco	1949-50
Schmidt, Bob	Tackle	Minnesota	1959-60
Schnelker, Bob	End	Bowling Green	1954-60
Schnellbacher, Otto	Back	Kansas	1950-51
Scott, George	Back	Miami (Ohio)	1959
Scott, Joe	Back	San Francisco	1948-53
Scott, Tom	Linebacker	Virginia	1959-64
Shaw, George	Quarterback	Oregon	1959-60
Sherrod, Horace	End	Tennessee	1952
Shipp, Bill	Tackle	Alabama	1954
Skladany, Leo	End	Pittsburgh	1950
Spinks, Jack	Guard	Alcorn A&M	1956-57
Stits, Bill	Back	UCLA	1959-61
Stribling, Bill	End	Mississippi	1951-53
Stroud, Jack	Guard-Tackle	Tennessee	1953-64
Sulaitis, Joe	Back	No College	1943-53
Summerall, Pat	Kicker-End	Arkansas	1958-61
Sutherin, Don	Back	Ohio State	1959
Svare, Harland	Linebacker	Washington State	1955-60
Svoboda, Bill	Linebacker	Tulane	1954-59
Swiacki, Bill	End	Columbia	1948-50
Thomas, George	Back	Oklahoma	1952

Tidwell, Travis	Quarterback	Auburn	1950-51
Toogood, Charlie	Tackle	Nebraska	1958
Topp, Bob	End	Michigan	1954-56
Triplett, Mel	Back	Toledo	1955-60
Tunnell, Emlen	Back	Iowa	1948-58
Weaver, Larry	Back	Fullerton	1955
Webster, Alex	Back	N. Carolina State	1955-64
Weinmeister, Arnold	Tackle	Washington	1950-53
West, Stan	Guard	Oklahoma	1955
White, Jim	Tackle	Notre Dame	1945-50
Wietecha, Ray	Center	Northwestern	1953-62
Wilkins, Dick	End	Oregon	1954
Wilkinson, Bob	End	UCLA	1951-52
Williams, Ellery	End	Santa Clara	1950
Woodward, Rick	Center	Iowa	1950-51, 1953
Yelvington, Dick	Tackle	Georgia	1952-57
Youso, Frank	Tackle	Minnesota	1958-60
Yowarsky, Walt	End	Kentucky	1955-57

10

Allie Sherman, the Second - Choice Coach

By the time 1959 arrived, Allie Sherman was a wanted man. He was wanted, for instance, by Art Rooney, the owner of the Pittsburgh Steelers. Rooney flew to New York several times and met with Sherman at the Manhattan Hotel in an attempt to hire him as Pittsburgh's future head coach—future because he would work for one year as the offensive coach under Walt Kiesling. Sherman, then 36 years old, wasn't sure he wanted to leave New York again, and he was very sure his wife Joan wanted to stay home.

Allie was wanted by Vince Lombardi, too, and it was perhaps one of the few times in that man's fabled career that he did not get what he wanted. Vince had just been hired as the head coach of the Green Bay Packers; Allie, then a scout for the Giants, was with him at a postseason banquet.

"Come with me," Vince snapped at Sherman. "I want to talk to you."

"He took me into the men's room," Allie remembers. "He

looked at me very sternly and said, 'I am taking the job in Green Bay. I need you to come with me. You can't say no because I need you. I have told the people in Green Bay you are my first choice as an assistant. When can you leave?'

"I was flattered, of course, but Green Bay? I had just made Joanie, a little Jewish girl from New York, live in Winnipeg, Canada, for three years while I coached the Blue Bombers. I was scared to death of coming home and saying Green Bay, Wisconsin, to her.

"But Vince was very insistent, and finally he told me why. 'Wellington Mara is going to call you and offer you my job on the Giants, and I'm afraid you'll take it. He knows what a great offensive coach you are. So do I. Come with me; we'll build championships together.'

"I was a little confused. Now I had the Steelers, the Giants, and Lombardi all wanting to hire me. I just needed time to think, and to tell the truth, I wasn't sure I wanted any of the jobs."

Football had been the major part of Allie Sherman's activities since his days at Boys High in New York City. Strangely, football stayed in Sherman's life despite several pointed reminders that, as a player, he was neither big enough nor good enough to make it.

Those who know Sherman agree that his two chief assets, and the two most obvious traits in his personality, are high intelligence and even higher intensity. Football has kept him intense, and even now, four years after a rude and unexpected firing by Well Mara, he has kept aware of all the changes and trends in pro football.

Allie and his intelligence might never have entered football at all had it not been for the T-formation. It was new, radical, highly complicated, and filled with boundless potential for those who could unlock its secret doors and passageways. It was the T-formation that made Sherman a quarterback, that got him the starting job at Brooklyn College, that interested the Philadelphia Eagles in him, and that finally got him to the New York Giants.

"I loved football when I was a kid," Sherman says. "But hell, I was just too small. How could I play?"

Lou Oshins thought the same. Lou was coach at Brooklyn College and regarded his 5-foot-8, 125-pound, left-handed quarterback candidate with more amusement than interest. But Oshins had decided to make the switch to the T in 1939, and once he heard Sherman expound on the new formation and execute the alien movements it demanded, he knew he had a quarterback.

"So what if he was kind of small?" Oshins once joked. "We didn't expect to play Notre Dame or Army, you know?"

Indeed, Brooklyn College had a football team that might not have passed for the freshmen substitutes at most larger universities. But when the opponents were City College, Adelphi, Yeshiva, and Hunter College, size mattered not as much as skill and savvy.

Sherman became a top quarterback, once leading Brooklyn to a 28-21 upset of a very good City College team. "I passed for 2 of the touchdowns and ran for the other 2," he remembers, "and I was as proud as if we had just beaten Ohio State. It's hard to explain what football meant to me. It was the challenge of doing things that worked, of figuring out what things would work and then being proven right. I guess even then I was unconsciously becoming coach-oriented."

Sherman's renown as a T-quarterback spread. Greasy Neale, a man who would play a major role in Allie's future, heard about this "punk kid from Brooklyn, and Jewish, no less." Neale, head coach of the Eagles, needed somebody who understood the intricacies of the T. He knew Sherman did, and he drafted him.

"Imagine," Allie remembers, "a Jewish kid from Brooklyn College getting drafted to be quarterback for the Philadelphia Eagles. I don't think anybody in my family believed it, and I know none of my friends did."

Having sprouted to all of 5-feet-10 and 160 pounds, Sherman nevertheless felt ridiculous when he reported to the Eagles, where runners were 225 pounds and linemen close to 300.

"Besides," he remembers, "Greasy never talked to me. All he did was yell when I did something wrong, which was roughly once every 30 seconds. Finally, I decided I was wasting my time, and I went to Greasy and told him. He was more sympathetic than I expected, and I told him I didn't think I'd ever make it as a pro quarterback. I was too small and too inexperienced.

"'Listen, kid,' Greasy said, 'you start to worry when I don't yell at you. That means I don't care. If I yell, I care. You are going to make it and make it big.'"

Sherman was more accurate than Neale. As a quarterback, he was seriously deficient:

> I remember lots of plays. I don't have full games to remember because I never played one. But in Los Angeles one time I came in for the regular late in the game, and I had a pass play in my mind. I had been watching the Rams' defense all game, and I knew it would work.
>
> So I called it. I'm not sure who the end was, Tom Miller, I think. Well, this damned play worked so perfectly he was 30 yards in the clear, waiting in the end zone. When I turned and saw him just where he was supposed to be, I got so excited I froze. There he was yelling and waving and there I was trying to get my arm moving, and by now the Rams started to figure out they had been fooled and were looking for the ball. Well, I finally threw it, and it was a high, soft cloudscraper that took forever to come down. There was poor Tom waiting for the ball and here came what seemed like 50 Rams, and it was a goddamned race.
>
> Well, the ball got to Tom just a second before the Rams did, and he caught the son-of-a-bitch but he got clobbered. I'll tell you, the play should have ended three minutes earlier. I think right there Tom was more impressed with my play-calling than my passing.

Augie Lio, now a sportswriter for the Passaic, New Jersey, *Herald-News*, was a teammate of Sherman's with the Eagles. He remembers well how Allie inevitably drifted toward coaching:

> I was the placekicker one year and he ' as my holder. I remember one game against the Giants, it was close and it was late and we were losing. As we walked onto the field for a field goal try, Allie whispers, "Let's fake it, Augie. I'll throw a touchdown pass."
>
> I looked at the little bastard and couldn't believe it. "You're nuts," I said. "The Giants will be looking for the fake first. You'll get killed." Besides, our line wasn't all that good, and there was every chance the Giants would bust through and block my field goal. But he insisted a fake would work, so finally I said I'd go along with it. Well, he got the play called in the huddle, and I was standing there facing the Giant defense while he called it. I saw them smiling, and I could hear them saying "fake, fake" to each other.
>
> "Allie," I said, "you are going to get killed." "Augie, shut up, will you? It's going to work." So we set up, the ball was snapped, and just as that little bastard started to get up to throw about 90 Giants fell on him. Honest to God, I didn't expect to see him on the ground when everybody else got up. I thought little pieces of him would be stuck to all their helmets and knees and shoulder pads.

Clearly, Sherman was a player who should have been a coach. But Neale was so dependent on Sherman's T-formation knowledge that Allie lasted five years with the Eagles, from 1943 through 1947.

In 1948 Allie was player-coach with the Paterson Panthers in a semi-professional league, but his reputation as a master of the T had not been forgotten. In 1949, when Steve Owen decided to add some of the T to his A-formation, he asked Greasy to recommend someone as a tutor for Charley Conerly. Neale said only Allie Sherman could do it. Owen contacted Sherman, and he was hired.

He remained as backfield coach through 1953, when Owen was fired and both Sherman and Jim Lee Howell were considered as the new man. "I told Well I wouldn't stay if I didn't get the job," Sherman said. "I wasn't trying to wedge him; it was just that I wanted to do more, and I had the job offer in the Canadian League. He said he understood, and when he decided to hire Jim Lee, we parted as good friends."

Sherman coached in Winnipeg for three years, and in each year he got the Blue Bombers into the postseason play-offs for the Grey Cup, Canada's older equivalent of the NFL's Super Bowl. "I really liked it up there," he says. "I was treated very well. I had a good salary, and they provided a home for us, and it was just a great situation. But Joanie was pregnant and homesick, and I didn't feel I should force her to stay."

In 1956 Joanie left for New York, and Allie stayed to finish out the final year of his contract. He already had informed the team he was leaving, and despite increased offers he would not change his mind.

"I really missed the family," he said. "One night Joanie called. She said she was at Marge Glickman's house [the wife of Marty, a well-known sportscaster, former Olympic medal winner, and one of Sherman's closest friends] and that she had to go to the hospital because her water had broken. You know how much I knew about that stuff? I asked if she couldn't put it off until the weekend, so I could get home."

Sherman resigned his post in Winnipeg and returned to New York, where he became a jack-of-all-trades. He scouted for the Giants on college football Saturdays, then worked the earphones from the press box on Sundays. In between he spent time at summer camp working with the quarterbacks and also had a job as a salesman, pushing packaging for men's shirts.

Then it got to be 1959, and the offers began pouring in:

I didn't tell Joanie about Vince's offer or Pittsburgh's

offer or Mara's offer because I hadn't decided what I wanted to do. But Well called the house one day when I was out on the road, and when he called back in 20 minutes Joanie got suspicious. She called me at the factory I was visiting, somewhere in Pennsylvania, I think, and told me Well had called. "What's so important that he'd call twice in 20 minutes?" she asked. "Are you going back into coaching again?" I told her I had the offers, but I hadn't made up my mind. When I got home, we had a little spirited discussion session.

I called Well back and he made me the offer to replace Lombardi. I told him Vince had asked me to go to Green Bay with him, and that I had promised I wouldn't commit myself yet. Well said he understood that and I should take some time to make up my mind. Meanwhile, I had ruled out Pittsburgh, so now it was New York or Green Bay. When I thought about the choice and considered Joanie, I had no trouble. I told Mara I would take the job, and I thanked Lombardi for his offer but turned it down. I thought it was ideal. I was back in coaching, I hadn't left New York, and I was just an assistant coach, so there was very little pressure.

The first thing Allie Sherman did when he accepted the job with the Giants was to disappear for seven weeks, taking with him films of every game the Giants had played over the last three years.

"I charted every pass the Giants had thrown during all that time," he said. "I figured out distances and patterns and situations and the score of the game at the time and how the defenses reacted to each kind of a pass. It was the most concentrated work I've ever done, but when I was finished I had a master chart of the pass routes that worked against every kind of defense and what the Giants' offense would be able to do."

Such diligence was quickly rewarded. The Giants became the top passing team in the league in 1959, won the Eastern Division championship, and played the Baltimore Colts for the league title, Allie's offense holding the lead until the defense collapsed in the fourth quarter.

In 1960 the Giants were still good, but the Eagles had grown better; Philadelphia's 10-2 record easily displaced New York as Eastern champions.

Then it was 1961, and Jim Lee Howell made good on his announcement that 1960 was his final year as the team's head coach. Well Mara tried hard to pry Lombardi loose from his Green Bay contract.

"Well told me he had made a promise to Vince," Allie said. "He told me he had committed himself to offer the job to Vince, but that if Vince couldn't get free I would be his only other choice. He asked me to be patient. He knew I had other offers, and he wanted to know I would be available if Lombardi couldn't take it. He was right. I had had four other offers, including another one from Art Rooney, and I knew that one way or another I would be a head coach in 1961."

Mara and Lombardi tried mightily to break the Packers' hold on their coach, but the effort was doomed from the start. Mara turned to Sherman:

We were in Mobile, acting as the coaching staff for the Senior Bowl, when he told me. It was at a buffet dinner, and I was standing at the food table when Well walked up, a plate in his hands. He winked, started to fork some roast beef or something, and then said, "It looks like Vince won't be able to get away. I'd like you to be the head coach of the Giants." No, I didn't drop my plate. I had expected it. But Well wanted to agree to all the terms right there, in two minutes. I know he had been able to do that with Owen and Howell, but I had a family, and I had to be sure of everything. I didn't mistrust him; I just wanted it spelled out. About a week later we signed the contract.

It was a 3-year contract for about $25,000 a year. It was what I wanted.

When he signed, Sherman was to find out just how understanding the Mara family of the early 1960s really was. "Jack Mara told me I didn't have to prove anything. I didn't have to win big to keep the job. He said they knew I was a good coach, and they were ready to wait for a team to be built slowly. But I wasn't sure we'd have to wait. I took all the films I could find and pulled another disappearing act. When I got out of my basement about two months later, I went to the team's offices and sat down with Jack and Well. I gave them my findings."

What Sherman's decision boiled down to was that the Giants could win it all in 1961 if they filled certain weaknesses and made a commitment to give up some of their future for older players who could make a contribution right away.

"You have to decide," he said, "if you want to do it my way. I think we have a shot at a championship, but I need your help."

To their credit the Maras took Sherman at his word. He gave them a list of what he needed, and Well set out to do his shopping.

"I said we needed another quarterback, a veteran, because I wasn't sure if Charley could make it another full season without help. I said we needed a fast wide receiver because we had no speed out there, and it limited our offense. I said we needed a cornerback, and I was hoping to get a tight end, too. I never thought I'd get it all, and I could not have dreamed I'd get who I got. But Well never made a trade without my approval, not then and not later when the trades backfired. I'll give him that. He never tried to take charge."

Well Mara, unknown to Sherman, had turned down an offer for a young lineman named Lou Cordileone in early 1961. San Francisco wanted the promising guard and was willing to surrender an old quarterback named Y.A. Tittle. Mara did not want Y.A. Tittle.

By August 1961 Mara wanted Y.A. Tittle. And, for the price of Lou Cordileone, he got him.

In 1960 a skinny split end named Del Shofner spent a frustrating season with the Los Angeles Rams. He was injured many times and in many ways. He suffered from ulcers. He caught just a dozen passes. Well Mara made overtures, found that Shofner was available, and, for a number-one draft choice, the popsicle-stick end became a Giant.

In Washington a diminutive tight end named Joe Walton was told one spring afternoon that his new team was the New York Giants. In Chicago George Halas telephoned Erich Barnes and informed the cornerback that he had been traded to the Giants. It was coming together, as Mara and Sherman mugged the rest of the National Football League.

When Tittle was introduced to Shofner and Walton, the chemical reaction was enough to stand the NFL on its head for the next three years. But more was necessary, and in this magical year of Allie Sherman's rookie season as head coach, more would happen. Everything would happen, and everything would turn out right.

Take Alex Webster. Sherman didn't want the veteran fullback in camp. He had been injured and slowed. The Giants were not at all sure Webster could make it, but the big redhead insisted he could, and because of so many services rendered he was offered another contract.

Jack Mara, understandably, was shocked at Webster's demand. "Write in a bonus if I finish in the top ten rushers," Big Red said.

Mara smiled, tried not to be cruel, and wrote it in. "I'm going to take your money," Webster warned, "and we are going to win a championship."

Webster knew where he stood. "Dammit, I wasn't even on the team's three-deep depth charts when summer camp opened," he said. "I knew I had to prove myself to Allie all over again. I was like a rookie. They didn't think I could do anything, so I first had to make the team, then get a starting job, and then hold it. I never worked so hard in my life. I had weighed 235 the last few years, but I sweated down to 215 to be in better shape and pick up some speed. Man, it almost killed me." Alex gained 928 yards in 1961, his career high and then the second highest total in Giants' history.

Gifford, who had sat out the remainder of the 1960 season after suffering a serious head injury when tackled by Philadelphia's Chuck Bednarik, decided upon advice from his doctors to sit out the 1961 season as well. Gifford was made a team scout, and Sherman had to make do without one of the league's most incredible athletes. But the number-one draft pick, a solidly built runner with great speed named Bobby Gaiters, was able to pick up some of the slack.

The Giants went to Salem, Oregon, for three weeks and came home with Tittle—an injured Tittle who would not be able to play for five weeks. On his first play in an exhibition game Tittle slipped and fell on the ball, and a horde of Los Angeles Rams fell on him, cracking two of his vertebrae.

"Still, we knew he'd be ready to open the season," Sherman says. "What bothered me more than his injury was how the team would accept him and the way Charley would take to him. I had to get the three of us together."

It was at Fordham University, a temporary training base after returning from Oregon, that Sherman called the meeting:

> We were in a tiny dressing room no bigger than an office. Just the three of us were there—Y.A. and Charley and myself. I shut the door, locked it, and then started to talk to them.
>
> "Guys," I said, "there are three men on this team who can decide the future of all the rest. We can win a championship or we can be broken into factions and cliques and bicker back and forth all season. Those three men are in this room right now. I need your help. I am in my first year as coach. Y.A. is in his first year with the Giants. Charley has been the Giants' quarterback for a dozen years. But I'm going to have to make a big decision, and I want you both to understand. I am going to have to pick

one of you as my starter, and I don't know when I can make that decision. It might be in a week or it might not be until the middle of the season. All I can ask is that the both of you be ready to play, be prepared to play, and be prepared to sit on the bench. I know that's a lot because you've both been starters for a long time, but the Giants can win a championship if I make the right choice, and I'll need all your help and understanding to make that choice and stick with it. Okay?"

Y.A. looked a little pale and nodded his head up and down. But Charley, bless his heart, he just smiled that crooked smile and drawled, "Sheeit, Al, you know all I want to do is win. Go ahead and do your damndest. I am always ready, and if old Y.A. here beats me out, I'll shake his hand." It was what I had hoped he'd say. I knew then and there we would win it because men like that, both in their late thirties, are just not supposed to be that co-operative.

The season opened with a loss to the St. Louis Cardinals engineered by a man with whom Sherman was quite familiar, quarterback Sam "The Rifle" Etcheverry, who that year had been lured down from Canada. He had been Player of the Year for the Montreal Alouettes (Webster's former team) several times and was a Canadian national.

Conerly started the second game, fell behind to Pittsburgh, and was rescued by Tittle, who threw 10 completions in 12 attempts, including his first 8 passes as a Giant. The following week the team was in Washington, and Conerly started. But he was struggling and the team was losing, and Allie asked Y.A. to warm up on the sidelines.

Shortly after Tittle began throwing casually, Charley was intercepted. Sherman yanked him and sent in Y.A. Conerly came out fuming, and the first crisis suddenly developed.

"Dammit, Al, I deserve better than that. I throw one damn interception and you take me out in front of everybody like that. Why don't you take your team and shove it?"

Sherman stood his ground. "You know better than that," he yelled. "Y.A. was warming up. I had already decided you were coming off, and the goddamned interception had nothing to do with it."

That night, after Tittle had won the game, Conerly was told by his wife that Tittle had in fact been warming up prior to the interception. The next morning Conerly reported to Yankee Stadium and apologized to Sherman.

But Tittle had won the job, and Charley faced a season on the bench. Right? Wrong.

Two weeks later, at home against the Rams, Los Angeles battled back from a 10-0 deficit to take a 14-10 lead with 3:45 to play. Tittle was terrible. Sherman was distraught. And Charley Conerly was ready.

"Get the hell in there," Sherman barked to his supersub. "Win this damned thing."

"Right, coach," said Conerly.

Charley Conerly went to work. He threw a 37-yard touchdown pass to Kyle Rote to put the Giants ahead 17-14, then hit Del Shofner with a minute to play to make it 24-14. The crowd of 63,053 had witnessed a remarkable performance and showed its gratitude by bellowing and celebrating into the dark night of New York City.

"I honestly had chills," Sherman said. "I had been in a lot of big games, and they never affected me. But I got chills for that old man. What he did was what makes sports so great. It was a miracle, and that old man lived up to everything he was ever taught. Honest to God, I got chills all over my body. I even think I wept a little."

Charley was to save yet another critical game as the championship race tightened. The Giants won the Eastern Conference with a 10-3-1 record to Philadelphia's 10-4; the tie was a 7-7 deadlock with Cleveland on the final day of the season—a tie for Christmas.

In 1962 and 1963 Sherman would take this aging team to Eastern Conference championships, and for two consecutive years he would be named NFL Coach of the Year. His acumen for the game continued to astound the experts and to impress the league's brightest lights.

"If I am watching a game between two ideally matched teams," said George Halas, "and if Allie Sherman is coaching one, that's the team I'll pick. He'll find a way to win it."

Lombardi, by then a hero and a championship coach in Green Bay, added his praise. "Year in and year out, the best prepared team we play is the Giants. Sherman does an outstanding job of getting his men ready. We can't catch him in anything, and he seems to anticipate what we're going to do."

Landry, another one-time Sherman associate and now the Dallas coach, was more upset. "The man is amazing," he said. "We'll play the first half, and he'll have stopped everything we wanted to do. Then we'll get into the locker at halftime and make several adjustments, only to find that he had anticipated every one of them and had us stopped again."

There were factors that could stop Allie Sherman. Age was one. Foolish draft choices was another. Incredibly damaging trades was a third. Combined, these forces led to the astounding collapse of the New York Giants, a collapse that was unprecedented in the team's history.

In 1964 the Giants were 2-10-2, having been 11-3 in 1963. In 1964 Sam Huff was no longer with the team, nor was Rosey Grier, nor Dick Modzelewski. All were gone, traded. The fans howled.

Huff was the big one, the man who had been taken into the hearts of the fans and who had become the personification of the Giants. He was their hero, their guru of violence, and when 60,000 of them chanted "Huff, Huff, Huff" on Sunday afternoons, their love was apparent.

But Sam Huff had become older and slower and somewhat spoiled by the rush of endorsements and money. Twice Sherman tried to sit down and talk with him, to convince him that he was hurting himself and the team, that he had grown soft. Twice Huff rebuffed his coach.

Fans would not have believed it, but Huff was offered around the league, and only the Washington Redskins expressed interest—providing the Giants would ask for no more than two average players, Andy Stynchula, a defensive lineman, and Dick James, an offensive-defensive back. Those two had always played well against the Giants. Sherman and Well Mara made the deal, and only the prophetic words of Jack Mara, who would die the following year, foretold the calamity to come. "On paper it's a good trade," Jack said, "but have you thought of the reaction of the fans? This might be one to forget about. We might want to let Sam just retire."

His brother and his head coach ignored him. "Jack was right, but I didn't see it," Allie said. "I know now I made a mistake, not by wanting to trade him, but by doing it."

The fans went wild. Protests and infuriated telephone calls ensued. Newspaper editorials shredded the Giants' stupidity and coldness. Huff himself was stunned, then bitter. He chose Sherman, not Well Mara, as the man responsible, and neither of them will ever forget a confrontation on a golf course that summer when Allie approached Sam with his hand extended, and Sam turned his back after muttering a vile oath.

Today, as an executive in the Marriott hotel chain, Sam is less vehement, and perhaps he has managed to see the logic of the trade. But when Sherman was fired in 1969 and replaced by Alex Webster, Huff made a point to visit the locker room, which he had not done since the day he had left in 1964.

In 1965 another major trade brought quarterback Earl Morrall to New York. That worked for a year or two, and the veteran led the team to a 7-7 record in 1965.

But it all fell apart in 1966, for Morrall, for Sherman, for Well Mara, and for the Giants. The record was 1-12-1. The defense allowed a league record of 501 points. It was a horror, a nightmare, and Sherman was in the middle of the mess. It changed him visibly. A man who had been quick to smile and ready to converse became quiet and morose, sometimes sullen, other times angry, often flying into tirades of unreasonable rage.

Morrall was finished. The Giants had to do something, and in 1967 they made another major trade, this time landing quarterback Fran Tarkenton from the Minnesota Vikings.

Tarkenton stuck around longer than Morrall, even longer than Sherman. In the end he, too, became a problem. He, too, balked at the losing, refused to accept any of the blame for it, and suggested to Mara after the 1971 season that he be traded elsewhere.

It couldn't help Sherman. He was fired nine days prior to the opening of the 1969 season, the morning after returning from Montreal, where the Giants had completed an 0-6 exhibition season by losing to Pittsburgh.

Now listen to Sherman's side of that story; it has not appeared before:

> We had been seven and seven in 1968, and it was starting to get better. I had decided before the exhibition season to go with as many of the rookies as I could so I'd know who could play when the season opened, when we really went to war. The losing didn't bother me. Hell, they were just exhibition games. But we had played well. The kids had done a good job. We were coming strong, and the veterans could see it.
>
> I'm convinced we could have won a few of those games that summer if I had kept the veterans in the game. We could have won that night in Montreal, and the veterans were aware of it. But we had decided to go for the whole pie when the season started. We were ready, and even walking off the field in Montreal that night we knew we had played a sound game. Tarkenton and Spider Lockhart were walking with me, and we all were smiling.
>
> I decided it was time for the players to hold a team meeting, asking the coaches and the press to leave the locker room. That's a common practice. You use a few of your dependable veterans because sometimes players can accomplish more among themselves than they can with a

coach yelling at them. I told Tarkenton as we got to the dressing room that a meeting should be called right away. Then I whispered it to Lockhart, too.

Well, they hit the room and started changing, and suddenly Tarkenton yells out, "Okay, everybody get out. The players need a meeting. That means all the coaches, too. Out."

I smiled and left, and maybe 20 minutes later it was over. Tarkenton came over to me and said, "Okay, coach, we're ready. It was a good meeting. We know why we lost the 6 games, and the players are willing to go along with it. They see what you've done, and they like it." Lockhart, too, was happy. "Coach," he said, "you're going to have it your way next week. This team is going to win right now."

The next morning I was fired.

What caused Sherman's dismissal, or at least what contributed heavily to it, was a 37-14 drubbing by the New York Jets in an exhibition game in the Yale Bowl in New Haven, Connecticut. Mara, who for years had fought the AFL, was forced in 1966 to agree to a merger. Then he had to swallow the Jets' fantastic success in the next 3 years.

Part of that success was the unbelievable victory in Super Bowl III, a 16-7 destruction of the vaunted Baltimore Colts. Green Bay had won the first 2 Super Bowls for the NFL with such ease and arrogance that the AFL owners were seriously considering canceling the postseason clash of league champions.

But the Jets turned it all around, and now it was the next summer and 75,000 fans crammed the Yale Bowl to see the Giants try to stop this band of brash and brassy players led by high-living, outspoken, and generally distasteful quarterback Joe Willie Namath.

The Giants were horrid. They allowed the Jets to score every possible way, from the return of a punt to the recovery of a kick-off in their own end zone. Namath was superb, hitting on 14 of 16 passes, and the Jets reveled in their virtuosity, putting to an end the 10 years of inferiority wished on them by the fans of New York City.

It was a cruel and telling day for Allie Sherman. He was distraught and had been so weeks before the game.

"We had 'em, we had 'em," he mumbled, over and over. "We had 'em right here," he said, pointing to the palm of his hand. "We had 'em, we had 'em," he insisted, finding an excuse for each incompetent error by his players. He was on the verge of a nervous breakdown.

Well Mara reacted as though someone close to him had died, which might well have been the case. His team, its integrity and its reputation, had been humiliated by the team he most disliked, the rival, pushy, newly rich New York Jets.

Well Mara left. He was gone for a week—"to think," he said. It was the first time in memory that he had left the team during summer training time. When he returned he had made up his mind to fire Sherman.

He denies that, to a point. "I really didn't decide until the night of the Montreal game," he insists. "I was sitting with Art [Rooney, the president and founder of the Steelers], and he saw I was troubled. He asked what was wrong, and I told him what I had on my mind. That was the first time I had spoken it out loud. We lost the game, and we flew home, and I couldn't sleep. Allie was my friend, just as Steve Owen had been my father's friend. But I couldn't see any other choice. There was no way out."

Sherman picks up the story now. "The kids had just gone to school," he said. "It was like 8:15 in the morning when Well called me. He said he hadn't gone to work yet and could I drive over and talk with him. I guess I had an idea what was going to happen. You know, you can't lose for a while without hearing rumors. But I never thought he'd do it. He knew what we were doing, and I thought he understood."

When Allie got to Well's home it was finished. "I feel like I should fire myself, too," Mara told Sherman. "I haven't been any help to you these last years. Maybe the day will come soon when we can both sit in the stands on Sundays and watch the team play."

Mara, of course, had no intention of replacing himself, and Allie knew it. "I had been after him for years to hire another man, someone to do a lot of the team administrative work," Sherman says. "Once Jack died and the NFL got so big and complicated it became clear Well couldn't handle it all by himself. He knew it, too, but Well is the kind of man who moves slowly, who takes a long time to make up his mind. But he never did interfere with me or force any trades down my throat. I just never thought he would do what he did. I was hurt, and so was Joanie. It didn't seem real, somehow. The season was about to start, and I thought I'd at least get to coach through the season, to see if my plans would work."

It was not to be. Instead, Mara went for a surprise choice. He named Alex Webster, who had just recently become backfield coach, to replace Sherman. In retrospect, it was a stroke of brilliance. Webster was too well loved, too popular, too much of a regular guy for the fans to boo him.

The fans had become particularly vicious in Sherman's last 2 years, and in addition to the expected ethnic insults from the Grand Old Guard of New York's monied class of morons, the 60,000 fans at each home game took to serenading Allie with a rendition of "Goodbye, Allie," sung to the tune of "Goodnight, Ladies."

It was cruel, vicious, and demeaning, and several times Joan Sherman left Yankee Stadium in tears. So did her children, who were treated to similar renditions in school by their classmates.

But who could be nasty to good old Alex? He was a fan favorite, a man who recalled days of glory and victory. Alex was a regular guy who drank beer and sometimes attended church and wasn't an egghead. Even the players liked Alex. What the hell, half of them didn't even understand Sherman. They were players, after all, not thinkers.

Allie Sherman was gone. He later formed a group that attempted to purchase the New York Jets, and the group drew as close as the final signing when Phil Iselin, president of the Jets, suddenly backed off.

"I didn't want to take another job in football where I would be in the position of getting fired," Sherman said. "That's why the Jets thing looked so good. Sure, I was very disappointed when it fell through."

What Allie Sherman accomplished stuck with the Giants and stays with them even today in their offensive concepts.

What Sherman accomplished throughout the league endures in the performances of those who sought his help— George Allen, head coach of the Washington Redskins; Don Shula, head coach of the Miami Dolphins; Tom Landry, head coach of the Dallas Cowboys; Dick Nolan, head coach of the San Francisco 49ers. "I had a lot of coaches come up to the house," he says, "and we'd spend all day talking about offense or defense or some other point of the game in theory. I never minded that. I was glad to help."

One who turned on Sherman was George Allen, who as coach of the Los Angeles Rams in 1966 oversaw a 55-14 destruction of Sherman's outnumbered charges and called time with seconds to play so that one more touchdown could be scored.

Flying back on the team's charter plane, Sherman was in a fit of rage and depression. "He'll never do that to me again," he murmured to me.

"But Al, the team did it, and to the Giants, not you."

He shook his head stubbornly. "No, George did it to me. Me. It won't happen again. These things have a way of coming back."

Ironically, Allen later did the same thing to the Giants of Alex Webster when as head man of the 1972 Redskins he called for time with seconds left to give Washington time for a meaningless touchdown in an already assured victory. Some men never change, or perhaps some men never lose the sense of insecurity that drives them to higher and lonelier pinnacles.

Those Giants who took the time to understand Sherman and his theories of football became believers. Tittle to this day remains one of Allie's staunchest backers, the result of a remarkable 17-14 victory in 1962 over a far-superior Detroit Lions squad.

Detroit had just played Green Bay on Thanksgiving Day of 1962, and Sherman watched as the fierce Lions sacked quarterback Bart Starr 11 times en route to a 26-14 victory. The Lions' next opponent was Sherman's Giants, an aging team still engaged in a fierce championship race.

For a week Sherman tossed between suggested game plans. For the first time in his career he did not have the game plan ready for the team's ingestion by the Tuesday before the game. Finally, he decided on a radical approach:

The Lions' best shot was their defense up front, the four studs on the line, and the best of those four were the tackles, Alex Karras and Roger Brown. There was no way we could buy time for Tittle to pass deep, and if he got nailed two or three times early we'd be finished. So I did something no other team had tried to do—I ran at Karras and Brown, doubleteamed them with guards and tackles and just took it to their gut. We had Webster and King, both 220-pound backs, and we just punched away. They had to react. They had to fight off the doubleteam blocks. Then I had Tittle throw, but not long ones that take time—short ones, quick outs and sideline passes and circle patterns to the backs. The team wasn't at all sure I was right, or even sane, but we won the game 17-14.

That night we were in Toots Shor's about midnight, Joanie and myself and another couple, when Y.A. walked in with his wife. He saw me, came over, put his arm around me, and said, "You little so-and-so, you made a believer out of me today, pal. You really pulled it off. That was the last thing the Lions ever expected."

Sherman's intensity turned off other men, including some who worked under him as assistant coaches. One was Jim Trimble, now the Giants' pro personnel director but then an assistant line coach.

Several times Sherman and Trimble engaged in screaming matches, and one time, after Sherman rejected a Trimble decision out-of-hand, big Jim yelled back, "Sherman, did you really invent football?"

Allie had problems with Webster, too. One misconception is that during that final game he coached, the mean-nothing exhibition in Montréal, Sherman and Tarkenton engaged in a bitter argument along the sidelines. What really happened?

"I was a peacemaker," Allie said, "between Tarkenton and Webster."

Apparently, Tarkenton had deviated from the game plan, and since the team was losing, Alex became upset. Words were exchanged to the effect that Tarkenton was disobeying the coaches, which led to Fran's observation that a man who doesn't know anything about the game should not attempt to coach it and should never criticize one who does.

"I just got in between and broke them up," Sherman said, "but the next day, after the firing, it was in all the newspapers that I was arguing violently with Francis and that I had lost control of the team."

Allie Sherman was too intense, and too driven, for his own good. When the Maras and their family-member scouts provided him with less than adequate talent, he could not tolerate the errors of the unfit. "Allie Sherman," said another head coach, "can make a good team great. But if he has a bad team, he can only make it worse. He knows so much he doesn't have the time to teach basics, and he can't realize some players simply don't understand him. They're bad players, and you can't make chicken salad out of chicken feathers. You need the meat."

Allie's intensity finally proved to be his undoing. As the situation worsened, he gripped the reins of authority more tightly, refusing to delegate any duties to his assistants, vainly striving to pull the team out of its death-dive single-handed.

Few men have been as touched by genius in this game. Few men have been quite as articulate when explaining what only they can conceive. Few men have been quite so equipped to win, and, paradoxically, quite so equipped to lose, for Allie Sherman's deficiencies came as companion flaws along with his assets and abilities.

He could not communicate to the lesser player or to the younger player, but when he had a team of veterans, he was a master.

"That little bastard taught us a hell of a lot of football," said the late Jimmy Patton, six times an All-Pro Giant safety. "He taught me more than I thought I could learn at my stage." Patton was already a veteran when Sherman became head coach—and Sherman's main duties were with the offense.

"Sure he got screwed," says another head coach. "If they tried to give me the kind of garbage they gave him and passed off as professional football players, I'd have quit. But he couldn't quit. His ego insisted that he could make winners out of the garbage."

When Allie was fired, he had 6 years remaining on a 10-year, $50,000-per-season contract. Well Mara had no choice but to pay it off, providing Sherman stayed out of football or any football-related endeavors. At the time of this writing Sherman was still being paid. He was also holding a position as an executive for a money-management firm with assets over $100 million.

"But there is nothing I wouldn't say about Well Mara for fear of jeopardizing my contract," he says. "The man was fair in all our dealings. I just didn't think he would become impatient at the end. We could have won."

The year Sherman left, the Giants slumped from a 7-7 season in 1968 to a mark of 6-8 under Alex Webster. With

Allie Sherman they might have done better. But the situation had deteriorated too far.

Tarkenton was blaming his failures on Sherman's coaching, as he would do two years later with Webster. The defense was as patchy a collection of nobodies as any head coach had ever been saddled with, and the attitude of losing had permeated all but the few professionals left on the squad.

A credibility gap already had begun to fester between the team and the press, between the players and the team's officials. Small incidents were blown all out of proportion. Smaller indiscretions became family scandals.

Sherman's presence could no longer be tolerated. It was a time to regroup and consolidate, and since Maras do not fire themselves—ever—the head coach was the only logical alternative.

And so it was, after all, "Goodbye, Allie." His firing, and all the complex, mysterious reasons that blended to make it inevitable, might finally have caused Well Mara to pause and consider. Changes were made, decisions were reversed, barriers were broken, and in 1970 and 1972 the Giants began to show signs of returning to football respectability.

Allie Sherman had sacrificed a great deal, and in the end he became the final sacrifice.

11

The Fifth Decade — 1960 - 1969

No man ever started a head coaching career more spectacularly than Allie Sherman. No man ever finished one more dismally than Allie Sherman. No man ever made such an impact on New York professional football as did this bantam coach, both for what he did, for what his teams did and did not do, and for the players he introduced to the metropolitan area.

In 1960 Jim Lee Howell was the head coach of the Giants. In 1969 it was Alex Webster. For the eight years in between it was Allie Sherman.

But it was much more. It was Y.A. Tittle and Del Shofner. It was Andy Robustelli and Sam Huff, Alex Webster and Jimmy Patton, Frank Gifford and Kyle Rote, Charley Conerly and Joe Morrison, Joe Walton and Rosey Grier. It was Jack Stroud, Rosey Brown, Homer Jones, Earl Morrall, Fran Tarkenton, Tucker Frederickson, Dick Lynch, and Erich Barnes.

It was glory and championship the likes of which had

seldom been experienced in the Giants' history. But it was disgrace and dishonor and travesty as well, and never had the Giants so embarrassed both themselves and their fans. The Giants of the middle and late 1960s were ludicrous. They were bad jokes disguised as football players.

But those men figured, too, in the twisting history of this franchise, and they, too, had names: Roger LaLonde, Mike Bundra, Allen Jacobs, Tom Kennedy, Joe Don Looney, Lou Slaby, Jim Prestel, Lane Howell, Don Davis, and Henry Schichtle.

Records of triumph were set by the good teams, and records of futility were set by the bad teams.

In 1961, 1962, and 1963 the New York Giants compiled a combined record of 33-8-1. They won the Eastern Conference championship each year. Sherman was Coach of the Year twice. Tittle was Player of the Year. Webster was named Comeback of the Year.

In 1964 the Giants were last in the East with a 2-10-2 record, their worst in the then 40 years of team existence. In 1965 they were 7-7, and then it went totally mad in 1966, when the team fell to 1-12-1 and surrendered a league record 501 points.

The decade began with the loss of a player and the loss of a head coach. Howell's departure had been announced. The fury of a Chuck Bednarik tackle, however, was a tragic surprise—Frank Gifford was one man the Giants would find impossible to replace.

The Giants lost two games to the Philadelphia Eagles in 1960 in consecutive weeks. It was in the first game with Philadelphia that the Giants lost Gifford.

Late in the fourth quarter, trailing 17-10, New York took the ball and began to move upfield. The Yankee Stadium crowd came alive with anticipatory glee, and when quarterback George Shaw cut loose with a pass to Gifford, New York's Golden Boy seemed to break loose. He veered toward the Eagle sideline and reached the Eagle 30-yard line. And then he was nearly killed.

Chuck Bednarik, a terrifying 250-pound middle linebacker, caught up to Gifford. Frank neither heard nor saw him, and the sudden jarring tackle sent him to the ground, unconscious before he hit the grass. To the 60,000 fans in the seats, Bednarik had long been a symbol of terrorism. Now, as he stood over the inert body of their hero and leaped up and down with unbridled joy, he seemed the personification of evil itself. A shower of boos cascaded down on the field, and the ball that had slipped from Gifford's hands, since recovered by Chuck Weber to insure the victory for Philadelphia, was forgotten.

Gifford, still unconscious, was removed to St. Elizabeth's Hospital. His injuries included a serious concussion, which was a breath away from a fractured skull. He was, as team doctor Francis Sweeny later admitted, "lucky to be alive."

Both Gifford and Bednarik defended the tackle as a clean, if violent, action. "He didn't mean to hurt me," Gifford said. "It was a clean tackle. It wasn't anyone's fault, but I sure did come close, didn't I?"

Gifford, proving that a team man is always a team man, refused to answer Bednarik's frantic phone calls at the hospital or to acknowledge the telegrams and flowers the concerned player sent. "Why should I?" he later grinned impishly. "We were playing them again the next week. I wasn't going to play, of course, but maybe I could get him so worried he'd play badly. I wrote to him right after the second game, just so he'd know what happened and how I felt."

Such psychology, however, did not have its desired effect. The Eagles beat the Giants again, 31-23, staging a remarkable comeback from a 3-touchdown deficit. Norm Van Brocklin was the quarterback, and he made the most of 4 interceptions recorded by his defense.

It was a defeat that all but sealed the Giants' 1960 fate, dooming Jim Lee Howell to a less-than-championship exit. The team even absorbed the ultimate humiliation before the season would end, a 31-31 tie forced by the fledgling Dallas

Cowboys, who to that date had lost all 10 games they had played and who finished the season with an 0-11-1 record. At the end of the season Philadelphia was in first place in the Eastern Conference with a 10-2 record. The Giants were forced to settle for second with 8-3-1.

And then it was 1961 and time for Allie Sherman, whose hiring as Howell's successor came only after Vince Lombardi tried to extricate himself from a Green Bay Packer contract.

"I knew I was number two," Sherman said, "and what I most wanted was to prove I was a better man, a smarter choice than Vince."

The route to Fairfield University in southern Connecticut takes the driver up the picturesque Merritt Parkway, twisting, manicured tapes of asphalt winding through foothills and valleys. Exit 44 becomes Black Horse Turnpike, and that takes the driver to the university, which is nestled off a minor road and set back into the hills of the affluent suburban area of Fairfield County. Here the New York Giants set up training camp in July 1961.

"We needed help," Sherman says. "Jim Lee might have been tired of coaching, but he also knew he had a veteran team that was aging. It was a very propitious time to retire, to give someone else the job."

Allie knew what he wanted. He never thought he would be able to convince Well Mara to get all of it. What he wanted included another quarterback, a tight end, a wide receiver, and a cornerback. "Not kids, players," he said. "Veterans who knew how to win."

That brought into play Mara's flair for trading, accented by strokes of fortune that should have tipped off everyone that the Giants were a star-struck team. From San Francisco came Tittle. From Los Angeles came Shofner. From Washington came Walton, along with a fullback named Jim Podoley who might have been a superstar had he not stepped in a hole at the Fairfield practice field and butchered his knee. From

Chicago came Erich Barnes. From the draft list came center Greg Larson, running back Bobby Gaiters, guard-defensive tackle Charlie Janerette, linebacker-tight end Bob Simms, quarterback-tight end Pete Hall, defensive back Allen Webb, halfback Joel Wells, and linebackers Mickey Walker and Larry Hayes.

From limbo came Alex Webster, who responded to the challenge of proving himself still capable with his finest season ever, a total of 928 yards gained rushing. He caught 26 passes for another 313 yards, and he scored a total of 5 touchdowns.

The season opened, and the Giants lost their home opener to the St. Louis Cardinals 21-10. A Canadian League expatriate, quarterback Sam Etcheverry, led the victory. Sam the Rifle, as he was called, had played with Webster in Montreal. They knew each other well, and Alex was more than just annoyed when Etcheverry's Cardinals beat his Giants.

The Giants considered that loss as just a fluke. That attitude turned into the hallmark of the team. "We honestly felt there was no way we could be beaten," Gifford says. "When we won, that was the way it was supposed to be. When we lost, the other team was lucky."

The team followed with five consecutive victories, a span of games that propelled Tittle, the newcomer, into the starting quarterback position over Conerly, the veteran and team leader. There were still moments of glory in store for Conerly, who would be playing his final season, but Tittle, the balding, bandaged, bloodied warrior, assumed the job and became a near-legend in New York.

The second game of the season was a 17-14 victory over the Pittsburgh Steelers, a game in which Tittle completed his first 8 New York passes, hitting 10 of 12 in the second half to overcome a Steeler lead and set up Pat Summerall's 19-yard field goal, which proved to be the winning edge. In Washington the next week, Conerly started again. But again it was Tittle who came in to save the victory, a 24-21 decision.

The Giants were 2-1, and the following week they were 3-1 with a 24-9 victory over St. Louis, avenging the opening-day loss. Then Erich Barnes turned around a game in Dallas, picking off a pass as the Cowboys were driving for the tying touchdown in the third period and returning it 102 yards for a touchdown; the Giants won 31-10.

The new quarterback was running smoothly, taking charge. In that Dallas game Tittle gave the ball to Gaiters, the talented but erratic rookie, on a fullback draw. Then he watched as Gaiters hesitated and picked up his head to look around before running and was smeared for a loss. "You stupid kid," Tittle roared. "I'm going to call that play again, and if you pick up your head I'm going to knock it off."

Gaiters stared at this bald, brilliant quarterback, 16 years his senior. "Yes sir, Mister Tittle," he gulped.

Y.A. called the play, and Gaiters, more afraid of Tittle than the Dallas defense, didn't pick up his head once, watching his feet as they ran for 20 yards straight ahead. Gaiters went on to gain 129 yards that day, his best performance as a Giant.

The 4-1 Giants were tied with Philadelphia atop the Eastern Division and had a game with the tough Los Angeles Rams coming up. It was as they feared—the Rams were good, very good, and in the fourth quarter Los Angeles held a 14-10 lead. Tittle? Well, he had been less than inspirational.

"Charley," Sherman yelled to Conerly. "Get the hell in there and win this. We can't lose it."

"Right, Al," Charley said. "Let's win."

So he won. He threw one touchdown pass to Rote and another to Shofner, and the fanatic crowd of 63,053 responded with a volume of noise seldom matched in Yankee Stadium.

But the Eagles were keeping pace, as were the Cleveland Browns, and when Dallas upset the Giants the next week 17-16, New York fell to second, tied with Cleveland and a game behind Philadelphia.

"That was our critical week," Sherman remembers. "We had a game with Philadelphia coming up, and if we didn't win it, we could have fallen apart."

Pete Previte won it for the Giants. No, Pete Previte did not play for them, nor did he coach. Nor was he a scout or a former player or a football strategist. He was the Yankee Stadium clubhouse porter. He cleaned shoes, washed uniforms, ran for coffee and cigarettes and sandwiches, and lived off the regular tips the Giants and the Yankees doled out to him.

"It seems to me," he mentioned that week to Sherman, "that when the Yankees need a run real bad, they put their fastest men on the bases. Why don't you put your fastest men on the field when you have to throw a long touchdown pass to get ahead?"

Sherman had no reasonable explanation. Sometimes the obvious gets lost in the complex.

So that Sunday, when the Giants felt they had to score to break the game open, they broke huddle on their 38 and set up on the line with defensive backs Jimmy Patton and Erich Barnes as two extra wide receivers. Then everybody ran as fast and as hard downfield as he could, and the befuddled Eagles, not knowing whom to cover, allowed Barnes to slip free. Tittle fed him a perfect pass, Erich made a perfect catch, and the Giants had a 62-yard touchdown play and a 24-7 halftime lead.

Philadelphia never moved much after that, and New York took the game 38-21, as well as a share of the Eastern Conference lead with the Eagles.

The next week they destroyed the Washington Redskins 53-0. Tittle threw for 3 touchdowns, and Patton scored on an interception thrown by a rookie quarterback named Norm Snead, the same Norm Snead who a dozen years later would lead the Giants back to respectability and become the NFL's leading passer.

Then New York was all alone on top. Cleveland beat

Philadelphia, and the Giants devastated Pittsburgh 42-21 on another 3-TD day by Tittle, his third straight.

Cleveland next, as 80,455 in cavernous Municipal Stadium on the shores of Lake Erie watched the Giants score 23 second-half points for a 37-21 victory.

Now it was December 3, and the Giants traveled to Milwaukee to play the Western Conference leaders, the Green Bay Packers. Green Bay against New York; Vince Lombardi against Allie Sherman; conference leader against conference leader.

And Alex Webster lost the ball.

"It was the most embarrassing moment of my career," the big redhead grins. "It had never happened before, and I know it turned the game around, and I felt like crawling into a hole and burying myself."

New York had built a 17-13 lead in the fourth quarter, Tittle and Gaiters scoring on the ground and Summerall adding a field goal. The Packers had had to punt, and New York took over on its 8. Tittle called for Webster on a power slant to the right, and Alex ground through a tight opening and suddenly hit daylight. He rambled up the sideline for 22 yards to the Giants' 30. A defensive back named Jesse Whittenton ran up to him, the two seeming to be on a collision course.

Webster veered a bit, and suddenly, in the best tradition of the Marx Brothers, the two passed each other and continued running in opposite directions. Did Whittenton miss Webster? Would Webster be able to continue, to score without another Packer catching him? How could Whittenton have avoided him and not even tried to tackle him?

Then Webster stopped, frantically pivoting and trying to reverse his field. And suddenly what had happened became clear. Whittenton had stolen the ball, had simply plucked it loose from the arms of the most experienced fullback in the league without either of them even breaking stride.

Whittenton would have scored, but he stepped out of

bounds on the Giants' 30. The Packers ran 5 plays before Jim Taylor scored from the 3. Green Bay 20, New York 17. It ended that way when the Giants lost the ball on a Gaiters fumble at the Green Bay 22 with 2 minutes to play.

The Giants had two games left, with Philadelphia and Cleveland, and one of those three teams would emerge as the Eastern Conference winner. On December 10 the Giants played Philadelphia in old Franklin Field, and Philadelphia was a foggy, murky, dreary city that day. The fog and mist grew so thick as to mask vision from the press box high atop the stadium, which now serves only as the University of Pennsylvania's home field.

It started out badly. The Eagles took a 10-7 lead in the second period, and Sherman yanked Tittle. "I had just taken him out for a minute or two so he could see from the sidelines what the Eagles were doing on defense. But then Charley got hot, and there was no way I could put Yat back in."

Conerly had, indeed, "gotten hot." He threw 5 passes and completed them all, the fifth going for a touchdown. He was to throw for 2 more touchdowns to Del Shofner, and the Giants were to win the game 28-24. They also needed a bit of Oscar-winning acting by the punter, Don Chandler. Late in the game the Giants, trailing 24-21, were forced to punt. The Eagles rushed, and Chandler held back for a second, in itself a risky move. Then, when he kicked the ball, someone brushed past him. He hit the ground, yelling and clutching at his right thigh. The official threw a flag—roughing the kicker. The Giants got possession and first down.

Later, in a jubilant locker room, a reporter asked Chandler who ran into him.

"I don't know," he said, grinning.

The reporter asked which leg was hurt.

"I don't know," he said, grinning.

The reporter wondered why he was grinning.

"No comment," he said, grinning.

Oh, the reporter suddenly realized—a trick, right?

"No comment," said Don Chandler.

In the Philadelphia locker room Eagle linebacker Bob Pelligrini tried mightily to smash down the door of the room where the officials were changing. "I'll kill the son-of-a-bitch, I'll kill him," a reporter remembers hearing Pelligrini scream.

Clearly, it was Pelligrini who was charged with running into and knocking down Don Chandler. Did he do it?

"I never got near him," he said. "Never close enough to touch him. Never."

The Giants had won the game 28-24.

There was one game left, in New York against Cleveland, and the Browns were out of the race because they had lost a fourth game. But the Eagles were a game behind, and should they win while the Giants lost, they would force a play-off for the Eastern Conference championship. A victory or a tie by the Giants would clinch.

They got the tie on December 17. The game quickly became known as "The Tie for Christmas."

The Giants scored on a pass from Tittle to Wells. The Browns scored on a pass from Milt Plum to Leon Clarke. Then the game became a defensive clinic, neither team gaining, neither offense working. One last-ditch bomb from Plum to Ray Renfro came within a fingertip of working—but the fingertip was Barnes's, and he deflected the ball into the right corner of the end zone.

On a late fourth-down play, staid old Paul Brown, coach of the Browns, chose to punt from near midfield. The Eagles sent up a roar 90 miles away that could be heard in Yankee Stadium. The Giants, in Allie Sherman's first year, were Eastern Conference champions. The Giants, old and wounded, crippled and lame, were champions. Tittle was named the NFL's Most Valuable Player. Sherman won the accolade as Coach of the Year. Webster, playing most of the season in agony from several injuries, including a seriously pulled groin muscle, won the Comeback of the Year. The championship game with Green Bay was two weeks off, on December 31, 1961.

Green Bay in 1961 was a small town, the epitome of Middle America. It had the bubbly enthusiasm of a small town, so alien to the sophisticates from New York. It had its Packers, the only source of community pride and recognition. It had a championship game.

Green Bay in December is cold, colder than most Giants had ever experienced or believed possible. As the chartered airliner proceeded west-northwest from Idlewild (now JFK) Airport, and as the neat squares of farms became visible below, the spectacle of snow began to impress the New Yorkers. Vast blankets of white seemed to stretch the width of the horizon, and the gray, slate-colored, late afternoon light gave an accurate indication of extreme cold.

When the plane set down at Green Bay's Austin Straubel Field, the temperature was 11 degrees. The sun was partially hidden by swirling snow, prompting tackle Rosey Brown to say, "Look, the sun is wearing a coat, too."

Phil King, the fullback who was killed in 1973 in a tragic accident while cleaning his pistol, was the first to deboard. "Stay there, guys," he yelled back. "It's too cold to breathe."

A bus took the team and the accompanying press to the Northland Hotel, a time-worn building that, contrary to popular belief, was not standing before the town was established. All along the route the visiting New Yorkers saw posters and stickers on store windows and houses and car bumpers, gold-and-green stickers that read "Titletown, U.S.A."

Huff thought that was funny. "How about that," he said, "the hicks don't even know how to spell Tittle."

It was the last bit of levity the Giants would know. The Packers ate them up. They might have been hicks, they might have been housed in a town small enough to be hidden in the Borough of Manhattan, but they had football players.

They had Paul Hornung and Jim Taylor as powerful,

punishing runners. They had the Mechanic, Bart Starr, at quarterback. The receivers were Max McGee and massive tight end Ron Kramer. Boyd Dowler was the flanker, and the offensive line offered tackles Bob Skoronski and Norm Masters, guards Fuzzy Thurston and Forrest Gregg, and center Jim Ringo.

Defensively, the Packers were stifling. Willie Davis, Dave Hanner, Henry Jordan, and Bill Quinlan were the front four. Ray Nitschke, Dan Currie, and Bill Forester were the linebackers. Hank Gremminger, Jesse Whittenton, John Symank, and Willie Wood made up the secondary.

The score was 37-0. The Packers dominated the Giants as no team since the 1940 Chicago Bears had dominated a championship game opponent. Hornung, on a weekend pass from the Army Reserves, scored a still-standing record of 19 points.

Rookie Greg Larson, now the Giants' veteran center, filled in at tackle that day. He remembers the fury with which the Packers won their game. "When we fell behind, they knew we had to pass. When they knew that, they came in with fists and knees and elbows. They came in screaming and screeching. It was absolutely terrifying. We had no way to stop them. It was unending. They were like wild men."

After Rote had dropped two passes out in the clear, one of which would surely have gone for a touchdown (and the other would have been close), the Giants were dead. Tittle tried. . .Conerly tried. . .they both failed.

Sherman's miracle had fallen short.

"I knew going in that we'd have to play over our heads just to stay close," Allie admitted much later. "That Green Bay team was possibly the best I've ever seen."

So ended the 1961 season. But more glory was to come, mixed with bittersweet disappointment for Sherman and Tittle.

The start of the 1962 season was eventful. Conerly had retired, and now no subtle conflict would continue between the two proud quarterbacks. Sherman, not satisfied with the meager talents of such backups as Lee Grosscup and Bubba Marriott, obtained veteran Ralph Guglielmi from the Washington Redskins. Summerall, too, had departed, and Sherman arranged for Ken Strong to tutor Don Chandler, the punter, in placekicking. Chandler was an apt pupil—he not only became the first 2-way kicker for New York in a long time but led the NFL with 19 field goals in 28 attempts, 47 of 48 extra point tries, and finished second (to Green Bay's fierce fullback, Jim Taylor) in total scoring with 104 points.

And Frank Gifford had returned. "I sat out the 1961 season because of that injury," he recalled. "I missed the hell out of the game, and it got to the point where I had to see if I could play again. I still wasn't too old, and I knew if I didn't try it then I would be wondering for the rest of my life. If I wasn't any good, I'd accept that and quit. But I had to know. I told Al and Well, and they agreed I should return."

Gifford, one of the most intense and high-minded players the Giants ever had, was moved to a new position. At the suggestion of the doctors, he would no longer be risked as a running back, for there was some fear that the constant pounding he would be exposed to might be fraught with danger. Instead, he became the flanker, replacing Rote, who also had decided to announce his retirement.

Rote as flanker had been superb. Gifford as flanker was perhaps even better. He caught 39 passes that season for 796 yards and scored 8 touchdowns in all.

Sherman thus had Tittle at quarterback, Webster at fullback, Gifford at flanker, Shofner at split end, and Walton at tight end. At the halfback spot—he had traded the promising but dense Gaiters to San Francisco for tight end-flanker Aaron Thomas—he alternated Phil King, Joe Morrison, Paul Dudley, and rookie Johnny Counts.

The offensive line had changed in position but not in names. Rosey Brown and Jack Stroud were the tackles,

Stroud having played guard in 1961. Darrell Dess and Greg Larson or Bookie Bolin played guards, Larson having been a tackle in 1961. Reliable Ray Wietecha, who was in his final season, was still an All-Pro center.

Defensively, the front four was the same—Robustelli and Katcavage at the ends, Modzelewski and Grier at the tackles; they were called the Ro, Ro, Mo, and Kat line.

Linebacker Cliff Livingston had retired, but a rookie named Bill Winter, from tiny St. Olaf College in Minnesota, came on strong, and at 6-feet-3 and 220 he played remarkably well as a starter in a pressure situation. Huff was still in the middle, and violent Tom Scott was on the right. The secondary was superb, with Dick Lynch and Erich Barnes at the cornerback stations, Jimmy Patton and Allen Webb at the safeties.

Again, as in 1961, there were other teams favored to win the Eastern Conference. There was Cleveland, for example, with the incomparable Jim Brown at fullback and with Jim Ninowski, Tom Wilson, and a rock-ribbed defense. There was Philadelphia, still tough, still poised, and still fuming at its half-game failure the previous season.

But at the end of the season the New York Giants were at the top of the conference with a 12-2 record. In second were the surprising Pittsburgh Steelers with a 9-5 mark. The Browns were 7-6-1; the Eagles were 3-10-1 cellar-dwellers.

What won it for the Giants? Many things, including the remarkable season enjoyed by Tittle, who completed 200 of 375 passes for 3,224 yards and 20 touchdowns; Webster's leg-churning running, which accounted for 743 yards and 5 TDs; Gifford's amazing comeback; the 53 receptions for 1,133 yards and 12 TDs from Shofner; a determined defense that overcame the retirement of Livingston, that played with a rookie at starting linebacker and still limited its opponents to 283 points.

But perhaps Sherman's coaching was the most critical factor, for the team that was growing old in 1960 had reached its peak and its limit. Sherman's coaching abilities were never more on display than in the sixth game of the season, against Detroit.

The Giants had lost their opener to Cleveland 17-7 but then bounced back to win 3 in a row. Then a fourth-quarter field goal by Lou Michaels won a game for Pittsburgh 20-17, and the Giants were 3-2 and starting to fade. Coming up was a game with Detroit, a ferocious defensive team with enough offensive weapons to beat anyone.

"It was their defense," Sherman remembers. "It was hard to believe. After we lost to Pittsburgh, I was not very optimistic about the rest of the season. I had watched Detroit do an incredible job against Green Bay. I think it was the first time they met, when the Packers won. But the score was close, and Detroit should have won. I can remember that defense, just smackin' the hell out of Starr all day. I never saw the Green Bay offensive line get beat like that. I really didn't think we had a chance of beating them, and that meant we'd lose two in a row and be three and three."

The defense that frightened Sherman so was mainly the front four, although linebackers such as Joe Schmidt and Wayne Walker and deep backs such as Dick LeBeau and Night Train Lane certainly helped. The men up front were Roger Brown, Alex Karras, Sam Williams, and Darris McCord.

Brown was gargantuan, weighing over 300 pounds. Karras, his companion tackle, was one of the NFL's best, among its quickest and clearly its meanest. Subsequently, he became one of its most outspoken critics, exhibiting a flair for crudeness and lack of tact as well as some self-serving controversy.

Sherman recalls the preparation for the game:

I had no idea about a game plan. For the first time I can remember we weren't ready with one on Tuesday before the game. I didn't know what would work, really. I knew Tittle would never have the chance to pass deep; we couldn't buy him that kind of time. So that meant we were going to have to use the 8-yard pass patterns. But with that obvious, the Lions were going to tee off on every play and just kill that old man. If he got nailed two or three times early, we would have been buried.

Finally, I decided to take a chance. Nobody had been able to run on them all year, but I wanted to try it. I had Webster and King [both over 220 pounds], and our offensive line was pretty good. Ed Kolman [the offensive line coach] put in what he called a Double Pinch blocking maneuver, in which the tackle and guard take one of the defensive tackles, the other tackle and guard get the other one, and we run it right down their throats.

I know, it all could have backfired. I could have looked bad. But if we went at them with what we normally used, we could have—no, would have—been buried.

So the doubleteam blocks were used, and the critical factor Sherman was counting on worked—Karras and Brown were too proud, too arrogant, to ignore the challenge. They were determined to fight off the doubleteam blocks, the Double Pinch, and they consumed time and energy in the effort.

Webster and King pounded at the two tackles. Tittle bought time to throw and started using sideline patterns. The Giants fell behind at halftime 14-7 but scored 10 points in the second half while holding the Lions scoreless. They had their victory 17-14, as a Yankee Stadium crowd of 62,856 screamed its banshee shrieks.

"Al made me a believer that day," Tittle said. "I never thought it would work. Being a passer, I just wanted to get back there and throw the damned thing all afternoon. But he taught me patience and strategy. I doubt any other coach in the league could have done what the little guy did."

The victory set the Giants off on a 9-game winning streak, the longest in their history. The next game, against Washington, showed the mental benefits accrued from the Detroit success. Tittle threw enough passes to gain 505 yards, the second-highest total in the history of the league, and he clicked on 7 touchdown passes, the most ever thrown in a single game in NFL annals. Joe Walton caught 3 of them, Morrison 2, Shofner and Gifford 1 each. New York won 49-34. The offensive was under way.

St. Louis fell 31-28. Then a 24-point second period put Dallas back on the drawing board 41-10. Philadelphia fell 19-14, followed by Washington again 42-24, Chicago 26-24, Cleveland 17-13, and Dallas again 41-31 in the season finale. Unlike the previous season, the final game meant nothing. Indeed, the game before that had been meaningless, too, since the Giants had clinched in the 26-24 victory in Chicago on 4 field goals by Chandler, the second time he had kicked that many in a game that season.

After the opening-game loss to Cleveland before a record crowd of 81,115, Dick Lynch had been interviewed. One of the questions put to him was, "Do you feel the Giants are finally through this season?"

He laughed, this handsome, cocky graduate of Notre Dame who in 1958 had scored the only touchdown in a 7-0 victory over Oklahoma that had snapped a 47-game Sooner winning streak. "Finished? We'll win 10 in a row yet, you'll see." He was wrong. They won only 9.

Now it was time for revenge. Green Bay had won 10 in a row, had finished with a 13-1 record, had scored 415 points, and had given up a paltry 148. It was, clearly, a super team.

"Bullshit," said Andy Robustelli, when told of Green Bay's superiority by a needling reporter. "All I need to remember is a score. The score is 37-0. I've never been as anxious to play a game as this one. We will absolutely kill the bastards. It's the only way I'll be able to forget the one last year out there. That one was the low point of my career. It burned into my brain, and the only way I can get rid of the memory is by returning the aggravation. It won't be enough to just win this game. We have to destroy the Packers and

Lombardi. It's the only way we can atone for what happened to us last year."

Most observers favored the Giants because of the home-field factor and because of Tittle's remarkable passing during the season. Surely the weather in New York could not be as bad as it had been in Green Bay. Surely Tittle would be able to pass easily.

The day, December 30, 1962, came up howling and icy. The winds tore at the fans, and the impossible air currents in Yankee Stadium, an edifice now more than fifty years old, swept up through the stands and down onto the field and turned everything to ice.

"It was the worst day I can ever remember for a football game," Vince Lombardi once recalled. "I was half sorry to ask people to play in those conditions. The ground was like concrete."

Starr and Tittle both experienced a new sensation. The two quarterbacks, whose experience as professionals, when added together, amounted to 18 years, found the football being blown back at them when they tried to pass.

The game became one of ground thrusts and vicious tackles. Green Bay had the 215-pound Taylor, and no tough-er man could be found in the league. New York had Webster and King, two of the biggest and strongest NFL fullbacks.

It was primeval, basic football. Taylor would hurl his body at the Giants' defense, and Huff, mostly, would hurl him back. Webster would plunge through the line to be met by Willie Davis and Ray Nitschke and Henry Jordan.

When it was finished, Green Bay had a 16-7 victory, and Taylor had a new enemy—Huff. "The man is the dirtiest player in the league," Taylor screamed. "He tried to cripple me. He used his elbows and knees when I was on the ground." Modzelewski claimed that Taylor had bitten him, and Robustelli was accused of all sorts of mayhem by half a dozen Packers. Grudges were born on that frozen field that live today.

For the second year in a row the Packers had taken the Giants in a championship game. Sherman, who was to become paranoid over his inability to beat Green Bay, began almost immediately to build for 1963.

"I didn't know how much longer that old team would hold together," he says, "and I wanted to see just what we needed to get one more championship shot."

He traded Grier, an incorrigible overweight problem, to Los Angeles for defensive tackle John LoVetere. Allie did not do as well when he believed the syrupy scouting report of one Peahead Walker, who claimed that a quarterback at Mississippi, Glynn Griffing, was "the finest quarterback in these Yewnited States." The Giants drafted Griffing, and he was to become a disappointment and a financial disaster to the Mara clan.

Another trade brought halfback Hugh McElhenny to New York, a man called "The King," whose broken-field running talents were spoken of in reverential terms by even the most accomplished of runners.

Then there was Tittle. As long as Y.A. remained, the Giants had the arsenal. In 1963 Y.A. enjoyed his finest season ever. He earned his second Player of the Year award, led the league in passing, and became the NFL's Most Valuable Player.

What he did was this: he threw 36 touchdown passes to set an NFL record. He completed 60.2 percent of his passes to set a team record that stood until 1972. He threw 367 times and completed 221 for 3,145 yards. He was intercepted only 14 times. And he did it in only 13 games, having been injured against Baltimore early in the season and forced to sit out the next one, against Pittsburgh, in which Guglielmi was himiliated 31-0.

Shofner caught 64 passes for 1,181 yards and 13 TDs. Gifford caught 42 for 657 yards and 7 TDs. Morrison caught 31, Walton 26, Thomas 22, Webster 15, and McElhenny 11.

King replaced Webster as team rushing leader with 613

yards in 161 carries, but Morrison was right behind with 568 in just 119 attempts, a laudable 4.8 per-carry average.

The defense functioned smoothly, and LoVetere filled in ably for Grier. "He was so good," Sherman says, "we felt we had gotten the best of the trade, and Rosey was doing a hell of a job in L.A." Two years later, however, LoVetere would suffer torn knee ligaments and then, through an unwillingness to go through the necessary rehabilitation, would be forced into an early retirement.

The Giants won it again, slipping past Cleveland with an 11-3 record, scoring an incredible 448 points, beating opponents by such scores as 37-28, 37-14, 33-6, 37-21, 42-14, 44-14, and 48-14.

It was a season in which they played a near-perfect game against a fearsome and capable opponent, and that, too, is Sherman's story to tell: "Cleveland had beaten us in New York," he says, "and it had been a particularly bitter game. [Jim Brown leveled charges at the Giants that Tom Scott had been instructed "to blind me, to gouge out my eyes."] They were hanging close to us all season after that, and we had a game with them out there. We knew we had to win it, but it was going to be extra tough. I was never more surprised at what we did, but we had spent so much time working on that game plan I don't think any of the coaches or myself or Tittle slept much all week. We had to know exactly what to do under any circumstances, and our defense had to be ready to stop whatever they did."

It worked. As a vast crowd of 84,213 watched in stunned silence, the Giants totally dominated the Browns. New York scored 17 points in the first period, turning a fumble recovery into a 6-yard Tittle-to-McElhenny touchdown pass, converting an interception into a 23-yard Tittle-to-Shofner touchdown pass, then adding a 29-yard field goal by Chandler, the first of 4 he would kick in that game. It was 23-0 at halftime. Cleveland was dead. It finished 33-6.

"I don't think any team I've ever coached played a better,

smarter game," Sherman said. "We did nothing wrong. We intercepted passes that should have been completions, we stopped Brown on running plays that should have worked well, and we completed passes to guys who were double-covered perfectly. It was a special, almost magical day. I'll never forget it, and neither will any of the men who played in that game."

The Giants, who fully expected to have a third meeting with Green Bay, were to be disappointed. The Packers, with an 11-2-1 record, were second to Chicago, an 11-1-2 team with a standout defense assembled by a young coaching assistant named George Allen.

So it was to Chicago, not to upper Wisconsin, that the Giants went at the end of December. But the result, sadly, was to be the same. It was Tittle's most disheartening loss. Let it be told in his words, some of which can be found in *I Pass,* an autobiography written with the help of Don Smith, the team's one-time publicity director.

"The losses to Green Bay in 1961 and 1962 were hard to take, but the one to Chicago was even worse. I was firmly convinced we were going to win that one. There was no doubt in my mind. It wasn't just for me that I was so disappointed; it was for a lot of guys who had battled through a tough season. We all had a stake in it. I wanted it because the memory of losing those games with Green Bay was still raw. I also was damned tired of hearing how I couldn't win 'the big ones.' We had a lot of older players, who maybe wouldn't be getting another chance, and I felt like I owed it to them, too."

The Giants prepared well. The Bears were a team with just barely enough offense; they relied on defense and won with defense. But what defense that year had been able to withstand the irrepressible passing of Y.A. Tittle?

"Al's theory was that games were won by the side that made the fewest mistakes, and so you do what you do best, even if it's simple. Defensively, Chicago was very good. But there wasn't a man in the league who could stay man-to-man with Del Shofner or Gifford. But I had to get hurt. Dammit, I had to get hurt."

What happened was named Larry Morris, a tough linebacker, and what he did was to hit Tittle across the left knee as Y.A. threw a 14-yard TD pass to Gifford in the first quarter. "But it was all right until the second period, when I passed to Gifford but slipped and fell on the hard ground, and as I fell there was Morris again, blitzing. He shot at my leg, and it was bad. It was like somebody stuck a knife in the joint of the knee."

Dr. Anthony Pisani sprayed the knee with a numbing chemical and then injected Novocaine. "I tried to play again, but I was way off," Tittle says. "I had to back-pedal instead of dropping straight back, and it was awkward and time-consuming."

The Giants had to send in a substitute, but Glynn Griffing was hopeless and lost, confused and unprepared. "The boy was a nice kid and all," Sherman says, "but he was not a quarterback. He was nowhere. We had trouble getting through to him, and it was just hopeless. If I left him in he was going to get plucked ⌐ intercepted ⌐, and we'd have been out of it for sure."

So Sherman did the only other thing he could do—he called on the badly injured Tittle, who was sitting on the sideline in agony (whether from his knee or from watching Griffing is not clear), and sent him back into the game.

Griffing would never play another game with the Giants. He not only was limited as a quarterback, but he had a "peculiar outlook" on football, according to Sherman and several others.

"He had a wedding date set that season," Allie recalls, "and we asked him to put it off until after the schedule, which he agreed to do. But then we had like two weeks to get ready for the championship game, and he left to get married. We arranged to give the team a few days off, and we told him he had that time. But he arrived two or three days late anyway, something about being caught in a snowstorm . . . or letting himself be caught in a snowstorm. Anyway, he was no use in the game. If he had looked any good at all, I might not have put Tittle back in, but we had a shot at the game and the kid would have given it up. We were handling them well defensively. We had to get some points."

But Tittle was crippled, and while even that much was worth more than Griffing healthy, it was far from enough. The game ended 14-10. The Giants had made it 3-for-3 in 3 straight years of championship games—3 losses.

It was to be the end of the line for the Giants; the ravages of age and stupidity made rapid and fatal progress through the team's lifeline.

Huff was traded. Modzelewski was traded. Robustelli retired. Walton retired. King was traded. Guglielmi left, having played in just two games the previous season. Those who remained had peaked and were starting the slide toward retirement, the ones named Webster and Stroud, Gifford and Brown, McElhenny and Scott, Patton and Shofner, and, yes, even Tittle.

"I was a bad quarterback in 1964," Tittle says. "It got so bad I knew it was time to retire."

Tittle's decision was hastened by two factors — his confusion at all the changes from the status quo and his dedication to excellence. He could not tolerate the errors of those who were left. "I tried to do everything exactly as we had done it in the three previous years," he said. "I asked myself, why break up a winning combination? I figured it would last forever."

In a moment of rare insight, Tittle slouched in an armchair at Fairfield University the year after he retired and recalled the difficulties of 1964: "I just figured it would never end," he said. "I figured Webster and King would be there to pick up the linebackers and Shofner would be flying way downfield somewhere and Gifford would be faking out a back and be standing there open and Walton would somehow get free for the third-down pass. I never thought we'd get old. And when we did, when we got to be old guys and washed-up athletes, I couldn't handle it. When something was not in its right place, I was mediocre, a loser. That's when I realized it was time to retire."

One other thing happened to Tittle in 1964 — John Baker. Baker was a 6-foot-6, 250-pound defensive tackle with the Pittsburgh Steelers. In the Giants' first game with Pittsburgh Baker broke through a young and inexperienced tackle named Lane Howell and got to Y.A. as he was about to throw the ball.

It was as vicious a tackle as has ever been made, and the older man slumped to the ground in obvious agony. For a while, from a vantage point high above Pitt Stadium, press box observers thought the worst. "My God, he looks dead," someone shouted; Tittle did not move. Baker was standing over the bald quarterback and seemed to be yelling at him. Webster was the first player on the field to get to the pair, but he says today he does not remember what, if anything, Baker was screaming. It was not pretty.

Tittle was helped off the field with head lacerations, chest bruises, and broken ribs. It was the second game of the season, and it followed a 38-7 opening-day loss in Philadelphia, a game that caused the Giants serious concern. The Eagles were not a good team. In 1964 they were to be 6-8. But safety Don Burroughs knifed through the offensive line time and again to harass Tittle into passing too quickly or to throw the valiant old man to the ground before he could pass at all.

It was disaster followed by disaster. The Friday night following the Pittsburgh game, when Washington came to Yankee Stadium, rookie Gary Wood of Cornell threw 10 times in the first half without completing a single pass. Tittle had to play the second half, heavily bandaged and with his rib cage strapped together. The Giants won 13-10 when

Wood ran for a touchdown late in the game, having come back for Tittle, who was in far too much pain to stand upright.

The defense disintegrated, and the offense disappeared. John Contoulis and Roger Anderson were playing defensive line where the year before Robustelli and Modzelewski had stood. Jerry Hillebrand was asked to fill Huff's position as middle linebacker, and Hillebrand was an abject failure. So, too, was his replacement, rookie Lou Slaby.

It all began to fall apart. The Giants' top draft choice, for example, had been a magnificent running back from Oklahoma named Joe Don Looney, a 6-foot-2, 230-pound prize package drooled over by many teams. But when Joe Don got to the training camp, he began to come apart emotionally. He refused to practice, ignored curfew, argued with teammates, coaches, and reporters, and engaged in fist fights and after-hours revelry. Finally, he was traded to Baltimore, not having played in even an exhibition game for the Giants.

"Joe Don began to crack one day at practice," recalls Don Smith, who was there and who saw it. "We had a tackling dummy that was built on a recoil spring to make it tougher to drive back. The players were instructed to hit it and get out of the way because it snapped back with pretty good force. Well, Joe Don didn't believe it. He was a physical fitness fanatic, always building his muscles and lifting weights, and maybe he didn't think a machine could knock him down.

"Well, he hit the thing and waited. Sure enough, it snapped back and knocked him on his rear end. He got up and hit it again. It hit him back again. He started losing control, hitting it and yelling at it and cursing at it, until finally he wrestled it to the ground and was kicking and rolling around and almost crying. It was a little scary."

The only sense Joe Don ever made in New York was his refusal to allow old Doc Sweeny to work on him. "You keep that crazy little man away from me," he warned, and since old Doc had by then become more of a character and a mascot than a healer, no one could argue with Joe Don's stand.

Few could argue with his twisted logic, either. "Why should I have to go to sleep at 11 o'clock if I'm not tired?" he asked. "Why do I have to practice if I know the plays we're going to work on?" It was a tip-off as to the direction the entire season was going to take.

So the team collapsed, Sherman became frantic, and the final record was 2-10-2, the worst in the history of the Giants.

In 1965 it was better for two reasons: Homer Jones and Earl Morrall.

Jones, who had been drafted by the AFL's Houston Oilers, had suffered a knee injury and was subsequently cut. He called New York, which had made him a twentieth-round draft choice, and asked for a trial. He got it.

The Giants tried to get through their exhibition schedule with Wood, Bob Timberlake, Henry Schichtle, and John Torok at quarterback. But all were hopeless. Finally, they had to effect a trade with Detroit and Cleveland in a three-way deal, sending Barnes to Cleveland for linebacker Mike Lucci, then sending Lucci and guard Darrell Dess to Detroit for Morrall.

It worked. Morrall gave New York respectability and a 7-7 record, and Homer Jones, a colorful, erratic character, gave the Giants a folk hero. He caught 26 passes for 709 yards that season, including the league's longest reception, an 89-yard touchdown.

Homer, from Texas Southern, kept the reporters in stitches. "I ran on a relay team once and came back with two batons," he said. But Homer never joked. He was deadly serious. He was also a superb athlete. At 6-feet-2 and 215, Homer had 9.3 speed — world class — in the 100-yard dash.

He had won a gold medal for the U.S. in a meet with Russia at Los Angeles in 1960, running the 220-yard dash in 20.7 — around a turn.

But it was Earl and Homer and nothing much more; the 1965 Giants scrambled to a 7-7 record.

By 1966, however, even that brief flirtation with normality was finished. The Giants crashed deeper and louder than any team had ever crashed before.

Most of their starters were bad jokes, and those who could play football well were injured. Tucker Frederickson, the NFL's first draft pick the year before, was a case in point. He stretched his knee ligaments in summer camp when hit by a rookie named Jeff Smith, then tore them three weeks later while reaching for a pass against Green Bay in an exhibition game. He was lost for the season.

The rookie crop — which had been carefully selected and then seduced away from the rival AFL teams that had drafted them — proved to be, generally, embarrassing. Offensive tackle Francis Peay was the number-one pick, a man for whom the Giants paid an under-the-table amount of $250,000. He played only sporadically and was eventually traded to Green Bay for 2 players who have since left New York, though Peay remained with the Packers until 1973.

The second draft pick was a hulking 6-foot-6, 260-pound defensive tackle from Los Angeles State named Don Davis. He was a honey, a killer. He was also a glutton, and by the time he got to training camp he had ballooned to 339 pounds. Sherman was nearly felled by a coronary when he caught his first glimpse of Davis waddling onto the field.

"I never saw anybody eat like that, or drink so much soda pop," said Well Mara. "Don was playing for the College All-Star team in Chicago, and we sent Rosey Brown out to watch him, to keep him away from the 'bottle.' So the kid would sneak sugar into his waterglass at meals."

Obviously, Davis never played worth a damn for the Giants. But he, too, was expensive — $150,000.

The other rookies offered little solace. Those who made the team and had a hand in the travesty that was to follow included linebacker Mike Ciccolella, running back Steve Bowman, tackle Charlie Harper, safety Phil Harris, defensive end Bill Matan, runner Randy Minniear, defensive back Bob Post, tackle Dave Powless, guard Randy Staten, center Joe Wellborn, tight end Freeman White, guard-tackle Willie Young, and, of course, Peay, Davis, and placekicker Pete Gogolak, who had jumped from the AFL Buffalo Bills to the Giants and who by so doing set off the ferocious player raids between the leagues that led to the eventual merger in June 1966.

The Giants were forced to play the 1966 season. They had defensive linemen like Mike Bundra and Roger LaLonde and anybody else who would volunteer. Linebackers? Carroll, Hillebrand, Bill Swain, Olen Underwood. None of them were able to do the job, nor could they do it when some of them, such as Swain and Underwood, moved to other teams.

The offense had rookie Chuck Mercein as its rushing leader with 327 yards, and after him came Morrison with 275. Morrall and Wood were equally ineffective in sharing the season. Wood played the final 7 games after Morrall broke a bone in his wrist in a practice-field collision with running back Allen Jacobs.

Defensively, additional problems were caused by the retirements of Patton and Lynch, though in Lynch's case his retirement was a blessing. He had been burned badly all through 1965 and had clearly lost the talent he had once evidenced.

The Giants were a joke. They surrendered a league record 501 points, allowing such single-game totals as 72 by Washington, 55 by Los Angeles, 52 by Dallas, 49 by Cleveland, and 47 by Pittsburgh. Their only victory was a 13-10 struggle with Washington, and they opened the season with their only tie, a 34-34 exercise in futility in Pittsburgh.

The loss in Washington, to the tune of 72-41, was the nadir

of the season. "I went to get a cup of coffee," said one of the players' wives, "and when I got back 4 more touchdowns had been scored. I was really embarrassed, and I put away my Giant banner."

The defensive lineup that day for the Giants, which deserves to be preserved, was as follows:

LE — Jim Katcavage
LT — Jim Moran
RT — Don Davis
RE — Glen Condren
LLB — Stan Szurek
MLB — Mike Ciccolella
RLB — Jeff Smith
LCB — Spider Lockhart
RCB — Wendell Harris
LS — Henry Carr
RS — Clarence Childs

"Can you imagine scoring 41 points in a game and losing by 31?" Sherman moaned. "I was speechless and ashamed. Never had I been beaten that badly."

Washington coach Otto Graham executed the final and supreme insult when he stopped the clock with 3 seconds to play so that Charley Gogolak, Pete's brother, could kick a 29-yard field goal for the final points. "He needed the practice," Graham protested, perhaps forgetting that the kicker had already made 9 of 10 extra point attempts.

Tom Kennedy, a quarterback purchased by the Giants in mid-season from the Brooklyn Dodgers of the Atlantic Coast Football League, tried to play that day. But he was powerless, as he had been weeks earlier in Los Angeles when in an attempt to stop the clock he had wheeled and thrown the ball out of bounds—only to be told that it had been fourth down and the Rams were about to take possession. The Giants should have known. Kennedy had showed up at the airport in New York carrying a Y.A. Tittle box game under his arm and had studied the little plastic men all the way to Los Angeles.

A game the next week in Cleveland, in which the Giants held a 33-7 lead and lost 49-40, simply brought them closer to the merciful end of the season. That came 2 games later, following losses of 47-28 to Pittsburgh and 17-7 to Dallas.

Obviously, the Giants were desperate. They had to make changes, if not to build the team then to stop the cancer, to bring back the fans.

It was done. The Giants obtained quarterback Fran Tarkenton from the Minnesota Vikings in the spring of 1967 for two first-round and two second-round draft choices. Those players became Clinton Jones, Ed White, Ron Yary, and Bob Grim for the Vikings.

Tarkenton, by then a six-year veteran in the NFL, had experienced his own problems in 1966. He could not interact with Norm Van Brocklin, the volcanic head coach, and had finally written a well-publicized letter to the team's general manager, Jim Finks, demanding to be traded or threatening to quit. When Van Brocklin resigned to take the Atlanta head coaching job, Tarkenton would not relent, saying the situation in Minnesota "had deteriorated."

So Francis came to the Giants. Ironically, he expressed great joy five years later when, after coming to a violent grudge match with Well Mara, he was traded back to the Vikings.

But in 1967 Fran the Scrambler, perhaps the most electrifying performer in the league, was pleased to be in New York. The Giants, for their part, were ecstatic to have him. He was capable of transforming them into, if not winners, at least respectable losers, not clowns.

Fran did it. He brought the Giants back up to 7-7. He enjoyed a super season, and he made the other players look better, if only because he took most of the offensive burden on himself.

Fran completed 204 of 377 passes in 1967. He threw for 3,088 yards and 29 touchdowns. He was magnificent, and as a runner he gained 306 yards in 44 carries, most of them frantic, spur-of-the-moment dashes out of the clutches of cursing, frustrated defensive linemen.

The Giants scored 369 points, more than 100 in excess of their 1966 total, and the defense showed an even greater improvement, following its 501-point nightmare by surrendering 379 points.

The Giants were better yet in 1968, though their record was another 7-7. They had, however, acquired some players who were to become significant in later years. They had further improved their defense. The performance of Tarkenton was again classic—he clicked for 21 touchdown passes, completed 182 of 337 attempts for 2,555 yards, and ran for 301 more yards.

Then came the summer of 1969. More specifically, then came August 17, 1969. The scene was the Yale Bowl in New Haven, Connecticut. The event was historic—the first clash between the Giants and their hated crosstown rivals, the Jets. More important, the Jets, through one of the great upsets in the history of all sports, would be met as Super Bowl champions. Behind Joe Willie Namath, a super quarterback with a mouth to match, the Jets had beaten Baltimore in Super Bowl III, 16-7. Now they were in New Haven to settle many old scores, many slights and insults and much ridicule, and they had the Giants in the best of possible circumstances—totally helpless.

It was no contest, and the 70,874 who jammed the hoary Bowl made sure the Giants and Allie Sherman knew how they felt.

Namath was invincible. He led the Jets to 17 first-period points and a 24-7 halftime lead. In the first half he completed 8 of 9 passes for 119 yards. He would finish the game with

14 of 16 completions for 188 yards and 3 touchdowns. He would throw 4 passes to Don Maynard, a man who had been cut by Allie Sherman as a rookie with the Giants in 1958, and Maynard would take those passes 75 yards. The devastation was complete. The Jets scored almost at will, and the crowd hooted and booed and sang its famous "Goodbye, Allie" chorus.

Namath, who missed only his first pass in each half, was not the only man who had a large part in killing the Giants. The Giants had several players who worked toward the same end.

A Jets rookie named Mike Battle took advantage of lazy tackling to return a punt 86 yards for a touchdown. Two Giants named Ron Blye and Henry Dyer booted a kick-off back and forth on their 2-yard line, each waiting for the other to pick it up, until a Jets rookie named Cecil Leonard recovered it. One play later the Jets scored.

It was humiliating. Sherman was as close to a mental and emotional breakdown as any man can get and still not teeter over the edge. Mara was livid, nearly paralyzed with shame and anger. The players—those who cared, those who were really players—were broken and mortified. The Jets were cruel winners, and their words and taunts stung deeply, to be remembered for a long, long time.

It was the end of Allie Sherman as the coach of the Giants, although Well Mara denies that the game signaled Sherman's dismissal.

But Mara left training camp for a week, an unprecedented move for him. The shock was complete, and all that Timothy Mara had accomplished from 1925 on, in the mind of his son Wellington, had been shattered. The Giants—Well Mara's Giants—had been exposed to public ridicule by a group of coarse newcomers.

Three weeks later, on September 11, the Giants traveled to Montreal for their final exhibition game against Pittsburgh. It was 10 days before the season would open, and the Giants were 0-5 for the summer. This would be their last chance to win before playing for keeps.

The score was 17-13 Pittsburgh. With 36 seconds left in the game Tarkenton, who had moved the Giants valiantly, threw a pass to Joe Morrison. Good old reliable Joe caught the ball at the Steeler 5. Then good old reliable Joe fumbled the ball. John Henderson recovered for the Steelers, and the Giants' sixth consecutive defeat was sealed.

"We did a lot of things well," Sherman said, perhaps as much to make himself believe as to convince the reporters on the team's charter-plane flight home. Then Allie went into some detail about a rumored finder's fee he had earned for arranging the merger of two businesses operated by friends of his. Then he left the reporters at LaGuardia Airport.

The next time any of us saw Sherman, he was unemployed.

It was 4:03 P.M. when the bulletin from Associated Press clattered across the country.

NEW YORK (AP) — Allie Sherman was dismissed as head coach of the New York Giants Friday, nine days before the start of the regular National Football League season. He was replaced by Alex Webster, offensive backfield coach.

Sherman had served as head coach for eight seasons during the time the Giants won three NFL Eastern Division titles.

"Since 1961," said Wellington Mara, the Giants' president, "all decisions affecting the operation of our football team have been made by Al Sherman and myself. Because I find recent results unacceptable, I have taken the following steps:

"I have asked Al Sherman to step aside as head coach, and I have signed Alex Webster to a two-year contract as head coach.

"Although I will continue to be the chief executive

officer of the Giants and, as such, will continue to have the ultimate responsibility for all decisions, I will appoint an experienced football man to assist our new head coach in the evaluation, selection, and procurement of players. It may not be possible to make such an appointment until after the football season, but actually few decisions of this nature remain to be made for this season."

Mara said that Sherman, who still has five years remaining on a ten-year contract, will remain with the organization. He did not say in what capacity.

Sherman was not present at the mammoth news conference at which his dismissal was announced.

It had been eight years. Only Steve Owen, in a different world and a different time, had been head coach of the New York Giants for a longer period.

Now Allie Sherman had been fired. Blunt, callous, cruel, ungrateful, thankless—all those words were used by the press to portray Wellington Mara's action. There was some reason to consider Sherman's dismissal, but not to do it so drastically. "At least," said Fran Tarkenton, "he should have been given the 1969 season to show if he had improved the team. I would think they owed him that. But it was the Jets game. He was a dead man the second the whistle blew."

Now the man unanimously considered to be a publicity stunt, the man who was said to have been "put up for sacrifice" until a "real coach" could be signed for the following season, began to make halting, unsure moves.

He was not qualified to be a head coach. What saved his coaching life was that he realized it.

"I have made no plans," said Alex Webster in his first public statement as head coach of the New York Giants. "I have called for a meeting of all the coaches tomorrow morning."

The season was nine days away, and Webster's struggle had begun.

GIANTS OF THE SIXTIES

Adamchik, Ed	Center	Pittsburgh	1965
Anderson, Bob	End-Back	Army	1963
Anderson, Bruce	End	Williamette	1967-69
Anderson, Roger	Tackle	Virginia Union	1965-68
Avery, Ken	Linebacker	Southern Miss.	1967-68
Barnes, Erich	Back	Purdue	1961-64
Blye, Ron	Back	Notre Dame	1968
Bohovich, Reed	Tackle	Lehigh	1962-63
Bolin, Bookie	Guard	Mississippi	1962-67
Boll, Don	Tackle	Nebraska	1960
Boston, McKinley	End	Minnesota	1968-69
Bowman, Steve	Back	Alabama	1966
Brenner, Al	Back	Michigan State	1969-70
Brown, Barry	Linebacker	Florida	1968
Brown, Roosevelt	Tackle	Morgan State	1953-65
Bundra, Mike	Tackle	Southern California	1965
Buzin, Richard	Tackle	Penn State	1969-70
Byers, Ken	Guard	Cincinnati	1962-64
Carr, Henry	Back	Arizona State	1965-67
Carroll, Jim	Linebacker	Notre Dame	1965-66
Case, Pete	Guard	Georgia	1965-70
Ceppetelli, Gene	Center	Villanova	1969
Chandler, Don	Kicker	Florida	1956-64
Childs, Clarence	Back	Florida A&M	1964-67
Ciccolella, Mike	Linebacker	Dayton	1966-68
Coffey, Junior	Back	Washington	1969-71
Collier, Jim	End	Arkansas	1962-63
Colvin, Jim	Tackle	Houston	1967
Condren, Glen	End-Tackle	Oklahoma	1965-67
Conerly, Charley	Quarterback	Mississippi	1948-61
Contoulis, John	Tackle	Connecticut	1964
Cordileone, Lou	Guard	Clemson	1960
Costello, Tom	Linebacker	Dayton	1964-65
Costello, Vince	Linebacker	Ohio	1967

Counts, John	Back	Illinois	1962-63
Crawford, Bill	Guard	British Columbia	1960
Crespino, Bob	End	Mississippi	1964-68
Crow, Linden	Back	Southern California	1958-60
Crutcher, Tommy Joe	Linebacker	TCU	1968-69
Davis, Don	Tackle	L.A. State	1966-67
Davis, Henry	Linebacker	Grambling	1968-69
Davis, Roger	Tackle	Syracuse	1965-66
Davis, Roosevelt	Tackle-End	Tennessee A&I	1965-67
Dess, Darrell	Guard	N. Carolina State	1959-64, 1966-69
Dove, Eddie	Back	Colorado	1963
Dryer, Fred	End	San Diego State	1969-71
Dudley, Paul	Back	Arkansas	1962
Duhon, Bobby	Back	Tulane	1969-72
Dunaway, Dave	End	Duke	1969
Eaton, Scott	Back	Oregon State	1967-72
Fitzgerald, Mike	Back	Iowa State	1967
Frederickson, Tucker	Back	Auburn	1965-71
Fuqua, John	Back	Morgan State	1969
Gaiters, Bobby	Back	New Mexico State	1961-62
Garcia, Jim	End	Purdue	1966
Gifford, Frank	Back-End	Southern California	1952-60, 1962-64
Gogolak, Pete	Kicker	Cornell	1966-72
Gossage, Gene	Tackle	Northwestern	1963
Grier, Roosevelt	Tackle	Penn State	1955-56, 1958-62
Griffing, Glynn	Quarterback	Mississippi	1963
Gross, Andy	Guard	Auburn	1967-68
Grosscup, Lee	Quarterback	Utah	1960-62

Guglielmi, Ralph	Quarterback	Notre Dame	1962-63
Gursky, Al	Linebacker	Penn State	1963
Guy, Lou	Back	Mississippi	1963
Hall, Pete	End	Marquette	1961-62
Harper, Charlie	Guard	Oklahoma State	1966-71
Harris, Phil	Back	Texas	1966
Harris, Wendell	Back	LSU	1966-67
Hathcock, Dave	Back	Mississippi State	1967
Hayes, Larry	Linebacker	Vanderbilt	1961
Heck, Ralph	Linebacker	Colorado	1969-71
Hernon, Don	Back	Ohio State	1960
Herrmann, Don	End	Waynesburg	1969-72
Hickl, Ray	Linebacker	Texas A&I	1969-70
Hillebrand, Jerry	Linebacker	Colorado	1963-66
Hinton, Chuck	Center	Mississippi	1967-69
Holifield, Jimmy	Back	Jackson State	1968-69
Horner, Sam	Back	VMI	1962-63
Houston, Dick	End	East Texas State	1969-72
Howell, Lane	Tackle	Grambling	1963-64
Huff, Sam	Linebacker	West Virginia	1956-63
Jacobs, Allen	Back	Utah	1966-67
Jacobs, Proverb	Tackle	California	1960
James, Dick	Back	Oregon	1964
Janerette, Charlie	Tackle	Penn State	1961-62
Johnson, Curley	Kicker	Houston	1969
Johnson, Gene	Back	Cincinnati	1961-62
Jones, Homer	End	Texas Southern	1964-69
Kennedy, Tom	Quarterback	L.A.State	1966-67
Killett, Charlie	Back	Memphis State	1963
Kimber, Bill	End	Florida State	1959-60
King, Phil	Back	Vanderbilt	1956-63
Kirby, John	Linebacker	Nebraska	1969-70
Kirouac, Lou	Guard	Boston College	1963

Koontz, Joe	End	San Francisco State	1968
Kotite, Dick	End-Linebacker	Wagner	1967, 1969-71
Koy, Ernie	Back	Texas	1965-70
Lacey, Bob	End	North Carolina	1965
Lelonde, Roger	Tackle	Muskingum	1965
Lane, Gary	Quarterback	Missouri	1968
Larson, Greg	Center	Minnesota	1961-72
Lasky, Frank	Tackle	Florida	1964-65
Lasse, Dick	Linebacker	Syracuse	1962-63
Leo, Jim	Linebacker	Cincinnati	1960
Lewis, Danny	Back	Wisconsin	1966
Livingston, Cliff	Linebacker	UCLA	1954-61
Lockhart, Carl (Spider)	Back	North Texas State	1965-72
Longo, Tom	Back	Notre Dame	1969-70
LoVetere, John	Tackle	Compton	1963-65
Lurtsema, Bob	Tackle	Western Michigan	1967-71
McCann, Tim	Tackle	Princeton	1969
McDowell, John	Tackle	St. John's (Minnesota)	1965
McElhenny, Hugh	Back	Washington	1963
Maher, Bruce	Back	Detroit	1968-69
Matan, Bill	End	Kansas State	1966
Mazurek, Ed	Back	Xavier	1960
Menefee, Hartwell	End	New Mexico State	1966
Mercein, Chuck	Back	Yale	1965-66
Messner, Max	Linebacker	Cincinnati	1964
Minniear, Randy	Back	Purdue	1967-69
Modzelewski, Dick	Tackle	Maryland	1956-63
Molden, Frank	Tackle	Jackson State	1969
Moran, Jim	Tackle	Idaho	1964-67
Morrall, Earl	Quarterback	Michigan State	1965-67
Morrison, Joe	Back-End	Cincinnati	1959-72

Murdock, Les	Kicker	Florida State	1967
Nelson, Andy	Back	Memphis State	1964
Nolan, Dick	Back	Maryland	1954-57, 1959-61
O'Brien, Dave	Guard	Boston College	1965
Owens, R.C.	End	Idaho	1964
Parker, Frank	Tackle	Oklahoma State	1969
Patton, Jim	Back	Mississippi	1955-66
Peay, Francis	Tackle	Missouri	1966-67
Pesonen, Dick	Back	Minnesota (Duluth)	1962-64
Plum, Milt	Quarterback	Penn State	1969
Podoley, Jim	Back	Central Michigan	1962
Post, Bob	Back	Kings Point	1967
Prestel, Jim	Tackle	Idaho	1966
Reed, Smith	Back	Alcorn A&M	1965-66
Riley, Lee	Back	Detroit	1960
Robustelli, Andy	End	Arnold	1956-66
Rote, Kyle	Back-End	SMU	1951-61
Schichtle, Henry	Quarterback	Wichita	1964
Schmidt, Bob	Tackle	Minnesota	1959-60
Schnelker, Bob	End	Bowling Green	1954-60
Scholtz, Bob	Center	Notre Dame	1965-66
Scott, Tom	Linebacker	Virginia	1959-64
Sczurek, Stan	Linebacker	Purdue	1966
Shaw, George	Quarterback	Oregon	1959-60
Shofner, Del	End	Baylor	1961-67
Silas, Sam	Tackle	Southern Illinois	1968
Simms, Bob	End	Rutgers	1960-62
Slaby, Lou	Linebacker	Pittsburgh	1964-65
Smith, Jeff	Linebacker	Southern California	1966-67

Smith, Zeke	Tackle	Auburn	1961-62
Staten, Randy	End	Minnesota	1967
Stits, Billy	Back	UCLA	1959-61
Stroud, Jack	Guard-Tackle	Tennessee	1953-64
Stynchula, Andy	End	Penn State	1964-65
Summerall, Pat	Kicker-End	Arkansas	1958-61
Sutton, Ed	Back	North Carolina	1960-61
Svare, Harland	Linebacker	Washington State	1955-60
Swain, Bill	Linebacker	Oregon State	1965-67
Szczecko, Joe	Tackle	Northwestern	1969
Tarkenton, Francis	Quarterback	Georgia	1967-71
Taylor, Bob	End	Maryland State	1963-64
Thomas, Aaron	End	Oregon State	1960-62
Thurlow, Steve	Back	Stanford	1964-65
Timberlake, Bob	Quarterback	Michigan	1965
Tittle, Y.A.	Quarterback	LSU	1961-64
Triplett, Bill	Back	Miami (Ohio)	1967
Triplett, Mel	Back	Miami (Ohio)	1955-60
Underwood, Olen	Linebacker	Texas	1965
Van Horn, Doug	Guard	Ohio State	1968-71
Vargo, Larry	Linebacker	Detroit	1966-67
Walker, Mickey	Guard	Michigan State	1961-65
Walton, Joe	End	Pittsburgh	1961-63
Webb, Allen	Back	Arnold	1961-65
Webster, Alex	Back	N. Carolina State	1955-64
Weisacosky, Ed	Linebacker	Miami (Florida)	1967
Wellborn, Joe	Center	Texas A&M	1966-67
Wells, Harold	Linebacker	Purdue	1969
Wells, Joel	Back	Clemson	1961
Wheelwright, Ernie	Back	Southern Illinois	1964-65
White, Freeman	End-Linebacker	Nebraska	1966-69

Wietecha, Ray	Center	Northwestern	1953-62
Williams, Willie	Back	Grambling	1965, 1967-72
Wilson, Butch	End	Alabama	1968-69
Winter, Bill	Linebacker	St. Olaf (Minnesota)	1962-64
Wood, Gary	Quarterback	Cornell	1964-66, 1968-69
Wright, Steve	Tackle	Alabama	1968-69
Young, Willie	Tackle	Grambling	1966-72
Youso, Frank	Tackle	Minnesota	1958-60

12

Alex Webster's Giants — 1969 - 1972

From a publicity standpoint Well Mara's decision to make Alex Webster the new head coach of the Giants was brilliant. So what if Well passed over more qualified men on the staff of assistants? What did it matter that Norb Hecker and Jim Trimble, who had actually been head coaches, were to remain as aides, working under a man who had little coaching experience?

Alex Webster was a fan favorite. He was a link to the past, to the days of glory and years of championship. He was one of the guys, a big, strong, bearlike man who laughed and drank and smoked and carried on, who always played with pain and always made the big play.

No way in the world for the fans of New York to boo him. No chance of hearing that cruel, acid "Goodbye, Alex" strain wafting through the air over Yankee Stadium. You just couldn't help but like Alex Webster.

Mara denied that his actions were based on the fans'

behavior in the previous three seasons, though he did not deny his displeasure with the raucous treatment he and his team had received from the Old Guard. "It is time to bring everyone back together again," he said.

Were it not for the absense of operating time, which was entirely Mara's fault, and the alleged refusal on the part of Helen Mara, Jack's widow, to give up a percentage of the team's stock, Vince Lombardi might have become the coach. But Vince, who had stepped down as coach in Green Bay and was bored with being simply a general manager, insisted on some ownership. When he finally went to Washington, it was with five percent of the franchise's stock. He would have settled for that—perhaps less—in New York. New York was, in every sense of the word, home.

But Lombardi was not to return to New York; Mara knew that as soon as Vince let it be known that he wanted stock. Instead, Well went for Alex Webster, the man no one could dislike.

"The Giants' organization has never been more closely unified than right now," Mara said. "The old magic isn't gone. It's coming back."

Unfortunately the Mara Time Machine Theory had a hole in it. The hole was the team. It was just not that good. Still, results were to be immediate and spectacular.

"It's a hard thing to believe," Webster said of his sudden ascension. "I never expected anything like this. I remember that Friday morning Well called me and asked me if I could come down to the offices. He said it was important. When I got there, he took me into his private office and told me to sit down. Then he said he was firing Allie, had fired him. Then he asked me if I would like to have the job. I didn't think I heard him right, and when I called home, I told Louise to sit down before I said anything else. I was afraid she'd pass out."

So Alex met the press, at a hastily called conference tinged with a feeling of urgency.

"Yes, I think I can do the job. I believe I can do it, and I hope the players can believe in me," Webster said, with a look on his face that clearly expressed the numbness, shock, surprise, and excitement churning within him.

"I'm going to meet with the other coaches. We still have a week before the season starts, and I guess we'll try to make some moves."

And so it began.

Webster's first official act was to release another All-Pro and a close friend, defensive end Jim Katcavage. "I hated to do it, but I had to," Webster says. What he doesn't say is that Kat was no longer functional as a player, nor had he been for a year or more prior to 1969.

Jim was, however, rewarded for his years of faithful service. A few days after his release, he was taken back into the family as an assistant coach in charge of the defensive line.

In addition to Katcavage, Webster pared four others from the squad, including punter Dave Lewis, who went to Cincinnati and has led the American Conference in punting ever since. For the record, the other three cuts were center Phil Sobocinski, defensive tackle Charlie Johnson, and linebacker Bob Sanders.

From Pittsburgh, for a draft choice, Alex acquired his first player—defensive tackle Frank Parker, a zero.

The first game of the season was played the following Sunday, September 21. It was in Yankee Stadium, and the opponents were the fierce Minnesota Vikings, soon to be Super Bowl participants.

A crowd of 62,920 welcomed Webster with a fierce and lusty clamor, and then they were rewarded by the Miracle.

The Miracle? The Giants beat the Vikings 24-23. They scored 14 points in the final 10 minutes of the game. They scored the winning touchdown with 59 seconds left in the contest after a reserve tight end named Butch Wilson caught a ball he wasn't supposed to be near. It was a Tarkenton pass intended for rookie Don Herrmann, but Herrmann wasn't there, and Minnesota's Earsell Mackbee swatted the pass away. Wilson lunged, and as he fell he reached out and caught the football. He was on the Minnesota 10-yard line, 33 yards from where the play began.

A pitch-right to Tucker Frederickson got nothing, but a pass to Herrmann got it all. Homer Jones went right, Herrmann went left, and Mackbee went with Homer. So Tarkenton, of course, went to Herrmann. It was over, 24-23, and the Giants carried Webster off on their shoulders.

"I still don't believe what happened," Webster screamed in the deafening locker room. "It needs time to sink in. But it was a hell of a way to start, wasn't it? I couldn't have made up any better ending."

The season, however, was to be no better than 6-8. In time some grousing began, and with it came some mumbled accusations. "If Sherman had this team, it would have won 8, 9 games," said one of the players, one of the few who was for Allie. But he was wrong. If Sherman had had that team but had not coached it before he might have won more games. Had he not been fired, though, the team would have collapsed. There was a great deal of anti-Sherman sentiment among the players. After all, athletes never blame themselves for losing.

Alex had signed a two-year contract, and so 1970 was his. Privately, it was felt that 1971 would certainly belong to someone else. The value of Mara's masterstroke had passed. It was time to hire a coach, a big name, proven winner kind of a coach.

But Webster screwed up all those theories. He had a 9-5 season in 1970, and had his team won its final game, the New York Giants would have been champions of the National Conference's Eastern Division. That final game was with Los Angeles, and the score was 31-3. After an early 3-0 lead the Giants were helpless. But 9-5 is 9-5, and no one gets fired after that kind of season—especially a man so adored by the public and the ticket-buyers.

Mara might have been the man responsible for the Giants' 9-5 season in the first place when he made a dramatic trade in January 1970. It all started when Art Modell, owner of the Cleveland Browns and one of Well's close friends, decided he had to have quarterback Mike Phipps of Purdue in the draft. In order to acquire a high enough choice, he sent fan favorite Paul Warfield, the league's most dangerous wide receiver, to the Miami Dolphins. He obtained their draft choice, and it was high enough for him to secure Phipps.

But the reaction in Ohio was instant and bitter. Art felt he had to do something spectacular, and who was more spectacular than Homer Jones?

He called Well Mara. "I want Homer Jones," he said.

"Fine," said Well Mara. "I want Jim Kanicki."

"Agreed," said Art Modell.

"And I want a linebacker, maybe John Garlington?"

"No, not him. Wayne Meylan."

"Fine," said Well Mara . . . and then he held his breath. "And I need a running back. What about Ron Johnson?"

"Okay," said Art Modell.

Okay. Ron Johnson, a 6-foot-1, 205-pound bolt of lightning, had played behind Leroy Kelly. He did not play very much, but Mara knew his potential. Well had been as high on him as on O.J. Simpson when both were college seniors the year before, and Mara wanted him badly.

Johnson was in New York now, to join an emerging team led by other offensive stars such as Frederickson, Tarkenton, Herrmann, and tight end Bob Tucker, who would blossom into an All-Pro in another year.

Ron Johnson became the first man to gain 1,000 yards or more in the history of the Giants. He gained 1,027 and was superb. He made Frederickson a better runner, he made Tarkenton an incredible quarterback, and he made the Giants' offense a thing of precision and danger.

It was a remarkable season. The Giants lost their first 3 games and then won 6 straight. They lost 1, then won 3 more, and with 1 to go they were 9-4. A victory would do it; a tie would do it. But the Rams, led by George Allen (it would be his final game as the coach of the Los Angeles team prior to leaving for Washington), were simply too much for a young, inexperienced, and, to be truthful, lucky bunch of Giants.

They had strolled through a soft schedule, playing teams either crippled by abysmal talent or by injuries. But they did win nine games, and Alex Webster was assured of another season.

By his own choice he received a one-year contract. "I don't want more than one at a time," he said, "because I never want to feel I'm in the way. If I don't do a good job, I don't want to stay. If I do all right, I won't worry about being rehired."

And in 1971 the Giants almost didn't let Alex keep his job.

They fell to 4-10, but there is far more to that record than wins and losses. The team began to fall apart emotionally. The players broke into cliques and began to bicker and feud. Webster began to lose control. Mara was more and more a specter, hovering over all of it, ready to . . . to what? He wouldn't fire Webster. He couldn't fire players. He was just ready, and his constant presence did nothing but increase the tension and compound the problem.

The problem involved two key players—Tarkenton and defensive end Fred Dryer.

There were many complaints about Tarkenton. He ignored game plans and coaches with equal disdain; he changed plays in the huddle; he made up plays; he refused to throw up the middle when such pass patterns were most propitious; he was abrasive and inattentive; and he aggravated the hell out of Webster. Several times they were overheard in Alex's office, screaming, arguing, tearing it all up.

By mid-season the team had quit, flat-out quit. They quit against the Eagles 41-27. They quit against Washington 30-3 and 23-7. They quit against Dallas 42-14. They quit against Baltimore 31-7.

Webster suffered through every game. He had experienced some problem with his coaching staff, and now Hecker, Trimble, Rosey Brown, and Ken Kavanaugh were gone. Hecker was gone, but the other three, loyal and honored employees, were simply moved around. Trimble joined the front office as Mara's assistant, and they called him the director of pro personnel. Brown and Kavanaugh were made scouts.

Alex was his own man now. He had installed a complicated, multiple-formation offense patterned in part after Tom Landry's in Dallas, in part after Hank Stram's in Kansas City, and in part after what he came up with himself.

He was in charge. He was growing into the job. He was more secure and more knowledgeable and more aware of the subtle struggles and competitions going on all around him.

"This is my neck," he said. "If we are rotten, it's me who gets fired. I am not going to let a bunch of players, or even a few assistant coaches, screw me. If I'm going out, I'm going on my own."

So he fought back. He argued with Tarkenton and insisted on certain things, and when it got to the final game of the season he sat Tarkenton on the bench and played Randy Johnson. He had had it with the scrambler, from the summer trouble when Fran left the team in a salary squabble through the season when he lost his touch—or said he did—and became less than half the quarterback he had been in 1970.

Tarkenton had a sound excuse. He did not have Ron Johnson. In June in his native Detroit Johnson had been involved in a harmless game of pick-up basketball. He was kneed in the thigh, and some internal hemorhaging occurred. The ensuing clot became painful, and when Ron reported to training camp in July, heat treatments were tried in an attempt to break up the clot.

It did not work, and finally, after weeks of stalling and

hiding the injury, the team announced that its surgeon, Dr. Anthony Pisani, would perform "simple surgery" to remove the clotted blood from the wound, a "lavage" procedure.

"Oh, nothing to worry about," said the team party line. "He'll be ready for the opening game of the season."

He was not, but by then most of the newspapermen were accustomed to such gaps in credibility between themselves and the publicity arm of the Giants. Johnson returned in mid-season, played half of one game and half of the next, and then was seriously injured. He suffered torn knee ligaments and was lost for the rest of the season. He had gained 1,027 yards in 1970. He gained 156 in 1971.

The dissension meanwhile spread and enlarged. Dryer began talking to anyone who would listen, and what he had to say made for sensational headlines in certain of New York's sensation-seeking newspapers. Defensive tackle Bob Lurtsema joined the chorus; he would soon be released.

Dryer's comments found themselves collected and interwoven in a series of columns written by Larry Merchant of the *New York Post*. Merchant, a most imaginative craftsman, titled the series "Maranoia." He did not identify his source, but he used quotes and information that made it crystal clear that he did, in fact, have a player's confidence.

The columns were an attack on Mara, an attack so specific and brutal as to send the president of the Giants into paroxysms of rage. He was furious, and so were many of the players. He had been held up to public ridicule and so had his team, and to make things worse the crosstown New York Jets were still getting the larger share of publicity and attention.

The *New York Post* became a dirty word. Mara and his wife Ann admitted that they no longer read the newspaper, the only afternoon publication in the city. Its regular correspondent (not Merchant, of course) bore the brunt of many insults and mistaken-identity confrontations. In the spring of 1973 the regular correspondent began to feel the sting of reaction from Timmy Mara for several "breaches of propriety" in his handling of an entirely different subject.

Merchant accused Mara of everything from being a meddler and a pest to interfering with players' private lives to threatening trades to less attractive cities at the first sign of defiance. Mara's several sons—all blond and all evidently about the same size—were ridiculed by the unidentified player as "a bunch of bats hanging from their heels all over the locker room and the field."

There is little doubt the player talking to Merchant was Dryer.

There was also little doubt as to the future of the two parties in this rift in the New York Giants—Tarkenton and Dryer. They were destined to be traded, to be banished by Well Mara for disloyalty. Some said they were victimized for honesty, but the only law was Mara's Law, and Mara's Law held that disloyalty, as he defined it, is punishable by trade.

Tarkenton was sent back to Minnesota, a move that overjoyed him and did not fit within the framework of punishment in anyone's mind. In return the Giants received the Vikings' first-round draft choice for 1972 plus their second-round choice for 1973 plus quarterback Norm Snead, fullback Vin Clements, and wide receiver Bob Grim.

"I feel like I'm 10 years younger," said the 32-year-old Tarkenton. "I feel like a real burden has been lifted off my head." He went back home to Atlanta, where he had founded a million-dollar corporation, and spent the off-season celebrating.

A visitor later that spring found him still chipper and pleased. "Listen, I'm going to a team that was 11-3, and I'm leaving a bad situation. I told Mister Mara that a complete rebuilding job was in order for the Giants, and that if it was all the same to him I didn't want to go through that again. I came up with the Vikings when they were an expansion team, and I went to the Giants when they were horrible. I have been in the league for 10 years, and I want a shot at a championship."

Tarkenton denied, however, that he had asked to be traded. "Listen, you don't have to say it in so many words," he explained. "When I told him I didn't want to be part of a rebuilding program, and when we still had the memories of my summertime walkout, I knew I'd be gone."

Dryer, too, was quickly dispatched, but with a bit more enmity. A son of sunny southern California, the 6-foot-6, 230-pound beach boy had asked to be traded somewhere on the West Coast. Since he was a defensive end of staggering potential, although a bit erratic in his thinking and lifestyle, all the California teams expressed great interest in obtaining him. So Well Mara traded him to the New England Patriots.

Dryer was just angry enough to threaten premature retirement. He refused to report to the Patriots, and he made that clear to general manager Upton Bell, who visited San Diego several times. Finally, in May, the Patriots traded Dryer to Los Angeles for a number-one draft choice and a player named Rick Cash. Dryer was where he wanted to be, no doubt angering Well Mara back in New York.

Thus the 1972 season was one of great concern to Webster. He was without his best quarterback, and the defense would have to be juggled. But Ron Johnson was coming back, and the mystique of Mara Luck would hold true more dramatically than anyone expected.

First, new defensive coach Jimmy Garrett (who had been the offensive coach in 1971) scrapped the standard 4-3 defense and installed a complicated new theory, which he called the Rover Defense. Basically, the defense revolved around one man—ostensibly the right defensive end—who would be free, under certain situations, to move around and become a tackle, a linebacker, or the left defensive end. The rover would pick what he thought was both the enemy's weak spot and the place most likely for the next play to be sent.

Then the Giants signed defensive end Jack Gregory as a free agent after he had played out his option clause with the Cleveland Browns. Gregory is 6-feet-5 and 250 pounds. He is as good a defensive end as any man in the league. He was what the Giants needed, but it took the fortuitous situation of Garrett's shift and his subsequent decision to go to the Rover to convince Gregory that New York was his kind of town.

"I never even thought about New York," drawls the native of Okolona, Mississippi. "I had places like Miami and Oakland and St. Louis and Los Angeles all picked out. Then Garrett came calling at the ranch and told me about the Rover. Then he told me about the money the Giants were willing to spend. It was more than anybody else, so I took it."

Gregory was to be worth every penny. He personally accounted for 21 quarterback sacks and led the defense to 37 such captures of the quarterback behind the line of scrimmage. The previous season New York's defense had totaled 18 sacks.

That was one plus. Another was Snead, the oft-tried, always disappointing quarterback taken as a throw-in to be used only as insurance behind Randy Johnson.

Snead had been in the league for 11 years, none of them winning seasons. In 1971 he could not win the starting job with the Vikings despite the fact that only Gary Cuozzo and Bob Lee were his competition. The Vikings had built an 11-3 record with defense; all 3 quarterbacks were deficient.

When the Giants opened their exhibition schedule Snead was the bench-rider. But then Johnson was hurt in a 31-31 tie with the Jets, and Norman finished out the remainder of the preseason games. Norman started the opener in Detroit, and he was awful.

So Webster, after a three-day period of soul-searching, announced that Snead would go back to the bench for the Giants' home opener against Dallas. Randy had his job back.

On the Giants' second play of the game, Randy had a concussion. Snead came back in, and except for a few brief appearances to mop up games already decided, Randy saw no further action in 1972.

The Giants had gotten lucky with Snead. They had traded

off Tarkenton and could have seen their season turn into a major disaster. Instead, they watched as a professional disappointment went through his first superior season in a dozen years.

No quarterback in the league was better than Norman Snead in 1972. The man who had been a first-round draft pick by the Washington Redskins in 1961 led the NFL's passers, some of whom bore names like Namath and Tarkenton, Brodie and Gabriel, Dawson and Lamonica. He completed 196 of 325 passes, a 60.3 completion percent that shattered the team record set by Y.A. Tittle. Snead threw for 17 touchdowns, amassed 2,307 yards, and was intercepted just a dozen times.

In a sweet quirk of fate, the NFL's top three passers were all touched by association with the Giants. Snead was on top. Then came Earl Morrall, now of the Miami Dolphins. Third was Fran Tarkenton, whose season's statistics could not prevent a defensive collapse in Minnesota that led to a 7-7 team record.

If, in January 1972, anyone had said Tarkenton would play for a team that had a record inferior to the Giants', he would have been dismissed as a fan too intense to be considered real. But it had happened. The Giants were 8-6. The Vikings were 7-7.

There was much more. Johnson responded with a season even better than 1970; he gained 1,182 yards and led the league with 14 touchdowns. Bob Tucker, who had led the NFC in receptions with 59 (for 791 yards) in 1971, came back with 55 for 764 yards and emerged as one of the finest tight ends to play the position.

The defense, led by Gregory, was extraordinary. Two rookie linemen—John Mendenhall and Larry Jacobson—became starting tackles. Three young linebackers—Pat Hughes, Ron Hornsby, and Jim Files—began to remind veteran fans of Huff, Livingston, and Scott.

The offensive line protected Snead better than any other

team had protected its passer, allowing him to be sacked just 10 times. The Giants finished as the best passing offense in the league and reached a peak of sorts with a late-season 62-10 victory over Philadelphia to set a team record for points.

More important, the 1972 Giants were inherently a stronger team than the 1970 Giants. "We learned how to win big games," Webster said, "and now we have to learn how to become champions. There is nothing else we need except the realization that we can do it."

With this maturation of a team, Webster has achieved his maturation, too. He is a qualified coach, perhaps not as cerebral as Sherman, Landry, or Stram, but better at relating to the players than any other man the Giants have ever had.

"He's one of us," said Tucker Frederickson on the day Sherman was dismissed. "Big Red is one of the players, and we'll play for him because he's the coach now."

As the Giants head into 1973, they promise to be contenders. But the other problems, the meddling and the insecurities of being evicted from Yankee Stadium and the threatened juggling of last year's starters by an overambitious coaching staff, could hurt.

"Left alone, we'll win," says one of the players, anonymous here because he is still with the Giants. "But if they make too many moves, they can really louse us up. We just started to play together. You don't need new faces every year. Just the same ones, if they're good enough."

Alex Webster's Giants, then, are anxious to win. They are in no mood to settle for interference—from anyone.

GIANTS OF THE SEVENTIES

Alexakos, Steve	Guard	San Jose State	1971
Athas, Pete	Back	Tennessee	1971-72
Baker, John	End	Norfolk State	1970
Banks, Willie	Guard	Alcorn A&M	1970

Blanchard, Tom	Punter	Oregon	1971-72
Brenner, Al	Back	Michigan State	1969-70
Brown, Otto	Back	Prairie View	1970-72
Butler, Skip	Kicker	Texas-Arlington	1971
Buzin, Richard	Tackle	Penn State	1969-70
Case, Pete	Guard	Georgia	1965-70
Clements, Vin	Back	Connecticut	1972
Coffey, Junior	Back	Washington	1969-71
Crane, Dennis	Tackle	Southern California	1970
Crist, Chuck	Back	Penn State	1972
Douglas, John	Linebacker	Missouri	1970-72
Dryer, Fred	End	San Diego State	1969-71
Duhon, Bobby	Back	Tulane	1969-72
Eaton, Scott	Back	Oregon State	1967-72
Ellison, Mark	Guard	Dayton	1972
Enderle, Dick	Guard	Minnesota	1972
Evans, Charlie	Back	Southern California	1971-72
Files, Jim	Linebacker	Oklahoma	1970-72
Flowers, Richmond	Back	Tennessee	1971-72
Frederickson, Tucker	Back	Auburn	1965-71
Gatewood, Tom	End	Notre Dame	1972
Gogolak, Pete	Kicker	Cornell	1966-72
Goich, Dan	Tackle	California	1972
Green, Joe	Back	Bowling Green	1970-71
Gregory, Jack	End	Delta State	1972
Grim, Bob	End	Oregon State	1972
Hanson, Dick	Tackle	North Dakota State	1971
Harper, Charlie	Guard	Oklahoma State	1966-72
Hazeltine, Matt	Linebacker	California	1970
Heck, Ralph	Linebacker	Colorado	1969-71
Herrmann, Don	End	Waynesburg	1969-72

Hickl, Ray	Linebacker	Texas A&I	1969-70
Hill, John	Guard-Tackle	Lehigh	1972
Hornsby, Ron	Linebacker	Southeast Louisiana	1971-72
Houston, Rich	End	East Texas State	1969-72
Hughes, Pat	Linebacker	Boston University	1970-72
Hyland, Bob	Guard	Boston College	1971-72
Jacobson, Larry	Tackle	Nebraska	1972
Johnson, Bill	Punter	Livingston	1970
Johnson, Len	Guard	St. Cloud	1970
Johnson, Randy	Quarterback	Texas A&I	1971-72
Johnson, Ron	Back	Michigan	1970-72
Kanicki, Jim	Tackle	Michigan State	1970-71
Kirby, John	Linebacker	Nebraska	1969-70
Kotite, Dick	End-Linebacker	Wagner	1967, 1969-72
Koy, Ernie	Back	Texas	1965-70
Lakes, Roland	Tackle	Wichita	1971
Larson, Greg	Center	Minnesota	1961-72
Lockhart, Carl (Spider)	Back	North Texas State	1965-72
Longo, Tom	Back	Notre Dame	1969-70
Lurtsema, Bob	Tackle	Western Michigan	1967-71
McNeil, Clifton	End	Grambling	1970-71
McRae, Bennie	Back	Michigan	1971
Mendenhall, John	Tackle	Grambling	1972
Morrison, Joe	End-Back	Cincinnati	1959-72
Norton, Jim	Tackle	Washington	1970
Orduna, Joe	Back	Nebraska	1972
Parker, Ken	Back	Fordham	1970
Reed, Henry	End	Weber State	1971-72
Roller, Dave	Tackle	Kentucky	1971

Rucker, Reggie	End	Boston University	1971
Shay, Jerry	Tackle	Purdue	1970-71
Shiner, Dick	Quarterback	Maryland	1970
Shy, Les	Back	Long Beach State	1970
Small, Eldridge	Back	Texas A&I	1972
Snead, Norm	Quarterback	Wake Forest	1972
Taffoni, Joe	Tackle	Tennessee-Martin	1972
Tarkenton, Francis	Quarterback	Georgia	1967-71
Thomas, Aaron	End	Oregon State	1962-70
Thompson, Rocky	Back	West Texas State	1971-72
Tipton, Dave	Tackle-End	Stanford	1971-72
Tucker, Bob	End	Bloomsburg State	1970-72
Van Horn, Doug	Guard	Ohio State	1968-72
Vanoy, Vernon	Tackle	Kansas	1971
Walton, Wayne	Guard	Abilene Christian	1971-72
Williams, Willie	Back	Grambling	1965, 1967-72
Young, Willie	Tackle	Grambling	1966-72
Zeno, Coleman	End	Grambling	1971

13

The Giants Go to New Jersey

On December 27, 1970, the *Star-Ledger* published the first of a three-part series suggesting that a 750-acre tract called the Meadowlands and located in northern New Jersey would be ideal for development as the site of a sports complex. The series invited both the Giants and the Yankees to investigate such a proposal.

Despite its stature as New Jersey's largest newspaper and one of the largest in the country, the *Star-Ledger* had no idea that such an investigation already had been undertaken by the Giants and New Jersey Governor William T. Cahill.

Less than a year later, on August 26, 1971, Wellington Mara appeared at a press conference at the Essex House Hotel on Central Park South in New York City. Present were Cahill, Joseph McCrane, and David (Sonny) Werblin. McCrane was Cahill's chief aide involving the Giants. Werblin, former president of the MCA Talent Agency and one-time president of the New York Jets of the American Football League (as such an enemy of Well Mara's), was the newly named chairman of the New Jersey Sports and Exposition Authority.

The conference was to announce the Giants' acceptance of a 30-year lease on the proposed Giant Stadium, a 78,000-seat structure to be erected on the East Rutherford-Hackensack Meadowlands.

The site of the new stadium was said to be a 15-minute drive from the George Washington Bridge and 9 miles from the team's offices at Columbus Circle in Manhattan.

"As my father and brother before me," said Wellington Mara, "I've considered it a privilege to have played in the Polo Grounds for 31 years and in Yankee Stadium for 15. But every family dreams of moving into its own house.

"Now I can say to my family that if you have a seat in Yankee Stadium, you will have a better one in Giant Stadium. If you have none, you'll likely get one. We will always be called the New York Giants," Mara added. That last must be amended. As of April 1973 a move in the New Jersey legislature was under way to get the Giants to change their name so as to give some recognition to the state that is so graciously planning to spend hundreds of millions of dollars on a new stadium.

Reaction was mixed but immediate, and there was no neutral ground. The opposition, which included Mayor John Lindsay of New York City, branded the Giants "traitors, turncoats, and carpetbaggers."

Those in favor of the move hailed the improvements the new stadium would bring, namely ease of parking, far more pleasant surroundings, and a minimum of traffic congestion, which had haunted and plagued weekly motorists to Yankee Stadium, which is set in the lower Bronx streets.

The situation since the Giants had moved to Yankee Stadium in 1956 was this: they paid rental fees to the Yankees, who in turn paid rental fees to the owner of the edifice, Rice University. The land was owned by the Knights of Columbus. Moreover, the Yankees reaped the full benefit of the income from the parking lots, concession stands, and even program advertising. The Giants got nothing but a place to play.

And what a place to play. The locker rooms were frequented by rats. The ceilings leaked when it rained and sometimes when it didn't. Constant painting had not prevented the general rundown appearance of the stadium from worsening. It was, after all, built in 1923.

Getting to Yankee Stadium was frustrating. Getting out of it, especially on days when the Jets were playing in Shea Stadium, was sometimes impossible. Seating was bad because any stadium built for baseball must be automatically less than ideal for viewing football.

Then there was the case of Shea Stadium. The city had built the new arena in a frantic attempt to win back National League baseball, namely the Mets, in 1962. It had then offered the Mets a lease in perpetuity for Shea Stadium at a minimal rental and with full benefits as to concessions, parking, and other income-producing sidelines. Finally, a clause was inserted giving the Mets full authority to approve or disapprove any other events held in the stadium during the duration of the baseball season.

Then the city offered the winter use of Shea Stadium to the Jets, who had just been purchased by a group headed by Werblin. The team, then in bankruptcy, had played its games in the ancient Polo Grounds under the name of the New York Titans, and when owner Harry Wismer fell into financial impossibilities, the Werblin group moved in at a purchase price of $1 million.

It wasn't the $500 that Tim Mara had spent, but in 1964 any major league sports franchise in New York City was well worth $1 million.

"It occurred to us," said Well Mara once, "that we had been in New York, and a part of New York, since 1925. It occurred to us that we had been paying taxes and rentals and helping the community with charity for all those years. And then it occurred to us that we hadn't been asked to move into a brand new stadium. We were to be left where we were. It occurred to us that this was not a fair arrangement."

But where else could the Giants play? The answer: nowhere.

At least, not until Bill Cahill decided to do something about New Jersey's second-class complex. Being too close to New York City for too long had turned most of central and northern New Jersey into a string of bedroom communities, places for the workers to live and sleep before going back to New York to work. The impression most folks had of the Garden State was of a 12-lane turnpike that connected Manhattan with Philadelphia.

Suddenly, New Jersey had the Giants, one of New York's most prized possessions.

"The Giants are moving to New Jersey. Who needs the Giants? Screw the Giants." That appeared in one of the New York newspapers.

Mayor Lindsay reacted with livid anger, as befits a man who must explain to his party leaders and his constituents just how he managed to lose a National Football League franchise that had lived in New York for almost fifty years.

But fans, both New York and New Jersey residents, were cheered. A fan from Bayside, Long Island, who had nothing but a longer drive to look forward to, was pleased. "The greatest thing that ever happened," he said. "Yankee Stadium is outmoded, outdated, and everything else. It's the worst place ever to see a football game. It'll probably be easier getting there than Yankee Stadium. The only way to fix up Yankee Stadium is to put an apartment house there."

Lindsay, however, was a man scorned, and he vented the full heat of his fury. He first instructed Chairman Emanuel Cellar of the House Judiciary Committee to conduct an inquiry into the matter by his subcommittee on anti-trust matters, and Lindsay asked for a meeting with NFL Commissioner Pete Rozelle with regard to a replacement franchise. He also threatened to start legal action to prevent the

Giants from using the name *New York* once they moved.

But what he really did was buy Yankee Stadium for $24 million and abrogate all leases, which meant that the Giants, whose lease extended through the 1974 season, were suddenly homeless after the 1972 season.

Not wishing to take the case to court, the Giants tried to convince Lindsay and other city politicians that they could make a peaceful settlement. They would be willing to renegotiate their lease, perhaps even to increase their rental fee.

Lindsay was adamant. Construction at Yankee Stadium was scheduled to begin with the conclusion of the 1973 baseball season, which meant the Giants would be able to fit in only two regular-season home games before moving out. The Yale Bowl, in New Haven, Connecticut, was their only alternative.

Mara was now concerned with placating his family of fans. At a welcome-home luncheon at the Americana Hotel on September 24, 1971, he made the following statements:

At this time,on this occasion,and in this company, I am going to discuss several subjects on which I have previously been silent and on which I intend to remain silent in the future. Recently, and especially since we announced last month that we planned to move to Giant Stadium in 1975, a new cult has sprung up in the news media. They have appointed themselves arbiters of public morality, and their banner reads, "Tell It Like It Is."

Actually, they are Merchants of venom, and their credo, as expressed by one of their number, really is, "You can't make any money writing nice things. You have to hit somebody."

Theirs is a nasal cacophony, which normally I neither hear nor heed, but at this time I want to give you an account of my stewardship.

Since 1925 the Giants have obeyed the law, paid our taxes, and remained sensitive to our duty toward the community. In support of the latter, let me point out that in the last three years we have played 17 preseason games, which have raised $1,700,000 for charitable causes. Of this amount $440,000 has been turned over to New York-based charities.

I believe we qualify as good citizens and as such have the right to fulfill our obligation of service to you, our patrons.

It has been said that our move will be made primarily for profit. Any thirst for added income could have been slaked merely by raising our ticket prices to the level of some of our neighbors in the NFL. . .In 1970 we were 21 on a list of 26 teams in average ticket price. . .However, we chose to go the route that promised the best service to you for the foreseeable future. We are going to stand by that decision.

The audience of 1,500 stood and cheered and offered Mara a long, deafening ovation. It must be said, however, that the 1,500 in attendance were, after all, Giant fans.

Mara at that time disclosed a survey of the mail and telephone calls that had been received since the announcement of the projected move a month earlier. A ratio of 36-1 favored the move. The far-flung areas were equally agreeable to the idea. Queens-Nassau-Suffolk showed 155 for, 16 against. Westchester County and Connecticut showed 190 for, 7 against.

Mara had been spurred to action. When it was disclosed that the Giants would get a 50 percent cut of all concessions in the new stadium and that they would pay an annual rental of 15 percent of the gross revenue from ticket sales, Mara let it be known that the Jets' arrangement in Shea Stadium and with New York City was as good or better.

Mara reprinted pamphlets of all the favorable comments clipped from newspapers serving the megalopolis and mailed one to each and every season-ticket subscriber.

Of course behind-the-scenes action was taking place before

the announcement to move to New Jersey. The City of New York was well aware of New Jersey's campaign and tried mightily to negate the tremendous impact of a new stadium and 78,000 seats. When New York City lost, its officials were understandably bitter.

A letter to the *New York Times* in March 1973, when the Giants' attempt to find a new stadium was at its most hopeless, read as follows:

As one of the participants in the early negotiations (1971-1972) with Wellington Mara and his associates regarding the future of the New York Giants, the city could not then be fully aware of the fact that if they decided to leave New York, the city could not rationally afford a costly delay in the renovation schedule to accommodate them.

Mr. Mara and his colleagues told me that they were not concerned because they already had interim stadiums lined up in New Jersey or Connecticut for that purpose. When I mentioned the possible inconvenience to their fans, Mr. Mara said their studies showed that most Giant fans lived outside New York City, and most of the others were automobile riders who would enjoy a drive outside the city. "Giant fans will go anywhere to see us," one of Mr. Mara's associates said.

In short, the Giants' dilemma is of their own making.

The letter was signed Richard Aurelio, who during the time of the New Jersey-New York-Giants negotiations was a deputy mayor under John Lindsay.

In the same newspaper a letter was printed from Norman Redlich, the New York City Corporation Counsel. In part he said, "I personally conducted all negotiations with the Giants and, at Mayor Lindsay's direction, rejected the urging of some people to take out on the Giants our disappointment of their planned departure for the Hackensack Meadowlands. The city has agreed to the Giants' playing one exhibition and two regular games at the Stadium in August and September of this year—again at the same rent they would have paid the Yankees. Do these acts show a 'vindictive' attitude or a 'vendetta'?"

Groundbreaking was held at the Meadowlands in November 1972, a ceremony delayed by such matters as court suits filed by ecology groups and hearings demanded by the state's thoroughbred and standardbred racing tracks because of the plan to finance part of the construction of the stadium with the profit realized from a state-run race track.

But groundbreaking was accomplished, amid much pomp and political expediency, and in April 1973 the first two contracts were let, totaling several millions of dollars. The target date for completion of Giant Stadium is still 1975. But the Giants will be homeless for part of 1973 and all of 1974.

It is a situation, perhaps, indicative of the intensity of feelings stirred by the New York Giants. No one, apparently not even governors and mayors, is neutral to the Mara Family Giants.

When it became clear to Mara that the Giants would have to find a temporary home, a frantic search was undertaken. It led the Giants to the Yale Bowl after considering Palmer Field at Princeton, New Jersey; Rutgers Stadium in New Brunswick, New Jersey; Michie Stadium, the U.S. Military Academy facility at West Point, New York; Baker Field, the stadium used by New York City-based Columbia University; and even the possibility of working out a share-arrangement for the new Veterans Stadium in Philadelphia.

At no time did the Giants consider Shea Stadium, for two sound reasons. The city that had kicked them out owns Shea, and the wintertime residents of Shea, the Jets, are still not on the Giants' Christmas list.

Had the Yale Bowl fallen through, the Giants would have had no choice but to become a road team for the remainder of the 1973 season. There is some possibility, however remote, of returning to Yankee Stadium for 1974 since the projected renovation-purchase of the edifice is going to cost

New York City upwards of $65 million. Since Lindsay ruled himself out of another term as mayor, his successor might be compelled to find better places in which to spend this staggering sum.

One city aide, however, indicated that any such move would bring about a legal action by the Yankees, who agreed to remain in the city and in Yankee Stadium only if the stipulated renovations were done.

One of the problems the Giants found when they investigated the Yale Bowl as a possible home site was the presence of a local television affiliate of the CBS network, channel 3 in Hartford, Connecticut. Because Hartford is outside the NFL-imposed blackout radius of 75-miles, an estimated 500,000 viewers had been getting all Giant home games in their living rooms for the 14 years prior to the 1973 season. If the Giants moved to New Haven, Hartford would then fall within the 75-mile radius and would have to be blacked out.

Not wanting to anger half a million people—perhaps with the thought that even one of them could turn Congress to new directions in the already sticky blackout controversy raging throughout the league—Well Mara tried to lift temporarily the blackout restrictions.

But he met with hurdles too difficult to clear. How could the NFL then keep Dallas from beaming games into Fort Worth, or San Francisco from beaming into Oakland? The Giants' actions, now as in 1930, affected the whole of the National Football League. Ultimately, an arrangement was made whereby the games would be televised if sold out 48 hours prior to kickoff.

Where the Giants are going also will have a significant effect on the NFL.

And what the Giants do will continue to involve upwards of 15 million people. They are clearly the most influential of all NFL franchises. They are loved and hated, censured and condoned.

They are the New York Giants ... yesterday, today, tomorrow.

Giants' Championship Years

1927—11-1-1.

1933—11-3-0; lost to Chicago Bears in title game 23-21.

1934— 8-5-0; beat Chicago Bears for title 30-13.

1935— 9-3-0; lost to Detroit Lions in title game 26-7.

1938— 8-2-1; beat Green Bay Packers for title 23-17.

1939— 9-1-1; lost to Green Bay Packers in title game 27-0.

1941— 8-3-0; lost to Chicago Bears in title game 37-9.

1944— 8-1-1; lost to Green Bay Packers in title game 14-7.

1946— 7-3-1; lost to Chicago Bears in title game 24-14.

1956— 8-3-1; beat Chicago Bears for title 47-7.

1958— 9-3-0; beat Cleveland Browns in division play-off 10-0; lost to Baltimore Colts in title game 23-17 (sudden-death overtime).

1959—10-2-0; lost to Baltimore Colts in title game 31-16.

1961—10-3-1; lost to Green Bay Packers in title game 37-0.

1962—12-2-0; lost to Green Bay Packers in title game 16-7.

1963—11-3-0; lost to Chicago Bears in title game 14-10.

Giants' All - Pro Selections

1931—Denver "Butch" Gibson, Morris Badgro
1932—Ray Flaherty
1933—Mel Hein, Morris Badgro, Harry Newman
1934—Denver "Butch" Gibson, Mel Hein, Bill Morgan, Morris Badgro, Ken Strong
1935—Bill Morgan, Mel Hein, Ed Danowski
1936—Mel Hein, Tuffy Leemans
1937—Mel Hein
1938—Ed Widseth, Mel Hein, Ed Danowski
1939—Mel Hein, John Dell Isola, Jim Poole, Tuffy Leemans
1940—Mel Hein
1941—None
1942—Bill Edwards
1943—Al Blozis, Ward Cuff
1944—Len Younce, Frank Cope, Ward Cuff, Bill Paschal
1945—Frank Cope
1946—Jim White, Frank Filchock

1947—Len Younce

1948—None

1949—None

1950—Arnie Weinmeister

1951—DeWitt "Tex" Coulter, Ed Price, Arnie Weinmeister, Al DeRogatis, Jon Baker, Otto Schnellbacher, Emlen Tunnell

1952—Ed Price, Arnie Weinmeister, Emlen Tunnell

1953—Arnie Weinmeister

1954—Tom Landry

1955—Bill Austin, Frank Gifford, Emlen Tunnell

1956—Rosey Brown, Frank Gifford, Andy Robustelli, Rosey Grier, Emlen Tunnell

1957—Rosey Brown, Frank Gifford, Andy Robustelli

1958—Rosey Brown, Ray Wietecha, Andy Robustelli, Sam Huff, Jim Patton

1959—Andy Robustelli, Sam Huff, Jim Patton

1960—Andy Robustelli, Jim Patton

1961—Jim Katcavage, Del Shofner, Jim Patton

1962—Y.A. Tittle, Del Shofner, Jim Katcavage

1963—Frank Gifford, Jim Katcavage, Y.A. Tittle, Del Shofner, Erich Barnes, Darrell Dess, Dick Lynch, John LoVetere

1964—Rosey Brown, Erich Barnes, Aaron Thomas

1965—Rosey Brown, Tucker Frederickson

1966—Carl "Spider" Lockhart

1967—Ernie Koy, Homer Jones, Fran Tarkenton

1968—Fran Tarkenton, Homer Jones, Greg Larson, Carl "Spider" Lockhart

1969—Fran Tarkenton, Willie Williams

1970—Fran Tarkenton, Ron Johnson

1971—None

1972—Ron Johnson, Jack Gregory, Norm Snead

Giants' Head Coaches

1925	Robert Folwell	(8-4)
1926	Joseph Alexander	(8-4)
1927-28	Earl Potteiger	(15-8-3)
1929-30	Leroy Andrews	(25-5-1)
1931-53	Steve Owen	(150-100-17)
1954-60	Jim Lee Howell	(53-27-4)
1961-68	Allie Sherman	(57-51-4)
1969-	Alex Webster	(27-29)

Giants in Hall of Fame

Mel Hein, center, 1931-45	Charter Member
Timothy J. Mara, founder	Charter Member
Peter (Fats) Henry, tackle, 1924	Charter Member*
Cal Hubbard, tackle, 1927-28	Charter Member*
Jim Thorpe, halfback, 1925	Charter Member*
Arnie Herber, quarterback, 1944	Inducted in 1966*
Steve Owen, tackle, coach, 1925-53	Inducted in 1966
Joe "Indian Joe" Guyon, halfback, 1927	Inducted in 1966*
Ken Strong, halfback-end, 1933-35, 1939-47	Inducted in 1967*
Emlen Tunnell, safety, 1948-58	Inducted in 1967*
Vince Lombardi, coach, 1954-58	Inducted in 1970*
Andy Robustelli, end, 1956-66	Inducted in 1971
Y. A. Tittle, quarterback, 1961-64	Inducted in 1971*

*Played or coached for additional teams

Index

283

1 2 3 4 5 6 7 ← P Y → 9 8 7 6 5 4 3

1 2 3 4 5 6 7 ← P Y → 9 8 7 6 5 4 3